UNDERSTANDING GENDER AT WORK

HOW TO USE, LOSE AND EXPOSE
BLIND SPOTS FOR CAREER SUCCESS

DELEE FROMM

For more information and to contact the author visit
www.deleefrommconsulting.com.

Library of Congress and National Library of Canada cataloging-
in-Publication Data available upon request of the author.

Tellwell Talent
www.tellwell.ca

ISBN
978-1-77302-900-9 (Hardcover)
978-1-77302-899-6 (Paperback)
978-1-77302-901-6 (eBook)

To my clients for their marvelous insights and stories and to the wonderful women in my life who have encouraged, supported, and mentored me.

By so doing, you have greatly enriched my life.

CONTENTS

UNDERSTANDING GENDER AT WORK

INTRODUCTION

Own it! Lean in! Create a Feminist Fight Club. Drop the Ball. Hardball for Women. Take the Stage. Advice for women on how to succeed in today's workplace is everywhere. Although such advice is valuable and well intended, it can be contradictory and confusing when used as "one size fits all" advice. Especially at a time when practical advice for working women is very much needed. Many young women tell me that they have become demoralized trying to play a fool's game and have left the workplace. They tell me it was making them into something they are not, so they dropped out. Perhaps this explains the current trend of female millennials to embrace traditional values by staying at home and having children; it allows them to go back to a time when things seemed simpler and clearer.

I understand the impulse. Rapid and accelerating change is all around us. Technology is greatly changing the ways we live and work; the amount of information available is staggering. I wrote this book to guide you through the information on how to succeed at work as a woman. Each approach offered to women – act more like a man, lean in, leverage you power, create a new game, join a fight club, help others to shine -- has value but needs to be placed in context. And that context depends on you - your age and stage, your personal gender approach and style, your career level, and your workplace. One approach does not fit all women -- we are too complex and diverse for that.

I wrote this book to help professional women. I workshopped this book so that I would better understand what you want, what is important to you, and what would help. It is understandable when ambitious women, who are just plain tired, leave the workplace. However, we need women in the workplace. We need them for organizational strategy. We need them for diversity. This isn't just the right thing to do, it's the smart thing to do. To ensure continued and increased gender diversity, we need strong women in numerous industries, professions, and businesses using their voices. And this means it is essential for women to remain a solid part of the work force.

I believe that the key to women remaining on their career paths and doing well is seeing with clear eyes. Women need to understand their value and worth and to know what is favoured in the workplace. Recognizing invisible hurdles and outdated organizational structures will help them navigate it successfully. They can then start to change these obstacles by ignoring old gender scripts. It means tapping into their power and knowing what options are available. It means having a career plan. And as part of this career plan, it means knowing when to pivot to a more comfortable work environment that is a better fit and aligns with their personal values - one that recognizes their value. It means understanding gender at work. This book provides options, strategies, and tools for women to find their way in the world of gender blind spots, habits, stereotypes, and bias.

In the meantime, these outdated and restrictive gender stereotypes are being used to determine workplace wages and promotions. Why is this still a thing?

WHY SO SLOW?

Current statistics and global trends indicate that the future favours traits associated with females; however, today's data on gender parity, especially on wages and senior leadership, suggest the opposite.[1] The gender wage gap remains large as does the low percentage of women at the top level of leadership. So why has the progression to gender equity stalled when almost everyone – both men and women – openly supports it? This is especially puzzling when economic evidence shows, and has shown for a while, the many significant benefits of gender equality globally, corporately, and politically.[2] One factor that makes great sense to me as a neuropsychologist, and explains why change for women in the workplace has been so slow, is the influence of unconscious gender blind spots and biases.

We all have gender blind spots and biases – those automatic and quick ways of making assumptions about others based solely on gender. Through early childhood learning they become our frames of reference; in adulthood they are unconscious. And using these automatic, cultural short-cuts is of great benefit most of the time. They pave the way for easier interactions with others *of the same culture*. We feel comfortable and assured as to how our behaviours, communication patterns, and social rituals will be perceived and interpreted. We know what is valued and rewarded. However at work, where the rules still tend to be masculine and the leaders predominately male, the man's way is favoured. Understanding gender norms and rules at work therefore provides a significant advantage for women.

WHY THIS BOOK?

The aim of this book, with its focus on gender blind spots and habits, is to support and encourage you with the following advice and information.

1. *Know the Rules of the Game.* To be effective and make your value visible in a masculine workplace you need to know the rules of the game. This includes knowing what is rewarded and viewed as successful, having organizational awareness, and expanding your repertoire to include those styles that may have been natural to you when you were young but were suppressed and discarded during childhood training. Unless you know the gender norms that are in operation at work, your skills, talents, and abilities will be lost in translation. This awareness is of particular importance to young women coming out of high school or university where knowing how to advance and succeed in those institutions was transparent. In school, their ideas were heard, their value was visible, and the environment was a true meritocracy.

2. *Know Your Value and Strengths.* Recognizing your value in the workplace and the power you have is crucial. To learn when a feminine style is effective and that your perspective is powerful. Often women feel powerless when, despite their best efforts, they are not successful at work. By recognizing when the game favours the man's way, you discover the disconnect and are able to move forward with more confidence and awareness. Future trends favour the feminine, so the approaches, talents, skills, and strengths learned as a girl in childhood are on the cusp of being the centre of the game.

3. *Know When to Switch It Up.* By knowing best practices and when feminine approaches work best, you can start to selectively and strategically use the styles most of us learned in childhood. You will also know when to switch to masculine approaches when needed. This ability to switch is a powerful advancement tool for women.

4. *Recognize Unfair Tactics and Gender Bias.* Once you know the rules of the game, you will be better able to spot gender bias when it's operating. It can be evident in organizational policies

that favour the man's way or corporate structures that align with outdated family structures. Gender bias might be at play when others use tactics to gain an unfair advantage, such as stealing ideas or interrupting. Once you start to recognize it you can begin to shine a light on it, perhaps by having that brave conversation with others or by pointing it out to leaders. You have to know the rules of the game to clearly recognize unfair plays and be able to call them.

5. *Appreciate When to Tap into Your Power.* It is vital to know when the fit is not good, when you are tired of contorting to the demands of a masculine workplace, when the rules don't work for you, or when your value is not being recognized. This knowledge allows you to leverage your power and pivot. This might mean moving to another position where the salary is better, the corporate values align with your own, and the work is more meaningful and fulfilling. Alternatively, this could mean starting your own company where you get to create organizational structures and policies that disrupt old gender scripts.

From coaching and training women I know that women who have this information are more likely to stay in the workplace, to succeed and advance, and to help others succeed and advance. Women with this information are able to understand how to play the game and avoid being blindsided. They can recognize the invisible hurdles that still exist and navigate them successfully, exposing and challenging biases to make the way easier for others. By recognizing when the fit is not good and pivoting easily, they discern options that leverage their power, actively manage their careers, and create plans that work for them. These career plans might involve knowing how to *Go Along to Get Along* in order to advance in their organizations, or when to move on and create their own workplaces. Aware women know when to throw away old gender scripts and disrupt. In short, they use the four career strategies provided in the chapter Plan with flexibility and adaptability.

WHY ME?

The man's way of doing things was not favoured by my first profession – psychology. I worked at a large psychiatric hospital where both male and female gender ways were valued due to the nature of the work. An indirect approach was not viewed by other mental health professionals as weak nor as indicative of a lack of confidence. Due to my ability to switch between feminine and masculine styles and approaches, I was offered a position as head of the department after just four years.

In my second career as a lawyer, where I worked at a large law firm, it quickly became obvious that there were different rules in play and invisible dynamics at work. These dynamics fascinated me, and I observed and reflected on them during my 17 years of legal practice. Since 2003, my company, Delee Fromm Consulting Inc., has provided consulting services on women's advancement to a vast array of international organizations. My perspective on what works for women is drawn from these two totally different careers, my experience as a consultant and business owner, and the examples, insights, ideas, and stories from my clients.

THE AUDIENCE

This book is for women who want to advance and succeed at work. It's for those who find themselves working below their level of competence, skill, and talent and who want to avoid having their careers stall mainly because they are women.[3] This book provides options, strategies, and tools for preventing this while waiting for organizational changes and societal shifts. Until a future that favours women arrives, women will benefit from understanding the invisible hurdles they face and learning how to deal with them. This book is for women who want to advance despite an unlevel playing field, and for those who want to work with others to level this playing field.

Although it is meant primarily for women, this book will also be helpful for men. Specifically, it will be useful for men who are mentoring or wish to mentor women, who want to support and champion women, and who want to be more aware of gender blind spots that exist in themselves and in their organizations. It is also for men who recognize the many benefits of diversity, and for men who have the power and seniority to enact changes. Suggestions for enacting concrete changes for gender parity are included in the section entitled, "What Organizations, Leaders, and Mentors Can Do," and in the Conclusion. The advice set out in this book will also be of benefit to men who don't follow traditional gender scripts and may be subject to gender bias as a result.

WHAT THIS BOOK IS NOT

Each individual – woman or man – is a mixture of feminine and masculine traits and styles. No one person expresses only one style; we are naturally complex and diverse. We do not fit neatly into categories and the same response can occur for a variety of reasons. We are a dynamic result of many factors - personality, national culture, profession, innate preferences, education, and generation - to list only a few. This book is not about stereotyping. So when I use the words women or men I mean most, not all.

The aim of this book is not to make women into men. Rather it is about understanding masculine and feminine styles and learning the invisible dynamics operating in the work world – organizational and interpersonal dynamics that are still based on the rules boys learned. This understanding and awareness will allow you to make choices about whether you should *act as a man would act* in those situations where it is critical to your success to do so or whether to harness the power of the feminine style. You will learn how to anticipate bias, avoid it, and manage impressions. This book is about expanding your options through awareness and skill development so you can adopt the approach that is the most comfortable, most effective, and most appropriate for the situation.

The focus on feminine habits in this book is not to suggest that women are responsible for the gender gap or for closing it. The reasons for gender inequity are numerous and complex, involving external factors such as organizational barriers and gender bias in the workplace. It does not suggest there is anything wrong with women or feminine styles. In fact, as you will see as you read this book, many feminine approaches are more effective than their masculine counterparts.

This book is not about blaming or shaming men. We all have gender blind spots due to childhood learning and the patriarchy has not been kind to men either.[4] The word "understanding" in the title of this book was chosen as it means appreciating, comprehending, and empathizing. We need everyone to focus on solutions and work together in order to achieve gender parity.

Finally, this book is written based on a gender binary framework with a primary focus on helping women understand and navigate gender blind spots in the workplace. It is not written as a book to help transgendered persons navigate their careers at work. If it turns out to be helpful in that regard, that would be wonderful, however that is not the focus of this book.

HOW TO USE THIS BOOK

You can read this book from cover to cover or you can pick it up for specific advice. I would suggest you read the first two chapters, Origins and Expose, before any of the skills chapters. In Origins the focus is on how mental blind spots are created based on findings from cognitive neuroscience. Early gender training is explored to show how gender biases and expectations arise. In the Expose chapter, six types of gender blind spots that are most significant for women at work are identified, along with how to reduce their impact.

Each subsequent chapter focuses on an important skill for women at work with a focus on gender blind spots. These skill-focused chapters will encourage and support you with practical tools and techniques to:

- proactively **plan** your career using four career strategies;
- **ask** for what you are worth and for opportunities to make your value visible;
- **communicate** in a way that is clear and confident;
- convey an engaged and confident **presence** that commands respectful attention from others; and
- **promote** yourself in a way that is natural, comfortable, and memorable.

The last three chapters provide advice on how to harness and use feminine styles in order to:

- **lead** with natural and effective leadership skills;
- develop social intelligence and positive organizational **politics**; and
- nurture yourself by managing energy and reducing stress to **thrive.**

If you are craving more detail than what is provided in this book, a list of books that I have found helpful is included at the end of each chapter. If you want more advice and materials from my seminars, please see my book, *Advance Your Legal Career: Essential Skills for Success*, published by LexisNexis Canada.

It is my hope that by shining a bright light on gender blind spots and increasing your awareness of them, you will be able to better understand

and navigate the invisible hurdles that may be holding you back. You will be able expand your repertoire of behaviours and strategies through skill development to adopt the approach that is most comfortable and successful for you. Through examination of best practices, you may discover natural skills and approaches you gave up in childhood due to gender training. You may uncover abandoned skills and approaches that allow you to function more comfortably, authentically, and effectively. You will be able to tap into your power to help yourself and others shine at work. You will start to have courageous conversations to draw attention to practices and behaviours that stand in the way of gender parity.

I wish you all the very best and every success on your career journey!

Delee Fromm

TERMINOLOGY AND CLARIFICATIONS

In reading about *gender fluidity* in National Geographic, I thought I had the perfect term to refer to the ability to use both masculine and feminine approaches with flexibility and versatility.[5] I was reminded by a friend that the term refers to sexual identity and orientation rather than gender culture behaviours, approaches, and styles learned in childhood. So to ensure clarity and avoid, where possible, any misinterpretation about terms relating to gender, sex, and culture, I thought it would be helpful to set out definitions. Blame the lawyer in me.

TERMINOLOGY

Androgynous refers to a combination of feminine and masculine traits. In this book it means being able to shift between feminine and masculine approaches and styles in order to use the most effective one for the situation.

Bias refers to an inflexible, often unconscious belief, which can be positive or negative, about a particular group of people.

Culture is the shared pattern of learning of a social group that allows a group to be distinct. It involves an acquired and transmitted pattern of shared meaning, feeling, and behaviour that is shared by that group.

Feminine refer to traits or attributes ascribed by society to females.

Feminine culture is used in this book to mean female gender culture.

Gender is often used to mean biological sex because for most people, biological sex and gender are aligned. However, gender is broader than biological sex. In this book, gender means the masculine and feminine traits and attributes that a society ascribes to being male or female. These traits and attributes are taught to children through gender culture.

Gender atypical or nonconforming refers to those individuals who show a predominance of the other gender's traits. A woman who predominantly uses masculine approaches and styles would be considered gender atypical as would a man who predominately uses feminine approaches and styles.

Gender bias is based on gender attitudes or stereotypes that influence perceptions, actions, and decisions. These often lead to inaccurate conclusions about a situation or person, usually to the detriment of women. When these attitudes and stereotypes are unconscious, it is called *implicit gender bias*.

Gender blind spots refer to the attitudes and stereotypes created through fast neural processing and based on gender culture training. These deeply held frames of reference about gender influence our actions, perceptions, and decisions as adults, often without awareness. Gender blind spots can manifest as gender bias, gender stereotyping, gendered expectations, self-limiting mindsets, and gender habits. They are abbreviated as GBS throughout the book.

Gender culture refers to the early childhood training of boys and girls whereby masculine and feminine rules and norms are learned through direct and indirect messages and images. This cultural training ensures that children are programmed to perceive, act, and think in ways that are consistent with the gender they are assigned at birth.

Gendered expectations arise when we expect men to show masculine approaches, attitudes, behaviours and styles while we expect women to exhibit feminine ones.

Gender habits mean the approaches, responses, and behaviour we learn as children through gender training and often use without awareness.

Gender stereotyping involves the automatic attribution of masculine traits and roles to men and feminine traits and roles to women based solely on their biological sex.

Masculine refers to traits or attributes ascribed by society to males.

Masculine culture is used in this book to mean male gender culture.

Sex means the biological sex of the person – either male or female. This categorization typically, but not always, correlates with genes, gonads, and genitals. Biological sex is used to assign gender at birth.

Negative Stereotype Threat means being at risk of confirming a negative stereotype about one's social group.

Situational gender triggers refer to those situations where consistent gender differences are demonstrated in negotiated approaches and outcomes due to gender habits, biases, and gendered expectations.

Stereotype backlash means the negative consequences women and men often face when they act counter to traditional gender stereotypes. These negative consequences can include relational, societal, and economic sanctions or penalties.

ORIGINS

When I started university in 1972, the prevailing attitude was that women could be whatever we wanted to be and do whatever we wanted to do. It was a heady and exciting time and I, along with my female fellow travelers, were certain that we were going to change everything. That was over 40 years ago. Recent estimates by the World Economic Forum indicate we won't reach global gender parity at the current rate of change until 2186.[6]

So what is happening? Why so slow? It is not that men and women have different abilities, skills, or talents.[7] Years of research and meta-analyses demonstrate that the myth of different abilities based on sex is false. It is not that women lack ambition. In fact it is the reverse - recent research suggests that women start out with loads of ambition but their ambition decreases the longer they are in the workforce.[8] And with organizations and society openly endorsing gender parity, why is change for women in the workforce so slow?

An important answer to the puzzle may be our brains. I am not referring to anatomical or functional brain differences between men and women - that has been debunked - but to the way humans mentally process information and make decisions.[9] We appear to do it two ways – fast and slow. The fast processing system is by far the most prevalent and has the most significant impact on behaviour. It is the processing system that creates mental blind spots. These blind spots cause us to act and judge quickly with little conscious thought. And as a result of the persistent, rigorous, and ubiquitous nature of gender training in childhood, gender blind spots are born.

THE CONSEQUENCES OF GENDER BLIND SPOTS FOR WOMEN

Gender blind spots (GBS) significantly impact women in the workplace by slowing their progress, reducing their ambition, and stalling their careers. Implicit gender bias is one of these blind spots. It is made up of unconscious attitudes or stereotypes that influence perceptions, actions, and decisions often leading to inaccurate conclusions about a situation or person. It is very tricky to detect implicit gender bias since unconscious gender attitudes and assumptions may be the opposite of the views openly asserted.

Gender bias is not the only type of GBS that negatively impacts women's progress. Others are the gendered styles, behaviours, and mindsets we soaked up as children that have now in adulthood become unconscious gender habits and limiting mindsets. They are also tricky to detect because they are so ingrained.

These hidden GBS can get in the way of understanding both our own behaviour and that of others. Using a female gender script we misread the behaviour of males who are using a male gender script, while they in turn misread our behaviour. GBS often impede or prevent personal skill development. I have seen huge breakthroughs by clients in the development of new skills, as well as the use of already existing skills, through insights gleaned from self and situational awareness. In most cases this involves taking off the brakes – stopping those unconscious self-limiting thoughts that slow us down or derail us completely.

To illustrate how GBS can create confusion and frustration, below is a description of a client's situation. She came to me for coaching as she was completely at a loss to explain or deal with what was happening. Can you figure it out? An analysis of this situation is included later in this chapter using a gendered perspective. See if that analysis matches yours.

> *Debbie (not her real name) is a leasing representative who helps landlords lease out their commercial properties. She is an intelligent and confident professional with an impressive resumé. When she returned to the workforce after maternity leave she started with a new company and accepted the salary and benefits that were offered.*
>
> *During her first year, another leasing representative was hired right out of university with no previous work experience. He demanded the title of Director of Leasing and Marketing and got it. He argued that he had to have it so that he could "better be able to do his job and perform to job expectations." Debbie's title of Leasing Representative remained the same although she was the one training him – so in reality he reported to her but his title suggested he was her supervisor!*
>
> *Then he left the company. At her annual performance evaluation, Debbie was offered a salary increase of 50%. She did not respond. Rather she waited in the hope that her title would be changed to the one her male colleague had been given. Eventually she accepted the pay increase and never requested a new title. At her second annual review, she was told she lacked initiative and she needed to take on more of a leadership role.*
>
> *That's when she called me. During coaching she discovered that the young woman she was training as a leasing representative, who had no previous experience, was making only $10,000 less than she was.*

So how does one begin to analyze the invisible gender dynamics at play in this situation? Understanding GBS and how the brain, through fast processing, creates them will help. By recognizing how the gender rules, roles, and behaviour taught in childhood develop into gender bias and gendered habits, women can see GBS for what they are and address them.

HOW BLIND SPOTS ARISE

Mental blind spots involve unconscious, automatic associations that are reflexive rather than reflective. Regardless of how self-aware we believe we are, we operate mentally blind, with many of our behaviours and judgements being automatic. And this is not an occasional thing. Several prominent neuroscientists put the percentage that the mind works automatically without our awareness at between 80 to 90%.[10] This means that while we believe we are rational beings with great awareness, the unconscious is running the show. We continuously operate with blind spots – displaying behaviours, habits, and approaches we are not aware of while making assumptions and judgements about people and situations that are entirely unconscious.

So how can we operate so blindly? It is due to our brain and how we mentally process information. The brain appears to have two types of systems for processing information – rational and instinctual. The first is slow and deliberate – the second is fast and automatic. And they each have valuable but different roles in processing information.

The deliberate, slow system controls the things we do consciously and analytically. When it is operating, we are thoughtful, considerate, self-controlled, and reasonable, like sensible and wise adults. However, this type of mental processing and focus requires a huge amount of scarce mental energy and resources, and takes time.

In contrast, the automatic system allows us to quickly process vast amounts of information. Some research indicates that our brains can process 11 million bits of information every second. The conscious mind deals with 40-50 of these information bits, with one estimate as low as 16 bits.[11] If we needed to be conscious of every bit of sensory data that floods our nervous system every second, we would be paralyzed. Like an overloaded computer, we would crash. Our slow deliberate system does not have the capacity to process vast amounts of data.

Fast processing allows us to seek and create patterns from vast amounts of data - patterns and conclusions about experiences that remain long after the experiences are forgotten. If an association is out there, the neurobiology of fast processing will make it. And due to the quick nature of this process, the associations we make are below the level of consciousness. It is impossible not to have biases or opinions due to this brain mechanism, and we are constantly using unconscious frames of references, or mental short cuts, to make sense of the world.

Using fast processing, we are able to make assessments in nanoseconds. It allows us to believe we know things implicitly – we feel certainty at a deep level. We make judgements about things and people very quickly without knowing or remembering the mental content for those judgements.

Perhaps you have been attracted to someone immediately without knowing why, or leery of someone without even talking to them. This happens because their features appeal or repel based on preferences and associations we hold unconsciously. Research shows we make decisions about whether we trust someone or not in nanoseconds. And this fast processing is the basis for knowing how someone made us feel immediately on meeting them again – even if we can't remember their name or what they said to us. Clearly the features of fast processing have some great advantages; however, the drawbacks can be significant.

ADVANTAGES AND DISADVANTAGES OF FAST PROCESSING

Unconscious fast processing has served us well for survival. Automatic associations based on fast processing work exceptionally well as navigational guides, directing us through new or challenging terrain. We trust them implicitly as they work quietly and quickly, saving both time and energy. Being able to act without taking time to reflect and plan a course of action is important when danger lurks. Using this *sixth sense* to intrinsically know when a situation is unsafe allows us to act quickly and escape. This navigation system guides us to make split second decisions based on associations we have learned over time - associations that have become automatic.

This same neural system now assists in more complex environments such as social gatherings – paving the way for easy and smooth interpersonal interactions. For example, when we are with others who share our cultural background and childhood learning, this automatic system allows us to use social habits smoothly and unconsciously. We understand the gender code of conduct implicitly. Quietly and quickly they form the invisible aspect of interpersonal dynamics, making our interactions easier and less awkward. It becomes easier to socialize and work with others who are like us as it takes less effort. And our fast processing is validated in such settings, making it a positive experience.

However, this fast system can also create significant drawbacks and unwanted consequences when we operate on autopilot in an environment that uses a different code of conduct. We may use habits and approaches that are accepted and understood in a certain way by one cultural group but are viewed and interpreted totally differently by others raised with different associations and different rules.

Fast processing can also trip us up by creating feelings of discomfort about certain behaviours or approaches. These false navigational guides, which feel perfectly valid, may cause us to avoid certain skills, positions, or projects. Thus at work, the very behaviours that are advantageous to developing our career and advancing may feel foreign and wrong; activities such as negotiating self-interests, leading others, or promoting ourselves. It is only once we are able to recognize the basis of the discomfort that we are able to broaden our skills, expand our repertoires, and become versatile.

Another disadvantage of the way fast processing creates a significant blind spot is implicit bias. The Implicit Association Test (IAT)[12] measures unconscious internal associations for age, race, and gender by timing how quickly we make external associations using pictures or words. If the external associations match our internal associations, the response time is shorter and fewer errors are shown.

Measurements of implicit gender associations reveal that men are implicitly associated with math, science, career, high authority, and hierarchy. Women, in contrast, are implicitly associated with liberal arts, family, low authority, and egalitarianism. Research conducted in 2015 using words relating to work and family reveals that approximately 75 percent of people think "men" when they hear career related words such as profession, business, and work and think "women" with words such as domestic, house, and household.[13] This research also reveals that the vast majority of people associate men with boss, CEO, and directors while they associate women with positions such as assistant, attendant, and secretary. Men are viewed as leaders and women as helpers. Unfortunately, these biased associations are not decreasing among millennials. Survey research in 2014 shows that younger male participants were more biased than their older counterparts.[14]

The Bern Sex Role Inventory reveals that gender stereotypes remain entrenched in the new millennium. This inventory was used initially in 1974. In 2004, an extensive study of gender stereotypes showed that despite the 30-year time span, the same results were obtained. In 1974, women were expected to be affectionate, sensitive, warm, and concerned with making others feel at ease while men were expected to be aggressive, competent, forceful, and independent leaders. In 2004, women were expected to be affectionate, sensitive, warm, and friendly while men were expected to be aggressive, competent, independent, tough, and achievement-oriented. Don't these still sound like the characteristics operating today?

Implicit gender associations on the IAT are shown by most people *regardless of what they consciously think about these associations*. Two creators of the test, Mahzarin R. Banaji and Anthony G. Greenwald, were shocked when their scores showed they were racially biased. Amazingly, people who think they have no bias have been shown to be the most biased.

That is why blaming or shaming others, especially males, for gender bias is misguided. Everyone is susceptible and we are all biased. For example, senior female lawyers at corporations have admitted that they prefer to provide work to male rather than female lawyers. They know it is not right but it feels comfortable. This is a clear example of fast processing and implicit gender bias in operation.

So how do we deal with and reduce GBS? Through understanding gender socialization, and the gender rules and roles we learned, we can see more clearly the gender mindsets, biases, and habits we all have. Let's start with gender socialization.

THE PROCESS OF GENDER SOCIALIZATION

How we were socialized and the rules we learned in childhood significantly influence and inform our relationships and how we operate in the world. One expert defines culture as "the collective programming of the mind distinguishing the members of one group or category of people from others."[15] Gender culture looked at this way involves boys being programmed to be men and girls being programmed to be women. These experiences and lessons from childhood about gender form the mental content for GBS.

Gender socialization starts early. Male and female distinctions are easy to make and are thus made very early – some by babies as young as three to four months.[16] Research shows that most young children, some as young as two years old, are able to categorize items such as fire hats, dolls, and makeup by the gender that uses them.[17] At this young age they also start to use gender labels and are able to say to which sex they belong. Research shows that by age seven unconscious gender bias exists.

Gender socialization is rigorous. It starts in very early childhood through the transmission of gender rules as to appropriate types of activities, games, toys, dress, and colours of clothes. These rules are reinforced in a myriad of ways by many people, including family members, friends, media (such as TV shows, commercials, video games, internet, films, and books) and society in general.[18] Research shows that gender training is even taught through peer pressure with preschool children receiving a cool reception from other playmates when they play in gender-inappropriate ways, such as boys playing with dolls.[19]

Gender socialization is supported and encouraged by the toys offered to children. Most parents buy gender specific toys within months of a baby's birth. Popular girls' toys such as Easy-bake ovens, tea sets, and baby dolls give girls practice mimicking their future caregiving role. On the other hand, boys' toys that fit the male stereotype, such as models, encourage problem-solving, self-confidence, and creativity.[20] And these messages from toys have been getting more pronounced over the past 30 years. The reason for this is gendered segmented marketing. Why sell one toy for both sexes when you can manufacture two separate ones and sell more? [21] This marketing strategy seems to be working brilliantly based on the number of pink and blue toys dramatically displayed in images on the internet showing entire rooms filled with pink toys for girls and blue toys for boys.[22] It's amazing to think that the gender designation of pink and blue was reversed in the early 20th century with blue for girls and pink for boys: pink was thought to be a stronger colour.

Gender socialization is ubiquitous. Children are born into a world in which gender is constantly emphasized through toys, colours, dress, appearance, language, segregation, and symbols. Even when gender rules are not taught directly, research shows that individuals soak them up through the hundreds of thousands of virtual and real life images viewed during childhood and adolescence. And these images inform thoughts, attitudes, and behaviours, and create biases. Even if you don't support the promotion of traditional gender roles, just by having lived in a society that is based on these rules and the social order they create, you have picked them up and most likely operate unconsciously with some of them.

GENDER RULES AND GENDER BLIND SPOTS

Through gender socialization, girls and boys learn beliefs, values, attitudes, and behaviour (together called norms) that are considered socially appropriate for their sex. And these norms are vastly different for each gender. From the playground to the classroom to the boardroom we have been socialized to communicate, interact, lead, and behave in gender-specific ways.

Gender roles and rules are learned so early and so consistently that they become gender habits. For instance, the ritualistic "sorry" used by women is such a deeply ingrained habit that it is typically offered without awareness that it is being said or why. In addition to habits, gender rules create mindsets from which personal injunctions arise – injunctions that make certain types of behaviour uncomfortable or even prohibited. One example is the extreme discomfort many men experience in asking for directions. This gender habit is a costly one. According to British insurer Sheila Wheels who surveyed 1000 drivers, the average male drives 276 miles (approximately 444 km) while lost each year, at a cost to him of about $3400 CAD in wasted fuel over a lifetime.[23] Although the learned injunctions still affect behaviour, the underlying rule is long forgotten but the feeling of discomfort remains.

Forgotten gender rules and lessons allow judgements about others to be made quickly and automatically when they behave in a certain way. We often don't know why the judgements feel right or wrong, appropriate or inappropriate. We have totally lost sight of the gender rules and stereotypes that our attitudes and assumptions are based on. But why does gender training create such a disadvantage for women? Why do most gender biases impact women negatively?

GENDER AND THE UNLEVEL PLAYING FIELD

Gender roles and rules are artificial constructs created by societies to instill social order and set parameters so individuals know how to act and interact within that society. Gender stereotypes reflect a narrow band of human traits and behaviours that are used to illustrate and differentiate masculine and feminine. Yet masculine and feminine roles do not reflect actual differences between the sexes and scientific research has failed to demonstrate any cognitive differences. The only truly consistent differences between men and women are genes, gonads, and genitals.[24]

The relatively recent development of gender roles for men and women around work and home shows their artificiality. Our current gender roles were created as recently as the Industrial Revolution with the shift in work from an agrarian to a manufacturing-based economy.[25] This new division of labour required men to be at work and women to be at home.

And lest we think this division of labour was based on older hunter/ gatherer roles, Angela Saini, in her book *Inferior,* debunks that idea.[26] She examines current day tribes where she finds examples of men who are hands-on fathers and women who "hunt" as well as "forage" for food. Saini concludes that there is no biological commandment that women are natural homemakers and unnatural hunters.

Despite the shift of women into the workplace after the Second World War, gender stereotypes have not changed significantly as shown by results from the Implicit Association Test (IAT).[27] People still associate men with work and women with home. And at work they associate women with helpers and men with leaders. And this carry-over of old gender stereotypes can disadvantage women schooled in female gender culture and working in a masculine work world.

Not understanding the rules and norms of gender culture at work is like traveling to a foreign country that looks exactly like the one you grew up in. Because it is so familiar you use the same interpersonal habits and rituals you learned in your home country. And these habits and rituals are cultural blind spots for you. You assume that you are operating in a shared culture where your behaviours and attitudes will be perceived and interpreted in the same way as they were back home. Instead your behaviours are misread and your talents, skills, and abilities are discounted. It is a culture clash that you are unaware of, and one that can be very detrimental.

To do well in the game of business, as in any type of game, you need to know the rules. Specifically, it's important to know which behaviours are valued and which attitudes are rewarded. The game of most businesses and professions still tends to be based on masculine rules and norms while most women have been socialized to operate using feminine norms and rules. Thus, if you have been raised as a girl you most likely don't know masculine rules. This erects powerful barriers for women that are often reinforced through organizational structures, practices, and patterns of interaction that inadvertently benefit men while putting women at a disadvantage.

Disappointment, confusion, and frustration can and often do result when a woman operates using only feminine styles. As the world of business and many professions still favour the man's way, she will not likely be rewarded for such behaviour, her performance may be questioned, and she may be told to show more initiative.

Being conscious of the feminine rules and values and learning about masculine ones is a huge advantage. This knowledge can accelerate skills development and help you recognize the invisible dynamics of success and advancement. It also makes for easier career planning and the use of career strategies. Similar to taking an international posting to give yourself more credibility and a broader perspective, learning to navigate using both feminine and masculine norms will also make you more credible in your organization.

Going through the values, rules, and behaviours associated with each gender has another benefit – it validates and confirms for women what they have observed and felt. "I am not crazy!" and, "It's so great to know I am not the only one thinking this" are common expressions of relief from many women in my seminars after learning how gender rules operate in the workplace. Being able to recognize the invisible dynamics that are operating in workplace situations makes it so much clearer. And if you decide not to change your style and approach, this awareness allows you to be aware of double standards and to have courageous conversations.

MASCULINE AND FEMININE STYLES

To show that everyone understands what is meant by gender differences, in my seminar I read out a list of words and ask clients to shout out which gender approach or attitude - masculine or feminine – best describes the word or phrase. Can you do it? I have yet to find a coaching client, group, or audience who does not identify them the same way.

Fitting In	Competitive
Standing Out	Cooperative
Relationship	Collaborative
Outcome	Indirect
Results	Direct
Winning	Collective
Helping Others	Independent
Self-Interests	Hierarchical
Other Focused	Equalitarian
Goal Oriented	Brilliant

It is important to again note that these words denoting masculine and feminine styles are social constructs and are used to describe not only individuals but the predominant characteristics of corporations, countries, cities, and cultures. In negotiation, these words describe national cultural approaches, with some national cultures preferring a more feminine style and others using a more masculine style.

Are you having problems with the word brilliant? If you guessed masculine you are in good company. New research shows that the majority of girls as young as six years old believe that brilliance is a male trait and that achieving good grades is due solely to hard work.[28] This belief is not held by five-year-old girls. The researchers assert that even at this young age, girls discount the evidence in front of them. These false beliefs mirror those of teachers and parents who attribute good grades to hard work for girls but to natural ability for boys. This gender bias has been found to be directly linked to lower numbers of both women and African Americans in areas such as software development, where it is believed that success depends on sheer brilliance.[29]

How did you do in dividing these words into masculine and feminine styles? In the sections below I let you know how these words have been divided by my seminar participants.

DISTINGUISHING GENDER STYLES

When we were born, we were assigned a gender based on our sex and, if we were like most children, were taught which gender style was best for us based on that assignment. Some of us rejected the gender style imposed because we were surrounded by the other style (like being raised with brothers only or having a mother who had a very masculine style) or the style was in conflict with our innate preferences and approaches. Notwithstanding these exceptions, the majority of men and women recognize and align with traditional gender styles. To help you understand where you fall on the masculine/feminine continuum, a questionnaire is provided at the end of this chapter based on the style or approach you use with various skills.

The words chosen by my clients from the word list to describe feminine style are as follows.

Fitting In	Relationship
Indirect	Cooperative
Helping Others	Collective
Other Focused	Equalitarian

The overarching priority that unites these words is **valuing the group**. In feminine culture what matters most is the collective or the group. As a result of this priority, the goal is to keep everyone happy and relationships harmonious.

From this priority of valuing the group comes another quintessential hallmark of feminine style - how power is shown. This is the norm that underlies and informs most feminine interpersonal dynamics and as such explains much of the difference between male and female gender culture. From an early age most girls learn in the playground that **power is equal and shared** by the group. Everyone is equal and no one is the leader. Decisions are discussed and decided together. A natural advantage of this approach is the creation of alliances and networks. Girls learn to use the power of the group to implement change and protect others.

To step out of that flat power structure has serious social repercussions. Girls develop rituals of interaction and communication that allow others to save face in the broadest sense of the word, to minimize their own accomplishments, and to support the good of the group. If a little girl decides to be the leader and starts to push around her playmates, she will usually find that her relationships begin to suffer: friends will call her bossy and will start to avoid her. Another sure way for a girl to hurt relationships with other girls is to boast or brag.

As adult women we forget this childhood learning about power but have an unconscious internal injunction about standing out or appearing superior to the group – even in circumstances where it would be appropriate and beneficial to make our value visible. Instead, when we are told by others (usually males) that we should stand out more, we are puzzled by it. And it is important to keep in mind that gender is not the only culture that values the collective. Consequently, many women raised in certain national cultures have a double injunction about standing out, and in my experience, are unaware of either. This injunction against bragging is so powerful that I changed the name of my self-promotion seminar from "Bragalicious" to "Branding" because women so strongly disliked the original name.

The social rituals of reciprocal compliments (you immediately give back a compliment upon getting one), deferring to the team (when getting praise for your work) or saying "sorry" are reflections of keeping the power equal, fitting in, and being part of the collective. These values also underlie women not wanting to brag or boast to other women. On hearing about this rule, a coaching client immediately understood why her boss was upset with her for not telling anyone, especially her team of women, about her new job perks. It made her appear unappreciative to him; meanwhile for her it was about keeping her power equal with that of her team. It was a huge "aha" moment for her.

These are the words representative of masculine style from the list.

Standing Out	Winning
Direct	Independent
Competitive	Results
Goal Oriented	Self-Interests

The priority and focus for how to be a man is quite different from those for how to be a woman. What matters most is **achievement and status**. That can mean achievement with a team or more impressively, as an individual. Successful outcome is thus highly valued in this culture. To stand out, win, successfully pursue self-interests, be competitive, be focused on the goal, and be independent are all parts of achievement and with achievement comes status. In direct contrast to the idea learned by girls that power should be equalized, boys learn a **vertical hierarchy** of power in the playground. They are either **one step down or one step up** on the ladder of power. There is no equal level. Boys learn it is important to stand out from the crowd, to tell others about their accomplishments and to lead others by telling them what to do. These behaviours gain them status in the group and allow them to be one step up.

As a consequence of this focus on hierarchy, most men assess their relative ranking in new social settings. As one senior professional woman in a seminar expressed it, men like to figure out "who's who in the zoo." One executive who had always been puzzled by the change of behaviour in her husband at social gatherings asked her husband if that was what he did. He was shocked and surprised that she knew what he was doing and immediately asked suspiciously, "who told you what I was doing?"

Another aspect of this ranking in masculine power is the pushback experienced by women who achieve something that male colleagues have not. One young female lawyer who had asked and been allowed to attend an important industry conference could not understand why the male colleagues at her level were ignoring her. Once she heard about the masculine style of power displays she understood. It finally made sense that this was pushback for her being *one up*.

Despite the operation of masculine rules at work, using only masculine styles or gender habits to the extreme is not the best way to succeed at work. Any gender habit can become inappropriate if used without awareness or to the extreme. In Marshall Goldsmith's self-help book, *What Got You Here Won't Get You There*, he offers advice to successful men with whole chapters on how to apologize, thank others, and listen.[30] Some of the detrimental masculine habits listed in the book include: trying to win too much and too often; making destructive comments; telling the world how smart you are; failing to give proper recognition; claiming credit that you don't deserve; refusing to express regret; and exalting your faults as virtues.

Furthermore, it is not a good idea to drop feminine style habits immediately and completely. One young woman who realized she was always apologizing decided that she was never going to say "sorry" again. However, switching from one extreme to the other is seldom advisable or even warranted. Rather, using "sorry" appropriately, consciously, and perhaps strategically – to indicate responsibility, to build trust, or as a ritual with other women – works much better.

It is important to note that the masculine way of viewing the world as *one up/one down* is not always easy. Every interaction creates opportunities to lose status and position – to move down the ladder. With this mindset, you are constantly on guard and ready to push back. If this approach doesn't come naturally to you, think of a situation where you have felt the tension of being on guard and perhaps you will have a better understanding of (and maybe even some empathy for) this way of viewing the world.

ANALYSIS OF MASCULINE AND FEMININE STYLES AT WORK

To more fully understand masculine and feminine values and priorities and how they may be displayed in work behaviour, let's revisit my client's dilemma described above. To help you appreciate the different gendered approaches, an analysis of the feminine and masculine styles and norms involved in Debbie's situation is offered below.

FEMININE STYLE APPROACH

Accept what is offered: Debbie accepted what was offered when she joined the company with the underlying assumption the company would not underpay her and the company would be fair to her as *the group takes care of its members*. And that was the same assumption she continued to operate with as she waited for her title to be changed. She did not ask but rather avoided talking about the situation with her boss as she expected him (the collective) to know what she wanted.

Everyone shares the same values: She felt betrayed when, for her loyalty and acceptance of low pay, she was rewarded by being told during a performance evaluation she needed to show initiative. To her, this was adding insult to injury. In Debbie's mind, relationships are important and people are not treated in such an insensitive way.

Don't ask: Debbie didn't ask for more money or a more accurate job title as this might have hurt the relationship she had with her boss. Research on negotiation shows that most women compared to men tend not to initiate negotiations and 20% avoid negotiating at all. In female gender culture the goal of negotiation is to be cooperative, keep everyone happy, and reach consensus.

MASCULINE STYLE APPROACH

Ask for what you want: Debbie's male colleague, in contrast, was very clear in knowing what he wanted and asking for it. He did not wait for others to give him what he wanted at work - he went after it. No one was surprised by this except my client.

It's all about success: Achievement and status is what matters most in the male gender culture so this junior male's behaviour was neither surprising nor odd. It was entirely in keeping with the rules. What was shown to the world was that he was the director even if it did not accord with the true reality of the situation. He had won and that was what mattered most. He had set a goal and reached it. And it must have been the boss' goal as well – or it would not have happened.

By understanding the different values and norms underlying gender culture it is much easier to recognize where behaviours, assumptions, and attitudes differ and may be misunderstood. Once my client saw what had happened based on hidden gender values she better understood her boss and was able to respond successfully to the feedback. She understood how her assumptions from childhood had blinded her into interpreting the situation in a totally different way than the way her boss saw the situation. Her boss wanted her to show a more masculine style; that is what she did once she understood what it meant. She started by negotiating a higher salary.

GENDER RULES

To help you more fully appreciate GBS, it is important to know the salient gender rules that underlie masculine and feminine styles and how these rules impact important interpersonal workplace skills such as leadership, communication, negotiation, promotion, and presence.

Knowing gender rules has helped many of my female clients understand male behaviour that has been puzzling to them, such as why all the men in senior management changed to colourful socks like the new CEO (hint: follow the coach) or why a male boss was confused when an employee did not talk about her new perks and promotion (hint: a clash of masculine and feminine differences in power display). It has also helped clients see how feminine style may be misunderstand by male colleagues – such as the misinterpretation of a lack of confidence due to not talking about or drawing attention to their great work but letting it speak for itself (see the rules for Career Plan, Presence and Promote in the chart below). Hopefully knowing these rules will help you understand some confusing masculine or feminine behaviour in your office or allow you to see how your own behaviour might be misinterpreted.

Awareness of gender rules and habits at work can also offer valuable personal insight. On one occasion, a woman approached me after a seminar with tears in her eyes. She had had an epiphany during the seminar. Due to working in the very masculine work world of investment banking, she had turned her back on her feminine side. She had not valued those strengths she had learned in childhood and was grieving for them. Those were her words – not mine. I congratulated her on having this huge insight. I was thrilled for her as I knew that in becoming aware of her neglected and underappreciated feminine attitudes and approaches she was well on her way to becoming a more balanced and whole person.

Gender Rules and Essential Career Skills

	RULES FOR GIRLS	RULES FOR BOYS
WHAT MATTERS MOST	Relationships/ Harmony	Achievement/Status
POWER	Power is equal and shared	Power is a ladder where you are either one-up or one-down from others
CAREER PLAN	Do a perfect job/ Work hard	Brag about your wins/ Get noticed/Ask for what you want
COMMUNICATION	Enhance and support relationships/Get consensus, give support	Maintain status/Give orders, information, and advice
PRESENCE	Fit in – reduce	Stand-out - expand
PROMOTE	It's all about the team – wait to be noticed	Brag about the wins
LEADERSHIP	There are no leaders/ Being bossy hurts relationships	There is only one leader/ Be the leader
POLITICS	Don't rock the boat/ It's all gossip, lying, and unfair advantage	Understand the organization to get ahead/ Know who's influential

These rules have been set out in a concise form in the hopes of giving you new understanding about your behaviour and mindsets. Are any hidden ideas, mindsets, or thoughts coming to light as you read them? Are any insights about your approaches or behaviour sparked by these rules? Do you see how the actions of others may be based on these unconscious rules? Ideally, this information will allow you to see any false navigational guides you may be using and to better understand the invisible dynamics operating at work. The next chapter deals with the six different types of GBS and how to recognize and reduce them.

EXERCISE

QUESTIONNAIRE: MASCULINE/FEMININE STYLES

Read each statement carefully. If the statement describes you, circle T and if does not, circle F. As you respond, your frame of reference should be your approach at work. The purpose of this questionnaire is to create awareness of your use of masculine and feminine styles and your ability to use both flexibly. If you are uncertain as to your use, ask a trusted work colleague. The questions cover the skill areas of communication, leadership, presence, asking, politics, and self-promotion.

1. I can leave out details and get to the point. **T F**
2. In a group I like to fit in and not stand out. **T F**
3. I use openings such as "maybe it is just me" or "I guess my question is..." **T F**
4. I find it easy to negotiate for the things I want. **T F**
5. I wait my turn to talk and seldom interrupt. **T F**
6. I usually take what is offered to me. **T F**
7. I like to figure out who's who at work so I know who to get to know better. **T F**
8. I like to lead by example. **T F**
9. Negotiation is about getting what you want. **T F**
10. I feel more comfortable crossing my arms and legs when sitting in a chair. **T F**
11. My voice is loud and clear. **T F**
12. I feel uncomfortable talking about myself and let others do it for me. **T F**

13. When given an unrealistic deadline, I generally accept it and don't negotiate for something more realistic. **T F**

14. When I go into a negotiation I am confident I will get what I want. **T F**

15. I like to tell others how to determine goals and how to achieve them. **T F**

16. I consider politics a four-letter word. **T F**

17. I know who is influential in my group and the organization. **T F**

18. When I have done something exceptionally well, I call attention to it. **T F**

19. If interrupted in a meeting, I actively seek to take the floor back. **T F**

20. I have problems asking as I think I will be negatively perceived. **T F**

21. I have always assumed that my work speaks for itself. **T F**

22. I often motivate others by listening and letting them figure out the answers. **T F**

23. I like to give clear instructions about what needs to be done, how it should be done and by when. **T F**

24. When sitting at a conference table I sit tall with my elbows on the table. **T F**

25. I believe to lead well you have to put people first. **T F**

26. I am comfortable questioning or debating my colleague during a conversation. **T F**

27. I feel "braggy" when I talk about my achievements. **T F**

28. When in a group I try to stand out and be noticed. **T F**

29. I ask questions to gather information and to enhance the relationship. **T F**

30. I make sure that I tell others about my successes and wins. **T F**

31. I enjoy creating harmony in work teams to allow for greater morale and connection. **T F**

32. I avoid politics and think it involves too much gossip. **T F**

33. When I am acknowledged for a job well done I let my boss know about it. **T F**

34. I try to understand the rules of the game at work and how things really work. **T F**

35. I feel uncomfortable showcasing my skills. **T F**

36. When stressed in meetings I start to fidget and check my phone frequently. **T F**

To score the questionnaire, circle the question number below that you answered true (only T answers are scored), then add them up to determine which style you favour, if any. Please note that no one approach is better, however, in business a masculine approach is most often used and valued.

Style	Masculine	Feminine
Ask	4	6
	9	13
	14	20
Communicate	1	3
	19	5
	26	29
Presence	11	2
	24	10
	28	36
Lead	8	22
	15	25
	23	31
Promote	18	12
	30	27
	33	35
Politics	7	16
	17	32
	34	21
Total Score		

KEY TO SCORING

The ideal score is equal numbers of masculine and feminine style responses for each skill. The goal is to become androgynous, fluidly moving between masculine and feminine styles. If there is a large difference between styles in a particular skill category, you may wish to read the chapter on that skill first. If you are using one gender style predominately, you will benefit from trying the other style. [31] This will allow you to use them flexibly and contextually.

WANT TO READ MORE?

Banaji, Mahzarin R. and Anthony G. Greenwald. *Blind Spot: Hidden Biases of Good People.* New York: Delacourte Press, 2013.

Fine, Cordelia. *Delusions of Gender: How Our Minds, Society and Neurosexism Create Difference.* New York: W. W. Norton & Company, 2010.

Kahneman , D. *Thinking, Fast and Slow.* Toronto: DoubleDay Canada, 2011.

Myers, Jack. *The Future of Men: Masculinity in the Twenty-First Century.* New York: Inkshares, 2016.

Vedantam, Shankar. *The Hidden Brain: How our Unconscious Minds Elect Presidents, Control Markets, Wage Wars and Save Our Lives.* New York: Spiegel & Grau Trade Paperback, 2010.

EXPOSE

Gender blind spots significantly impact women at work. They create a disparity in the work experiences of men and women. They chill efforts by women to achieve career goals, cause them to stall, reduce their efforts, and even cause them to drop out. They negatively affect women's opportunities and hinder women in attaining leadership positions. Being able to recognize gender blind spots (GBS) allows you to keep moving forward, effectively deal with them, and reduce their power.

GBS are based on traditional gender roles and stereotypes: those artificial social constructs of masculine and feminine attributes that tell us how men and women should and should not behave. It is from these stereotypes that gender biases, limiting mindsets, gender habits, and gendered expectations are born. Behaviour that deviates from these stereotypes often causes feelings of discomfort in both the actor and the observer. Both people feel that something is not right because there has been a deviation from the expected script or pattern. And since these assumptions are often unconscious, we don't examine them or rationally challenge them.

So how does this play out at work when gender mismatch occurs? When women use masculine approaches, unconscious negative impressions are created. On the other hand, when women use feminine approaches they are not seen to be up to the job since the workplace tends to favour a masculine approach. Another consequence is that masculine behaviour is viewed totally differently for men and women. Masculine behaviour at work shown by men is a match with gender assumptions, so all is well. The same behaviour shown by women, even when effective, is not a match and thus is deemed unacceptable by others.

This double standard can be very confusing and frustrating for women who are not aware of the underlying bias. And motherhood, which places a woman fully within the societal construct of what is feminine, is often viewed as being out of synch or in conflict with work. The result? Many negative myths and biases about working mothers arise to disadvantage them.

This chapter examines GBS in detail. The six GBS of particular importance for women in the workplace include

- Common Biases (external and internal)
- Self-Limiting Mindsets (internal)
- Gender Habits and Rituals (internal)
- Misreading Gender Habits (external)
- Gendered Expectations (external)
- Negative Stereotype Threat (internal)

These six GBS include both external blind spots – the biases of others that affect how they treat us - and internal blind spots – personal biases that determine our own behaviour. Although external blind spots are the GBS most often highlighted, recognition of internalized gendered beliefs is also important. Recognition of all types of GBS is important so you can identify them and reduce their effects. It's good to recognize when you can deal with them, when they should be dealt with by others, and to be able to shine a light on them. This recognition also allows you to select career strategies to outplay and outwit GBS while waiting for a future that favours feminine approaches and characteristics. This chapter focusses on the career strategy, *Shine a Light*, while the next chapter, Plan, addresses all four career strategies.

TYPES OF GBS

COMMON GENDER BIASES

Many of the biases listed in this section are based on the same gender beliefs and stereotypes and thus the descriptions may seem to overlap. They are often subtle and not blatant, so the aim of these descriptions is to help you easily recognize these biases so you can bring them into the open for yourself and others. Although there are many biases described in this section, this list is not exhaustive.

Prove it Again. Studies show that for positions traditionally held by males, men are assumed to be competent but women have to prove their competence through achievements over and over again. This bias allows men to be promoted based on future potential while women are promoted on past performance. People who operate using gender stereotypes typically have low expectations of women at work and their potential. The saying that "women have to work twice as hard to get half as far" relates to this bias. This is supported by the experience of transgendered men and women who, having been both genders, report that being a man at work is so much easier.[32] Some women who recognize this bias learn to use it by playing into it. For example, they report their accomplishments and their team results to the CEO each and every quarter. They *go along to get along* and succeed.

The Tightrope. Acceptable behaviour for women in the workplace is narrower than for men since masculine rules are favoured and considered the norm. This bias underlies the tendency to label agreeable and collaborative women as not assertive enough or too feminine, and to label assertive women as aggressive, not collaborative, or too masculine. Many executive women I coach have been told they are too direct when they speak assertively. I offer suggestions for managing this behavioural tightrope in the chapters Ask and Communicate in this book.

Double-Standard. This bias is operating when the same behaviour from a man and a woman is judged differently, with the woman being judged negatively. Examples of double standards are: *she's aggressive and he's a go-getter; she's selfish and he's too busy; she's abrasive and he's incisive*; and *she's a shameless self-promotor and he knows his own worth.* From a women's perspective, it is also known as the *damned if you do and damned if you don't* gender bias. This can be the most damaging of all biases for women in leadership or seeking leadership positions due to association of leadership with the masculine. Paradoxically, research shows that leaders who use feminine styles are more effective.[33] Survey data collected in 2014 shows that the public prefers these leadership styles as well.[34]

The In-Group Bias. We have a natural preference for others that are like us, whether they look like us, share our interests and opinions, or have similar upbringings or educational backgrounds. This is a bias shown by everyone. This means that people are more likely to hire or promote others like them and overlook those who have a different background. As most leaders or gatekeepers in business are men, particularly in certain industries, the in-group bias leads to the same group of people being hired and promoted up the ranks.

Positional Bias. This gender bias operates by dividing men and women into different careers, professions, and positions based on traditional gender roles. As a result, it can affect both career advice and hiring. It is evident when career advice is based on external characteristics, such as race and gender, and not on a woman's strengths, talents, and interests. In law, for instance, Asian law students get counselled to work in corporate and finance areas. Female law students are generally steered away from litigation practice. This does not mean that advisors are trying to be unhelpful or have bad intent. Rather it is evidence of implicit bias.

We are all subject to this bias. Research shows that although we seem comfortable with female leaders in a variety of positions, we revert back to traditional gender roles for roles such as engineers, Fortune 500 executives, financial advisors, lawyers, or President of the United States.[35] This bias has been shockingly demonstrated on long-haul flights where female doctors are routinely treated with disdain and even hostility by cabin personnel. Highly trained physicians have been told to return to their seats or to remain in their seats after offering their help because the flight attendants refused to believe the women were doctors.[36] This particular blind spot makes it even more important to know how to manage and plan your own career.

Testosterone Rex. This is the false assumption that evolution, brains, hormones, and behaviour are responsible for sexual inequities. It's the notion that men evolved to be risk-taking and competitive for reproductive return, and these traits propel them to the top at work. And, as the logic goes, since sex differences are innate, this inequality cannot be changed. Counter to this assumption, there are no essential male or female characteristics. Using solid scientific evidence and meticulous reasoning in her entertaining books *Delusions of Gender* and *Testosterone Rex,* Cordelia Fine debunks ideas about gender differences and sexual inequities having their origins in biological differences. Angela Saini does the same in her book *Inferior.*[37]

Different means Lesser. This bias is based on the assumption that biological differences between the sexes translate into differences in innate cognitive skills and abilities. And by raising gendered differences we raise the unconscious assumption that women are not as capable as men.

When I first started teaching women's advancement courses there was pressure from other women not to talk about gender differences. It was based on a fear of this bias. Fast forward 15 years and scientific facts have dramatically debunked this bias. Meta-data analyzes show that there are no innate cognitive differences between men and women.[38] It appears that most, if not all, existing differences are grounded in gender training. And this cultural programming can be reversed. Some women have used this bias to their advantage by outplaying and outwitting those who are blinded (pun intended) to women's abilities and underestimate them (see details in the "Use It" section in this chapter).

Maternal Wall. Women who become mothers tend to face the worst career penalties. It is assumed they lose all career focus and interest now that they are mothers. The specific negative biases about women who become mothers include: they will put in less effort, be less motivated for advancement, and will prioritize home life over work life. In short, they will be less available to career demands than men or women without children. And if they aren't showing the appropriate amount of commitment to family, or are very committed to their careers, they are viewed as bad mothers. The tightrope bias of narrowly acceptable behaviour for women relates to motherhood as well. (For a full list of gender biases facing mothers, and the facts debunking each, see the section entitled "Maternal Break" in the next chapter, Plan).

A Woman's Place is in the Home. With all the women in the workplace you might think this bias is long gone. But you would be wrong and here is why. Most workplaces were initially created for a fully supported male worker - someone who had a wife to manage and organize the home. Despite huge changes in the make-up of the work force, organizations and society still operate on this assumption. The result? Working women are shouldering heavier responsibilities than ever (see the next section, "To Have It All, We Have to Do It All"). The psychological repercussions are that when men do housework, they feel they are helping out whereas when women do housework, they feel they are doing their job.

The assumption that a woman's place is in the home has other negative implications as well. Current research shows that males with wives at home have an unfavourable view of women in the workplace, think workplaces run less smoothly with more women, view workplaces with female leaders as less desirable, and consider female candidates for promotion to be less qualified than comparable male colleagues. Who are the males with the most resistance? Those populating the upper echelons and occupying the more powerful positions.[39]

To Have It All, We Have To Do It All. The false belief underlying this bias is also that a woman's place is in the home. Working women still do significantly more housework then men. Studies show that 76% of women who work still do the majority of housework, cooking (65% vs 39%), driving of children to events, scheduling of home repairs, and paying of bills (82% vs 65%).[40]

A related and equally pernicious belief is that to be successful at work means being a superstar at home. According to Time Magazine, approximately 80% of millennial moms believe that it is important to be the perfect mother.[41] This belief can create *Home Control Disease* – where women still focus obsessively on everything about the home and feel the compulsive need to ensure that it is all done their way.[42]

Sexual Harassment. It may seem odd to include this behaviour as a blind spot but it is due to the false assumption that it has disappeared from the workplace. Consequently, sexual harassment is not recognized when it occurs and is often overlooked. In some industries, such as tech and start-up companies like Uber, sexual harassment is rampant and goes unchecked.[43] The stories I hear as a coach make it clear that it is still very much around. And to add to the confusion, some leaders talk about sexual assault as if it were normal and not a serious criminal behaviour, or minimize it by calling it "locker room talk"or saying, "boys will be boys."

These biases set up significant invisible and visible hurdles at work and home that make it harder for working women to advance and succeed. Many of these biases are used to provide excuses for gender inequities. They create differences in how the same behaviour by men and women is perceived and the assumptions made about it. They create gaps in wages and the ability to advance. They cause women to focus their attention on how they are being perceived instead of allowing them to put that effort into doing the job. They make it difficult and sometimes impossible for women leaders to lead. They create and support a gap between numbers of men and women at the top of organizations. It is important to be able to recognize these biases in action, whatever the form, and be able to reduce their effects.

RECOGNIZE

Gender bias can take many forms in the workplace. Some of these biases are obvious and easy to spot in action: the same type of people being hired and/or promoted resulting in very little organizational diversity, the inability to see a woman in a leadership role regardless of how accomplished she is, and the idea that any behaviour - regardless of how sexist - is just "boys being boys."

Sometimes gender bias is at play through subtle differences in how women are treated. A current term for less obvious or subtle forms of discrimination is *microaggressions*. These forms of discrimination can include objective rules being applied strictly to women but leniently to men; the attribution of an idea to a man although made by a woman; constant interruptions of women in meetings; and the acceptance of women when it makes work life easier and more comfortable for men. It may even include a difference for men and women in the amount of informal feedback.[44]

Another form of *microaggression* is mansplaining. This is when men explain something to women - usually something the women already know - slowly and with simple words. And as ridiculous as it sounds, it is common. Fifty percent of women report being mansplained at least once a day and it is estimated that this annoying behaviour costs $200 billion a year in lost revenue.[45] Please don't be fooled by the descriptors subtle or micro. Current research shows the negative effects of subtle gender bias on career success and satisfaction, stress, turnover, performance, and physical and mental health symptoms are as bad as, if not worse than, overt discrimination.[46]

So how do you recognize gender bias? The process below sets out three steps for revealing unconscious bias. It requires the help of a slow and careful neural processing system in the analysis of evidence and data. Objective facts versus subjective perspectives allow for exposure. Note that this process works for uncovering others' biases as well as our own.

A Process for Identifying Unconscious Bias

Recognize	When actions or decisions of others are blatantly unfair or discriminatory against you, you will likely know. Micro-aggressions may be more difficult to spot so if you are feeling isolated, discouraged, or disconnected, start watching for hints of subtle bias and unfair treatment. Confirmation by others, such as colleagues, both to bias and micro-aggressions is often valuable to ensure that you are correct. It is also crucial to pay attention to your own thoughts, decisions, and actions for signs of bias.
Evaluate	Where an action or decision does not seem fair, examine the decision or action objectively. (Such decisions can include awarding bonuses, promotion, hiring, assignment of a special project, or an appointment to a committee). What impact does this decision or action have on an individual? Does it negatively influence the perceptions of others about this individual? What are the facts or hard evidence that support it? Is it based on evidence or on a subjective assumption?
Confirm	Ask others if they would have made the same decision. Do they think that the decision was biased in any way? Are they able to validly challenge your thinking about this? Ensure that you have all the facts and information. There may be facts or additional evidence that change your evaluation.

REDUCE

Diversity training does not appear to reduce gender bias. In fact, early indications are that such training makes it worse by allowing bias to be excused and gender inequities normalized.[47] Clearly, understanding bias does not automatically provide tools for dealing with it, but it does suggest certain techniques.

Different techniques from multiple sources are put forward in this section. The first three - name it, question it, and correct it - are used in negotiation to neutralize or counter competitive tactics. Competitive tactics are employed in negotiation to create an advantage for the person using them. Since gender bias also provides an unfair advantage for the person using it, even if used unconsciously, it is appropriate to use strategies that counter such effects.

Name It. The best way to reduce the impact of gender biases is by recognizing and exposing them. If you see something, say something. You might say, "This type of behaviour is standard in this department. Why are you calling me aggressive? This sounds like a double-standard." Name the bias and challenge its use. For example, a woman's reputation has been shown to take a hit by helping other women. As a woman, mentioning this bias while you advocate for another woman reduces the effect of the bias. Interestingly, a man's reputation is enhanced when he helps women, so if you are a man reading this, know that helping women helps you.[48] Naming a bias or microaggression to help others is a wonderful way to use social intelligence and to increase it.

Question It. This technique involves exposing the bias by questioning it. If you have had enough of mansplaining you may question the behaviour in the moment or later in the person's office. Ask calmly and put the onus squarely on them by saying something like, "What makes you think that I don't understand this concept or this material?" You may want to ask them how they would respond in your situation to such behaviour. The intent here is to make them explain (not mansplain) why they are treating you in a biased manner. The point of questioning is to show how irrational the behaviour is.

Correct It. It can be helpful to explain the disconnect between facts and a decision or action. Where a woman has been passed over for promotion due to the same type of behaviour that supports a man's promotion, challenge the decision. Use an objective assessment or data. It may also involve pointing out the advantages obtained by others based on the biased decision or action. By using objective and hard data, the bias will be revealed for what it is – incorrect and unfair, benefiting some and not all.

It often takes great courage to name, question, or correct biases. There tends to be a disconnect between a company's stated priority for diversity and what employees see being done. For example, 70% of companies say they are committed to diversity but less than a third of their workers see senior leaders held accountable for improving gender outcomes. Similarly, over 90% of companies report using clear, objective criteria for hiring and promotions but only half of female employees believe they have equal opportunities for growth. Due to this disconnect, many employees are afraid to address bias head on. If less than a quarter of employees see their managers regularly challenge gender biased language or behaviour, it makes sense that employees are reluctant to do so.[49]

Although there appears to be a recent surge in awareness about the GBS of unconscious bias, people aren't being shown how to have courageous conversations. So if you are afraid to expose a bias or challenge a decision or action based on it, it is understandable. Wait until you feel comfortable and, until that time, consider using some of the following strategies instead.

Building alliances. Talking with others who agree and support you will make it easier to have courageous conversations about gender bias; you not only get support but you also harness the power of the collective. Talk with and enlist colleagues, sponsors, and mentors, possibly including people with seniority and influence in the organization. With others supporting you and confirming your view, it will be easier to be brave. You may want to approach someone in HR. Typically, but not always, this is a group that is very aware of, and sensitive to, gender bias and sexual discrimination, particularly when it is overt.

Third Party Questioning. Having outsiders challenge the lack of diversity in a company and point out how this bias handicaps the organization can be an effective way to shine a bright light on gender bias. The firm I worked for as a lawyer was sensitive to the vast number of women who were corporate counsel and ensured that files were staffed with women. If a client challenged the lack of diversity of an all-male team, the critique would be heard and changes made. In the process of publishing this book and creating a new website, I used my power as a client to ask to work with women. They were available in each case. And if they had not been available, I would have questioned why not. Women helping women is a great way to start to be a part of the change.

Use Behavioural Design. Studies have shown that gender blind assessment and the use of objective criteria in hiring practices result in the selection of more women. Symphonies had a scarcity of women musicians until screens were introduced in the auditioning process in the 1970s resulting in gender blind auditions. The result was a rise in the percentage of women in orchestras from less than 5% to over 35% today.[50] Similar results have occurred with gender blind assessment of software coding showing that when people are assessed on pure ability, women are more likely to make the cut.[51] Iris Bohnet in her book *What Works: Gender Equality by Design* argues that in addition to women's empowerment initiatives, solutions from behavioural design should be used. This includes replacing intuition, informal networks, and traditional rules of thumb with quantifiable data and rigorous analysis. Many corporations are now operating their HR departments like their finance or marketing departments – based on evidence. Their HR departments have become people analytics departments. Using this approach of objective and gender blind assessment will greatly help reduce the effect of gender bias in the selection and promotion of individuals.

Use Technology. Anti-bias apps now exist to circumvent unconscious gender bias. For example, *Textio* scans job postings and flags phrases that would repel women; *Gap-Jumpers* hides identifying information until job applicants perform a skill test; *Blendoor* allows job seekers to check out recruiters on diversity ratings while recruiters get to see the skills and experience of job seekers without information about sex, race, or age; and *Unitive* guides managers through the hiring process and finds ways to prevent them from acting on bias. Look for ways to incorporate technology so that decisions will be gender blind.

Use it. This strategy entails recognizing gender bias and using it to your advantage. It has been called "stereotype tax" by Annie Duke, a poker player, to refer to male poker players who are so blinded by gender bias that they underestimate a woman's abilities. The result? She wins! And what works in poker works in negotiation. Examples from negotiation include: being relentlessly pleasant, using the iron fist in a velvet glove tactic, using cooperative strategies, and invoking relational and communal approaches. Some women in C-suites routinely send a list of their recent results and that of their team to their CEO every six months. They openly recognize they were hired to produce results.[52] This strategy of playing into the bias or stereotype works best where: the organization is unlikely to change anytime soon, it is very unlikely you can create change on your own, you need your job and fear penalties if you speak out, or you don't feel comfortable using the other strategies discussed.

This strategy is not for everyone, so if it feels disingenuous, use one of the others described here.

Try Humour. A senior business woman attending a seminar on leadership told the group that she deals with gender bias and inappropriate comments by saying in a lighthearted tone, "Do I have to call the diversity police?" She says it does the trick and makes the offender aware they have crossed a line. The use of humour can be tricky as it can easily turn into sarcasm or even anger, so tone is important. To appear lighthearted, you might want to try divorcing the substance of the comment from the demeanor. A C-suite woman from a very male dominated industry revealed to me that she often used competitive language with a smile and a laugh. Although she may have been issuing a command or demand, her tone and non-verbal language were not threatening. Imagine a light tone used with the phrase, "ah, the lovely smell of testosterone in the morning" followed by a light chuckle. Or "are you still using that outdated command and control approach?" If you know your audience and do it in a socially intelligent way, it can be a great way to signal that the behaviour is not appropriate while showing you are a good sport about it all. This is social intelligence at its finest.

Persuade them. Use principles of persuasion to change biased policies or procedures. If the person you need to persuade adheres to principles of fairness, use that in the discussion. If they are persuaded by economics, use the bottom line or data showing cost savings or profit. If they are swayed by efficacy, then prove your contribution with data showing your results. If they are swayed by what others think or do, use social proof. You might even use unconscious triggers of persuasion as they are very powerful tools.[53]

Disrupt. The essence of this approach is to act as if the future has arrived and GBS don't exist. In the "Trainwreck Files," Sady Doyle says that Hillary Clinton has always acted as if a woman could be the President of the United States.[54] Women who are disrupters move us forward by living possibilities and not accepting the limitations of the present. They let us believe that change is possible. To be a disruptor is not easy; society often takes many years, sometimes hundreds of years, to catch up to the change. One current example of potent gender disruption is shown by young people who insist on non-binary gender identification.[55] Disruption is one of the four career strategies I put forward in the chapter Plan.

For more suggestions on how to expose and defeat gender bias, I strongly recommend Jessica Bennett's insightful and witty book *Feminist Fight Club: An Office Survival Manual (For a Sexist Workplace).* If you are like me, the cover alone will have you smiling.

IMPORTANT INSIGHTS ON RECOGNIZING AND REDUCING GENDER BIAS

- Be open to recognizing bias in yourself. We are all socialized with traditional gender norms to some degree. No one is immune.
- Do not excuse or normalize bias even though we are all complicit. It is discriminatory and creates an unfair advantage for one group.
- Treat people as individuals and avoid automatic assumptions based on their race, gender, age, sexual orientation or other identity markers that categorize them as a member of a particular group.
- Replace subjective methods for decision-making such as intuition, informal networks, and traditional rules of thumb with the use of objective and quantifiable data.
- Establish clear, transparent, and objective criteria for making decisions about salary, bonuses, promotions, and hiring.
- Recognize that unconscious gender bias does not necessarily align with openly held beliefs. Most people openly agree with gender parity but are biased.

- Be aware that biases flourish when decisions are rushed and competition is high. Allow adequate time for making decisions and reduce competition between employees.
- Sponsor, mentor, and coach employees who are not like you.
- Get curious about others and avoid assumptions based on external characteristics.
- Know that attempts to reduce bias by suppression or repression are not effective and may amplify them.
- Remember that biases are not permanent – they can be changed with intention, attention, and new facts.

SELF-LIMITING MINDSETS

Self-limiting gender mindsets are based on internalized gender beliefs that result in women putting limits on themselves. They are unconscious admonitions and injunctions about what women should or should not do. They prevent women from trying things at work or developing skills that will advance their careers because they violate a gender rule or stereotype. Here is an example from coaching that illustrates the powerful and often puzzling effects of these GBS.

A woman with an important interview coming up approached me for coaching. She found it challenging to talk about herself in interviews. Even stating the facts of her accomplishments was difficult; she always responded by saying that everything was in her resumé. As a prominent lawyer who had coached many young lawyers, she had great confidence generally, so this limitation was especially puzzling. When asked about her childhood, she revealed that from a very young age she had been taught that humility was essential and bringing attention to herself was sinful. With this one powerful insight, she was able to overcome her issue and talk easily about herself in the interview.

Self-limiting mindsets often generate feelings of discomfort that prevent us from acting. These mindsets can cause us to downplay our credentials or give us the sense we are imposters so that our skills, talents, and experiences are never sufficient for whatever is required.

Self-limiting mindsets often result in missed opportunities at work. They, unfortunately, lend credence to the perception that women lack confidence, motivation, and ambition. So in addition to being passed over due to gender bias, women are less likely to raise their hands for a job or promotion. They might pass on a leadership position because they don't think they can lead. Women have to be asked to run for elected office a total of six times before seriously considering it.[56] There are many good reasons why women choose to scale back their career ambition such as personal goals, stage of life, or responsibilities. However, the limits women place on themselves are ingrained through gender training and prevent them from taking on positions with more responsibility or asking for opportunities.

Another way a mindset can hinder and limit working women is through gender beliefs about what they should be doing. These beliefs, often transmitted from mother to daughter, take the form of women believing that they have to do everything at home and that it won't be done right or managed well enough by others. Tiffany Dufu describes this particular mindset in her book *Drop the Ball: Achieving More by Doing Less*. She even gives it a name -- Home Control Disease.[57] This can allow women to sense they have control and power when feeling powerless. However, this mindset and behaviour often results is the opposite effect - feeling even more out of control and powerless. As Tiffany and other women have realized, trying to do it all is impossible.

Self-limiting beliefs often seem valid and correct to the holder as they get confirmed through the holder's selective perception and memory of events, experiences, and information. This is called confirmation bias. In other words, we see and remember what we believe. This bias makes self-limiting mindsets very difficult to recognize.

RECOGNIZE

One important way to recognize a self-limiting mindset, particularly as it relates to career skills, is through feelings of discomfort. If you experience these as you engage in a skill that is advantageous for you to develop, reflect on the situation. If the feelings don't make sense or are out of proportion for the situation, these feelings are most likely based on outdated associations and messages from childhood.

The hardest part of changing your mindset is recognizing your underlying beliefs. Tiffany Dufu made a realization about her own limiting gender belief, House Control Disease, when her husband gave her a book by Allison Pearson, *I Don't Know How She Does it*. The main character was so familiar that a light bulb went on and Tiffany recognized herself as having the same struggles. Often others can more clearly see the mindsets and outdated beliefs we operate by, just as we are able to see theirs. If you are struggling to find a hidden gender belief that is limiting you, ask a trusted friend, mentor, or close family member. They will know.

REDUCE AND REPLACE

Sometimes all it takes is a flash of insight to illuminate the limiting mindset and cause a behavioural reset. Often it requires more. Using the analogy of cultural training as computer programming, new coding is required. Detection of the malicious code and replacement with a functional one - one that allows you to think differently – requires some work on your part. Your beliefs are yours, you have control over them and what you have learned, you can relearn. You can replace limiting mindsets with others that are beneficial for your success.

If you feel uncomfortable doing an activity although you know objectively it would be good for you to do, try to identify why you have the discomfort. Once you have identified the beliefs that are limiting you and causing uneasiness, write them down. Make them visible and conscious.

Then select a new belief that is more realistic, beneficial, and suitable. Write it down. It might be the belief that telling others about your accomplishments is important as it makes your value visible.

Remind yourself that a belief is just an idea or thought that you keep repeating and reinforcing. Beliefs shape your behaviour and your judgement. Imagine what it would feel like holding the new belief. Think about how much easier the activity would be, how good it would feel, and how you might behave differently.

Beliefs shape our behaviour and structure learning experiences. With new beliefs we do different things, see different things, and remember different things.

Once you recognize that beliefs are subjective and can be changed, you can start to look for tools that support your new beliefs. With the realization that your beliefs are creating assumptions and attitudes that don't work, you are on the way to changing them.

GENDER HABITS AND RITUALS

Unconscious gender habits are approaches, responses, and behaviour we learn as children through gender training and use as adults, often without awareness. Gender habits can be very detrimental to a work reputation. During a communication seminar a woman shared a recent experience she had with a gender habit. After she had finished a presentation at work, a colleague told her that she had added "Okay?" after every single slide. Interestingly, she was totally unaware of doing it. This is a clear example of an unconscious gender habit appearing under stress. In this instance asking "Okay?" was about connecting with the audience and getting their approval. The audience, made up of men and women, most likely went away with the impression that the presenter was unsure about the substance of her presentation.

It is not just feminine style habits that can get in the way. Masculine style habits have the potential to alienate the speaker from the audience - such as acting overly confident, being too much of an expert, not connecting with the audience, or winning points at the audience's expense. So it is important to be aware of your particular gender habits so that you can recognize when they occur and stop them from creating negative impressions.

RECOGNIZE

Feminine habits are often difficult to recognize because they tend to be used unconsciously and often when we are under stress. They tend to be our default mode and make us feel comfortable. Unfortunately, they can also reinforce gender bias and play into gender stereotypes. So it is important to be aware of what they are and how they can show themselves at work. Some common ones include

- Not asking
- Taking up less space physically
- Using tentative language patterns
- Avoiding conflict
- Blaming yourself for failure
- Negotiating well for others but not yourself
- Avoiding leadership positions
- Not self-promoting

- Asking questions for rapport not information
- Avoiding office politics

In contrast, masculine habits include[58]

- Trying to win all the time
- Interrupting others
- Acting overconfident and appearing entitled
- Making destructive comments
- Using bantering to communicate
- Preferring command and control style leadership
- Using expansive postures to signal authority
- Negotiating well for self-interests
- Knowing and aligning with the goals of the organization
- Telling others about successes and wins
- Blaming others for failures

You may have noticed in reading the lists that not all of the habits are detrimental. Gender habits are neither good nor bad – right nor wrong. They depend on the situation and the people involved. And because humans are complex, males and females display both masculine and feminine habits. The habits we have depend on our upbringing, the messages we received, the role models we had, and the images we saw.[59]

So how do you become aware of your particular gender habits? Like the woman who added "Okay?" to each slide discussion, you may be fortunate to have colleagues who tell you about your habits. If not, ask. Perhaps the habit involves tentative language patterns that don't synch with your otherwise confident professional demeanor. Perhaps it relates to negotiating well for others but not for yourself. Whatever it might be, find out.

REDUCE

Each skill chapter of this book aims to help you become aware of gender habits you may have. Once you have identified them, you can consciously reduce those that may be getting in the way of your career success and advancement. Gender habits can also be a great strength when used contextually and consciously, so being able to identify beneficial ones is also important.

MISREADING GENDER HABITS

Gender habits and approaches from one gender culture are interpreted by members of the other gender culture based on the rules they learned in childhood. Consequently, such habits are often misread and misinterpreted. Since status and achievement are paramount in masculine culture while relationships are key in female gender culture, feminine behaviours often suggest a lack of confidence when viewed through masculine lenses: behaviours such as being modest, not bragging about successes or promotions, working to fit in with the group, and reducing physically are all behaviours that run counter to showing higher status.

To be clear, such behaviour rarely has anything to do with a lack of confidence, competence, skill, talent, intelligence, or ability, and everything to do with gendered patterns that are learned in childhood.

To illustrate the confusion that can result, a coaching client who is a director of communication and marketing in a tech company worked quickly and quietly behind the scenes to create presentations and videos that were consistently rated as excellent not only by the employees of the company but by the executives as well. She was therefore puzzled and hurt when one executive, with whom she had a wonderful relationship, advised her that she needed to make her value more visible. In his opinion she needed to do a victory lap after a great presentation and in failing to do so, she appeared to lack self-assurance. My client was puzzled, confused, and even offended until I explained his masculine perspective. Making her value visible to others in the organization would not be achieved only by getting the work done well but also by ensuring others were aware of it. According to her colleague, she needed to promote her accomplishments to be accorded the status she was due.

RECOGNIZE

To help you understand and recognize this type of blind spot, I have listed some common masculine misinterpretations of feminine behaviours revealed by clients below.

- Being new on the job and asking questions of a male boss was the method used by one of my clients to build rapport with him. When he told her that she seemed to lack the knowledge and competence that he knew she had, she came to me to figure out what was going on.
- The only woman manager at an aeronautics plant was a great puzzle to all the other managers as she negotiated the highest salaries in the company for her team but the lowest for herself. They could not figure out why she showed such inconsistent negotiation skills.
- One woman in a seminar told me that she prefaced all of her questions with "this may be a dumb question" or "it may just be me ..." to avoid any pushback and ribbing from her male colleagues. When she realized that they most likely viewed her as uncertain and lacking in confidence as a result, she decided on the spot to drop the preface and instead deal head on with any possible pushback.
- The only woman on a professional panel consisting of older men started her presentation by downplaying her experience in comparison to the illustrious panel. A male in the audience

took her literally and later prefaced a question to her with an explanation of a very well-known legal case. The female audience members who recognized the mansplaining told me they gasped audibly as the man asked his question.

Many feminine habits are often misinterpreted as a sign of low confidence, or even of low competence, using masculine norms. In my experience this misinterpretation of a lack of confidence is the number one reason women are referred for coaching by corporations and firms.

This is a true clash of gender cultures when those who value the group (as well as input, feedback, feelings, and ideas) are viewed by those who value individual achievement and status as lacking in self-confidence and personal power. And since these judgements come from fast processing, the misinterpretations are often made quickly and unconsciously. That is, the assessor may not even know what behaviours were involved but the overall impression is a lack of confidence or competence. And the impression is typically very strong and lasting.

REDUCE

The skill chapters in this book provide information about feminine habits that are frequently misread and misinterpreted, together with tools and techniques for behavioural change. Information about feminine gender habits is provided so you will feel less frustrated and more in control as you anticipate gender bias and manage impressions. These skills will ensure that when you speak, lead, or negotiate you are doing so in the most effective way and you can avoid triggering any gender stereotypes that will lessen your power, message, or brand. This information will allow you to recognize and reduce any habits that may get in the way of others seeing you as competent, confident, and socially intelligent.

GENDERED EXPECTATIONS

Expectations of appropriate gender behaviour based on gender stereotypes are very powerful. They are so powerful that they cause male basketball players to act irrationally and throw foul shots in the least effective way. Almost every single basketball player in the NBA uses the overarm technique, a technique that is far less effective than the alternative – the underarm shot. The latter method involves shooting from between the knees and flicking the wrists. It allows for more control of the ball and statistically is much more successful. Wilt Chamberlain, a famous American basketball player and holder of numerous NBA records in scoring, rebounding and durability, stopped using the underarm shot despite improving his stats of successful shots from under 40% to over 60% in just one game. When asked why he stopped using it, he said, "I felt silly. I felt like a sissy even though I knew it was wrong not to use it." Interestingly the underarm method is called the "granny shot" and tends to be viewed with disdain by the crowd. And Wilt is not alone in feeling the pressure. All NBA players (except for one) currently use the less effective method of foul shooting in a sport that is all about making shots.[60]

The power of gendered expectations also caused female students at Harvard Business School (HBS) to adopt less academically successful behaviour. Research shows that the women who started out with equal academic and career achievements to the men received significantly fewer academic honours upon graduation than their male classmates received. What was the difference in behaviour between men and women? Although the women prepared more for class than the men, they participated less. The reason? In order to balance social and professional relationships, many women admitted to self-editing in the classroom to manage their out-of-classroom image. They did not want to violate traditional feminine stereotypes by arguing forcefully in class.[61] Bright young women censored themselves so they would not be disliked outside the classroom.

The power of gendered expectations is not just psychological. Research shows that when women act in a way that is counter to gendered expectations they may also experience social and economic sanctions.[62] Assertive women were found to receive lower wages and fewer promotions than assertive men. And the managers responsible for such promotions and wage increases were found to be totally unaware of this sanctioning – showing yet again the unconscious nature of these GBS. Similar economic sanctions, although less severe, were found to apply to men who were friendly, relationship-focused, and cooperative (gender atypical traits). Thus, implicit gender bias affects both men and women in the workplace when they act counter to gendered expectations.

RECOGNIZE

Recognizing gendered expectations and understanding the potential consequences of violating them allows you to anticipate these biases and respond more appropriately. The following is a list of situations where the women recognized in real time the gendered expectations being placed on them and were able to respond well.

- A young woman lawyer who asked for a higher starting salary *based on the criteria used by the organization* was met with an "awkward silence." She recognized the reason and held firm during the negotiation.
- A group of junior women recognized that their supervisors - men with wives at home - did not provide work to them due to their different lifestyle choice of working. As a result, they looked for work elsewhere.
- A female executive was told during a performance evaluation that she was too direct in her communication style and should

learn from other women in her company how to communicate less directly. She challenged the assessment citing examples of males at her level who were even more direct.

· A brilliant young student was advised by a high school teacher that she was too aggressive and that boys would not like her. She was undeterred by this traditional gender advice and went on to become a successful criminal defense lawyer who has managed to use her competitive nature to great advantage.

Being conscious of gendered expectations and understanding the perspective of others is a powerful way to change these GBS, as well as a great start to becoming socially intelligent and politically savvy.

REDUCE

The same strategies that work to reduce and diminish the effect of gender bias allow you to respond well to gendered expectations. Early identification and selecting the best counter strategy for the situation are key. You may decide to name it and correct it: "There seems to be a double standard operating here. There are many men who are Senior VPs that are even more direct than I am." You may decide to reduce its power by questioning it: "You seem to be taken aback by my asking for a fair salary based on your own criteria. Why is that?" Or you may talk to others about it and build alliances for change.

Still another way to deal with expectations is to consciously play into them. Learn to ask in a way that is gender typical. Numerous examples are provided in the chapter Ask. Employ words associated with a feminine approach to align with other's expectations. Use "we" instead of "me." Wherever possible, ask what you can do for them. Talk about your team or colleagues and how much you enjoy working with them. This strategy is the opposite of disrupting whereby you make others comfortable by behaving in expected ways – you consciously *go along to get along*.

NEGATIVE STEREOTYPE THREAT

A negative stereotype threat (NST) occurs when a gender stereotype negatively influences a woman's cognitive performance. This is a true mind bug. When people are faced with a cognitively challenging task and they identify with a social group that does poorly on that task, they perform poorly. The perceived threat activates emotional brain regions, which in turn raises stress levels and interferes with attention and concentration. Not surprisingly, performance suffers. An NST can be based on race, socioeconomic status, age, gender, or a combination of these.

Research shows that both female and male performance can be selectively affected by bringing gender identity to the fore, including describing sex differences in performance at the beginning of test sessions. A classic example involved giving women a math test after reminding them that women aren't as good at math as men are. The result was that women consistently underperformed. When no description was provided about performance, men and women had the same level of results.

The tasks that activate gender NSTs are those generally thought to show gender differences in performance, such as verbal and social sensitivity tasks for men, and math and mental rotational ability for women. However, the research showing cognitive sex differences is being challenged by the examination of other factors, such as age and culture, and the use of meta-analysis.[63] Based on this, it appears that gender stereotypes create cognitive sex differences rather than the other way around.

Of particular concern is the finding that the effects of a stereotype threat may emerge as early as kindergarten.[64] Still another disturbing finding is that an NST can be activated in women using subtle cues, including: having to indicate your gender on a form before a test session, being the only female in the room, experiencing the implicit sexist bias of an instructor, and watching "air-head" females in commercials. And subtle triggers have a greater effect than blatant cues.[65] Thus, NSTs may be more of an issue now than they were decades ago when blatant discrimination was more prevalent. It has even been suggested that NSTs may account for generally elevated stress levels in working women.[66]

How does an NST play out in the day-to-day work environment? If you notice you are the only woman on a team heading into a boardroom you may start to have thoughts about your worthiness, skills, and abilities even without being aware you are having them. Gender training and fast processing cause you to think thoughts that accord with negative stereotypes about women.

In addition to diminishing performance, NSTs have also been found to activate a defensive mindset. A person may become cautious, careful, and conservative in an attempt to avoid failure, and cease being bold, innovative, and creative.

A new NST that I am seeing in young women who are coaching clients is the negative stereotype associated with age. Young millennial women are worried that when they question their career choice or their fit within an organization they are seen as a "typical complaining and lazy millennial." As a result of this NST based on age, they are paralyzed to move on or to consciously analyze their situation to make good choices. Negative stereotypes are never helpful, so early recognition is key to stopping the impact and effect of this type of threat.

RECOGNITION

The belief that you will not do well on a task for no rational reason is a sign of an NST. This belief will likely cause anxiety and may stop you from doing the task altogether. The triggering of an NST can be subtle and so anticipating where it can arise and noting when your performance level dips are good places to start looking for it. Do you have a pattern of lowered performance that is inexplicable? Get curious and figure out why. The reason may be an NST.

Another sign of an NST is feeling like an imposter. Women tell me this feeling arises when they are the only woman in a meeting. They feel they will be exposed as a fraud. When in the grip of this thinking, the defensive mindset is activated; women hesitate to be bold and creative and instead hold back on higher order cognitive functions to fit in.

Another trigger for an NST is exposure to the masculine habit of testing. Males tend to strive to know where everyone ranks in terms of status and achievement. Due to gender bias, it is generally assumed that women rank one down. This masculine tendency to test, coupled with a lack of women at senior levels in most organizations, can easily create psychological feelings of isolation and low self-worth – fertile ground for the activation of an NST. Once you recognize when you are being tested, it will make it easier to avoid having negative thoughts about yourself and prevent an NST.

REDUCE

The reason early recognition is so important is that once the emotional brain is activated by an NST, it is difficult to deal with it using mental will alone. Cognitive control of the emotional brain is almost impossible and trying to suppress or dismiss negative thoughts uses precious mental resources, distracting you from the task at hand. In short, suppression makes it worse. When you are in that skittish, anxious space, try to take a break - go to the washroom or get a coffee. As you do this, clear your mind and focus on your breath. In other words, meditate. Meditation has been shown to be an effective way of dealing with negative thoughts and extreme emotions. As you relax, your concentration and focus will improve.

The best ways to reduce the effects of NSTs are to anticipate and prevent them. Here are research-based suggestions for doing this.[67]

- *Identify with a high-status group.* When individuals feel secure in their abilities and comfortable about their place in the group, they have less stress and can concentrate on tasks with ease. NST research confirms that individuals primed to identify with higher status groups, even when they belong to low status groups, perform better.[68] So focus on those aspects that elevate you: your intelligence, skills, experience, potential, and talent. If you have a senior position, focus on the status you have. If you have an advanced educational degree or degrees, focus on your level of education. This is a strategy used by people as they age. Age bias is the strongest negative bias and research shows that people avoid NST as they age by not seeing themselves as old but instead identifying with younger groups.[69] If this sounds like a weak strategy, remember that we are dealing with an irrational mind bug and this approach does outsmart it.
- *Anticipate and Debunk.* Approach tasks associated with gender NSTs as calmly as you can and recognize anxiety as being due to NSTs and not as a reflection of your abilities. Arm yourself beforehand with the facts about those tasks and skills so you don't buy into false negative gender stereotypes. For example, a feminine approach is often most effective in negotiation and leadership despite the widespread belief that a masculine style is superior for these skills.
- *Reframe the Situation.* Think of the task as a way to improve your abilities, expand your skills, and enhance your experience. This frames the task as a positive experience rather than a negative one in which you won't do well.
- *Disrupt Negative Gender Stereotypes.* Surround yourself with powerful and positive women, and seek mentors who support

your success. Being around such women will change the unconscious negative stereotypes you hold – stereotypes that have been
transmitted to you during childhood and are no longer valid.

In order to reduce gender NSTs at a societal level, rigorous scientific
studies are needed to debunk research that claims cognitive sex differences. Furthermore, successful women need to be showcased to create
positive images and new gender associations for boys and girls. By dispel-
ling the myth of gender differences, we can provide new associations for
the fast processing system of generations to come.

CAREER STRATEGIES

It is understandable if you feel frustrated or overwhelmed in reading
about these many forms of GBS. Be reassured that just by becoming
aware of them you are on your way to successfully dealing with them.
The next chapter, Plan, sets out four career strategies for dealing with
GBS to help you better navigate the gender minefield at work.

The interest and passion of men and women at all levels to make gender
parity a reality is encouraging. Here are some practical suggestions in
working towards this goal.

WHAT ORGANIZATIONS, LEADERS, AND MENTORS CAN DO

COMMIT TO GENDER PARITY

- Hold yourself and your organization accountable for improving gender outcomes.
- Open the door to women. Put them in senior roles and give them the support to succeed.

- Be open to feedback and learning about implicit bias – gender, race, and age.
- Be a role model and confront inequities head on through organizational strategies.
- Call out any biased practices, policies, or behaviour. Shine a light on any that penalize or disadvantage women. If you are silent you are complicit.
- Encourage a culture of courageous conversations and exposing biases.
- Be part of the movement to sign the Women's Empowerment Principles, an initiative of UN Women, and the UN Global Compact to guide businesses in promoting gender equality.
- When gender differences in promotions, salary, performance evaluations, and leadership positions exist, figure out why. Use data.
- Ensure a metric of equality – make success measurable and attainable.
- Level the playing field when hiring by removing demographic information from job applications and using objective tests and structured interviews to assess candidates.

CHAMPION WOMEN

- Sponsor women colleagues. Use your influence to advocate for them, speak up for them, and support their advancement in your organization.
- Showcase women who have succeeded, making their success obvious and ensuring that women are well-represented at each level.
- Appoint highly qualified women to the higher levels of leadership in your organization including executive teams, corporate boards, managing partners, and C-suite positions.

- Ask women what would make them feel more included.
- Conduct exit interviews for women. Include questions about what made them feel included, anything that made them feel excluded, and what can be done to specifically attract and retain women.
- Use microaffirmations on a daily basis that recognize an individual's value and contribution.

WANT TO READ MORE?

Bennett, Jessica. *Feminist Fight Club: An Office Survival Manual (For a Sexist Workplace)*. New York: Harper Wave, 2016.

Bohnet, Iris. *What Works: Gender Equality by Design*. Cambridge: Belknap Press of Harvard University Press, 2016.

Fine, Cordelia. *Testosterone Rex: Myths of Sex, Science and Society*. New York: W. W. Norton & Company, 2017.

Goldsmith, Marshall. *What Got You Here Won't Get You There*. New York: Hachette Books, 2016.

PLAN

I was persuaded by young women to include a chapter in this book on career planning. The reason? The career advice they have received has largely been based on their external characteristics and not on their individual interests and strengths. They have experienced positional bias, which is bias that comes from the faulty belief that certain groups are better suited to specific positions.

I received advice based on positional bias 30 years ago when I wanted to practice litigation and ended up in commercial real estate. At the time, I did not recognize the advice for what it was. In a similar vein, women in finance are being advised not to go into investment banking and capital markets. This does not mean that advisors are trying to be unhelpful or have bad intent. Rather it is evidence of implicit bias. This gender blind spot (GBS) makes it important to know how to manage and plan your career.

Another significant factor making career management and planning imperative for everyone, not only women, is rapid change. We are living in a time of rapid shifts in business. New services and products rapidly become ubiquitous – disrupting and making obsolete the old way of doing things. How did we ever live without smart phones? It seems like computers have been around forever. The cycle for new products, ideas and services has become shorter and shorter. And this impacts the landscape of work and employment. The average employee tenure now is four to five years. For workers aged 25 to 34 years of age it drops to three years.[70] Positions that you hold now may not exist in five years, and positions that you will hold in five years most likely don't exist now. The only thing that is certain is change. So how do you plan and manage your career with such accelerated change? Is it even possible?

Not only is it possible to navigate the accelerated pace of change, but learning to do so provides a significant advantage. Having a road map allows you to identify when changes are necessary and determine how to leverage your skills in a positive and knowledgeable way. Having the right tools and techniques (T&T) for assessing and making career changes and corrections allows you to reap the rewards of flexibility, freedom, and opportunity.

In this chapter, four career strategies for dealing with GBS are discussed, as well as three key stages in career management including the initial years, maternity pause, and finding the right fit.

CAREER STRATEGIES: TOOLS AND TECHNIQUES (T&T)

The selection and use of the four career strategies set out in this section can be based on objective factors such as age and stage, profession, position, and workplace, as well as subjective factors including feelings of discomfort or frustration, personality preferences, and natural traits. You may use one consistently, or mix it up, using different strategies for different situations. You may find one that works well for you or you might want to try out several. Reading the descriptions will help you recognize the strategy you may be using now.

T&T: GO ALONG TO GET ALONG

Most women, especially in the initial years, try to fit in with the gendered expectations of the workplace without awareness of GBS. Going along with these expectations as a strategy, however, requires awareness of GBS and of the masculine rules of the game. Using this strategy tactically requires spotting gender bias and recognizing how your approaches may be misinterpreted through a masculine lens to your detriment. It is about managing the impression you make to allow your value to be made visible, and to avoid gender minefields. In order to use this strategy, you need to be aware of what is rewarded and how success is measured in your organization. Your goal is to be able to switch fluidly from feminine to masculine styles for greatest efficacy and best practices. Most of the chapters in this book focus on this strategy.

T&T: SHINE A LIGHT

This strategy is based on recognition of gender bias and stereotypes in operation in the workplace. Awareness allows you to identify this bias, name it, and point it out to others. Through this strategy, you acknowledge that everyone has gender bias but you don't let others use that fact to excuse or normalize it. You are hard on the problem of bias but soft on the people. You are not afraid to have courageous conversations or identify your own self-limiting mindsets. By dragging gender bias into the light, you reduce its impact and start changing attitudes and perspectives. Details on how to use this career strategy are given in the chapters Expose, Ask, Promote, Lead, and Thrive.

T&T: PIVOT

This strategy involves finding creative solutions to an unlevel playing field. You recognize when the load you are shouldering at home is too heavy and you negotiate for changes with your partner. You develop techniques for enlisting others, co-creating, and learning to delegate with joy.[71] At work you recognize when the fit is not good, the rules don't work, or when your value is not appreciated. You pivot and move to where the salary is better, the corporate values align with your own, the work is more meaningful and fulfilling, you create the organizational structure and policies, or you own the business. Or you may drop out of the workforce completely to find passion and purpose in other endeavors. For more information on this career strategy see the section entitled "Finding the Right Fit" in this chapter.

T&T: DISRUPT

This strategy involves throwing away old gender scripts. It requires that you create new ways of working based on human abilities and skills, not gender stereotypes. You fully recognize the limitations of gender beliefs and norms imposed on you, others, and society, and you choose to work as if they don't exist. In doing so, you show other women the possibilities. As a woman using this strategy you find opportunities to reduce gender bias by working with leaders and organizations to change policies, or starting your own company with policies that promote gender parity. You support and use objective systems for hiring and promotion that are gender blind. You call out gender bias and unfairness when you see it. By understanding the restrictions and delusions of gender created by society, you lead with authenticity.[72]

CAREER STAGE: INITIAL YEARS

The initial years at work are about building expertise, building relationships, and building networks. They can be the most challenging years as they involve the steepest learning curves. Not only are you learning substantive skills and knowledge, you are learning the social codes of conduct for your workplace or profession. This is usually the stage where the *Go Along to Get Along* career strategy works best. You ensure that you make your value visible to others using styles and approaches that align with masculine norms. You see the value in knowing both masculine and feminine styles and are learning to use them flexibly and fluidly.

T&T: TIPS FOR DOING WELL

Keep Learning: In 2015, women of all ages surpassed men in obtaining university degrees.[73] This love of education and continued learning is even more important today as the pace of change keeps accelerating; young women are driving the change. Millennial women list "lack of opportunities for learning and development" as the second most common reason for choosing to leave an organization.[74] Continuous learning is necessary for acquiring the latest skills, and smart companies are increasingly committing to educating their employees. If your workplace does not offer it for you, make sure that you seek out your own professional learning opportunities.

Connect and Observe: It is helpful to talk to and, if possible, work with well-regarded and experienced senior people. Spending time with those you admire and who inspire you gives you a chance to learn good work habits and ways to approach and solve problems. Become socially intelligent and organizationally aware. See the Politics chapter for T&T related to this point.

Ask for Feedback: Men provide more informal feedback to other men than to women. It tends to be more casual, explicit, micro-feedback.[75] Women, in contrast, tend to get more vague feedback like not being asked to work on projects or attend important meetings. Thus it is important for women to ask for specific feedback. If the comments are negative, don't take them personally or get defensive - feedback is how you improve your performance. Be seen as someone who is keen to advance and develop.

Set Boundaries: You want to develop and maintain good working relationships in your initial years, however, this does not mean becoming everyone's gopher or working yourself to the bone to make everyone happy. It also does not mean frequently working around the clock to be a team player. I hear about this all too often from younger women who don't set boundaries and are generally exhausted and in poor health. I recently spoke to a young woman who suffered a concussion due to exhaustion from work. If setting boundaries is challenging for you, then commit to working on this skill for your own health and well-being. See the chapter Thrive for details.

Get Mentoring: In addition to watching successful individuals, talking to them and getting their advice is important. It can involve a formal mentoring system set up by your employer, or a more casual process where you approach someone you feel at ease with and admire. Don't stop at one mentor – try to have one from within and outside your group. If possible, try to have a female and male mentor. With more than one mentor, you have the gift of multiple perspectives.

Initiate Career Dialogues: Start conversations about your career goals and motivations with your immediate boss or supervisor. This will allow you to learn about opportunities and possibilities in your organization, as well as letting your employer know what you would like to achieve.

Make Your Value Visible: It is important for others, especially influential others, to know the value you bring to your organization. Having a champion who broadcasts your skills and talents is pure career gold, but don't rely on this happening. Make sure that others know about your successes. See the chapter Promote for more details.

Have A Game Plan: Although most women don't have a career plan, it can be extremely useful. Thinking about where your career is headed can help you know if you are on track and allow you to see opportunities that you might otherwise miss. Setting goals allows you to know your priorities so you can say "no" more easily and authentically to work that does not advance your career or align with your goals. A career plan allows you to work smarter, not harder.[76]

T&T: CREATING A GAME PLAN

If you have a clear focus for where you want to go in your career and how to get there, consider yourself fortunate. If not, a Career Development Plan is included at the end of this chapter to help you create a career road map. In this section, key questions from the plan are discussed.

WHERE AM I NOW?

- *Am I developing the expertise I need?*
- *Am I developing the relationships I want?*
- *Am I meeting and working with the people I want?*
- *Am I progressing like others at my level?*
- *Am I achieving the benchmarks for success at my level?*
- *Does this position fit my priorities/needs/values?*

It is good to be curious and to ask purposeful questions relating to your career. Depending on the organization, an evaluation will typically be part of your formal development assessment. Ask trusted colleagues about where they are and how they are developing. Find out what is valued by the organization, perhaps from a mentor if you have one, and use this information to determine where you want or need to be. Know what success is at your level in quantifiable terms. Know the benchmarks so you can aim for them and recognize when you have achieved or exceeded them.

If you answered "no" to the last question about fit, you may wish to read the section "Finding the Right Fit" below.

WHERE AM I GOING?

- *Where do I want/need to be? What is the next level?*
- *What specific changes or improvements do I hope to achieve?*
- *What are the goals that will get me there?*

When answering these questions, be detailed and clear about what it is you want to achieve. For example, in developing expertise, what area or skills in particular do you need? What would you be able to do once you reach the next level that you are not able to do now? Perhaps it means working on bigger or more complicated files or projects. It may be useful to divide larger goals into more manageable sub-goals that can be realized more quickly. Sometimes career development involves developing a particular skill. In that case, you may wish to use the plan set out below. Ask for help from a mentor or a trusted colleague if you get stuck or don't have all the relevant information.

HOW DO I GET THERE?

Each goal or sub-goal typically involves a series of concrete steps or actions to be taken to move you closer to the goal. Actions should be doable and measurable. Detailed actions help to determine what resources you may require. Below is an example of a plan setting out the sub-goals and actions relating to the overall goal of making your value visible to others at work.

Goal: Make My Value Visible

Sub-goals: Show expertise to clients and colleagues.

Actions:

1. Write a quality article for clients.
2. Speak at an event where clients are in attendance.

3. Start a social media blog on current topics and developments in area.
4. Become the head of a section for a professional or industry association.

Sub-goals: Get on a committee.

Actions:

1. Get a list of organization committees.
2. Gather information about the process for getting on the committees.
3. Talk to people on the committees I want to join.

Sub-goals: Work with a senior person.

Actions: Discuss my interest with my mentor or, where appropriate, talk to the person directly and ask for work (yes, it can be that simple).

WHAT RESOURCES DO I NEED?

Once you have achieved this level of detail regarding sub-goals and actions, the resources needed become clear and the next part of the plan can easily be fleshed out. Each action should be associated with one or more resources. Resources include people, activities, information and/ or training that will help you get where you want to be. Below are suggestions for determining the best resources for accomplishing your goal.

Find a Mentor or Coach. Mentors can protect you from discrimination and help you navigate rocky patches and obstacles. Most women who succeed and reach positions of influence credit having a mentor. It is always good to have individuals you can talk to about work, and a mentor is a great place to start.

Ask Others. Talk to trusted colleagues or, if you have a mentor or coach, ask about the steps they followed and the resources they used to get to where they are now. You might even involve them as a resource in achieving the goal. Workplaces can be competitive, so ask trusted colleagues only. If you can't ask, then observe those who have achieved a similar goal to yours.

Ask for What You Need. Determine the resources you need and ask for them. By negotiating for what you need to achieve your goals you may get valuable resources; and even if you don't succeed you will have practised asking. See the Ask chapter for details on how to ask.

AM I THERE YET?

Evidence helps you recognize when you have achieved the actions you outlined, and ultimately your goals. It is important to make the actions as concrete as possible so that resources are easily determined and achievement is clear. Determine what successful completion looks like before you get started. Use the Career Development Plan template at the end of this chapter to help you further assess where you are, where you want to go, how to get there, and when you have arrived.

CAREER STAGE: MATERNITY PAUSE

Mothers in the workplace often face gender stereotypes and false gender assumptions. For many ambitious professionals, a career is ideally continuous; through this lens, a maternity leave, which is a career break or gap, is viewed as unusual. Similarly, career progression is viewed as being linear and upward, like a ladder. These outdated views and lenses need to be challenged. Rather than being a gap or a break in a career, a maternity leave should be viewed as a pause - very similar to a medical or educational leave. Maternity pauses, like other career and life transitions, are a normal and healthy part of life.

With the emergence of flatter organizational structures in recent years, the concept of a career ladder is being replaced by a more apt image of a career lattice. With the lattice image, career progression involves more than one direction and can include horizontal, vertical, and diagonal movement. The success of "returnships," a form of work experience that helps women return to the workplace regardless of how long they have been away, reinforces the idea of a career lattice.[77]

The type and extent of planning for this type of pause, and the complexity of your maternity plan will depend on various factors, including your position, work responsibilities, and the organization for which you work.

Another important factor in planning your maternity pause is your organization's relevant policies, procedures, and planning. If your organization has a culture of care, its process for maternity or paternity pause will most likely be well thought through. If this is the case, then the amount of planning and preparation required by you will be greatly reduced. If there are minimal or no policies in place, then the practical suggestions set out below will help you plan. Suggestions for each of three periods - before, during, and after maternity pause - are provided. Also, several excellent books on planning for a maternity pause are listed at the end of this chapter in the section "Want to Read More?"

T&T: BEFORE THE PAUSE

During this time, most organizations will help you prepare for your temporary absence, recruit your replacement, and create a clear plan regarding changes in workload. Career dialogues, which are an important tool throughout your career, are of great value at this time. These dialogues allow for an exchange of ideas and information around career goals, motivation, and opportunities. Here are some other specific actions and tools to ease the transition before the pause.

Establish a communication plan. Determine whether, and how often, you will communicate with your supervisor while you are away on pause. Be clear about what will be discussed, and when and how communication will be maintained.

Return-to-work plan. Ensure you have a clear plan before you pause. This plan provides details of the parameters of your pause and, as such, may include date of return, reintegration actions, roles and responsibilities, work schedule, and career options upon returning. It may also include the extent of your contact with clients and customers. This information allows you to discuss the details of your role and options upon returning.

Interviews with direct reports. Set up individual meetings with your team to discuss your expectations and clarify any concerns or issues they may anticipate. You will also wish to meet with those who are covering for you during the pause.

Make use of mentors or a buddy system. If possible, pair up with someone who has gone or is going on a pause. They can provide you with valuable information about the pause and what to expect upon your return. You may be able to keep in touch with them during your pause to find out how they are doing and to help you transition more easily back to the workplace.

Exit interview/career dialogue. Before your pause, ensure that you have any questions answered and concerns addressed. Review expectations about the pause, such as whether you have all of the necessary resources for leaving and returning to work. You may review the return-to-work plan. If career dialogues have been ongoing, this might also be the opportunity to talk about your career goals and motivations.

T&T: DURING THE PAUSE

This is a time when you will be adjusting to changes brought on by motherhood and, depending on your work circumstances, your involvement in work related activities will be minimal.

Use the communication plan. If the organization does not follow the established plan, you may want to take the initiative and call them. This allows you to keep current on any changes to the organization, any upcoming events or announcements, and any potential training opportunities that have come up. It is important to stay in the loop as an essential member of the organization so you may also find other ways for keeping current, such as having colleagues provide you with this information.

Go into work and be seen. This is part of keeping in touch. It does several things – allows you to stay current with news and changes, and keeps you on the radar of colleagues. You will need to determine how often is appropriate and what works best for you. Perhaps it means going into work before meeting up with a colleague for lunch. It will keep you connected to the workplace and smooth the transition back to work. Note that going into work is optional in most cases, so if it does not feel right or does not work for you, don't do it.

Stay current by attending professional groups and network events. Many mothers like to stay current by attending events hosted by groups they belong to. This has the added advantage of allowing you to network and can make the return to work after the pause easier.

T&T: AFTER THE PAUSE

As the time approaches for your return to work, you may feel anxious about being out of the loop even if you have kept current with colleagues. The following activities can make reintegration easier.

A back-to-work interview. Having an open dialogue about any changes in roles and responsibilities will be good for you and your supervisor. It will allow you to communicate effectively and to share goals and career plans.

Step-by-step reintegration plan. Depending on the changes you will face upon returning, such as not coming back to the same position or working with new members on the team, a detailed plan for reintegration should be available. This will allow everyone involved to be clear on any changes and thus make your transition back smoother.

Discuss flexible work arrangements. This may have been discussed and arranged before your pause. If not, these options should be canvassed to afford you the opportunity to effectively manage your work and family life. If your workplace does not have a flexible or agile work arrangement in place, you may want to advocate for one.

Comeback coaching. This type of coaching provides career transition support that most mothers can benefit from it. It may begin weeks prior to your return to work and may continue into the first few months. It allows you to gain clarity on your career goals and provides support in re-establishing a career dialogue with your employer.

T&T: DEBUNKING COMMON BIASES AND MYTHS

There are many biases about mothers at work; in order to expose them, you must first understand and recognize them. It will help you and others from implicitly buying into them. Traditional gender roles of men at work and women at home are at the heart of most of these biases. Societal assumptions are that working mothers stay at home to raise their children and, if they return to work, their focus and commitment to work is lessened. One of the most egregious results of these biases is lower wages. A Trades Union Congress report in 2016 reveals that fathers earn, on average, a 21% wage bonus compared to men without children. In stark contrast, women who become mothers before the age of 33 typically suffer a 15% pay penalty.[78]

It is imperative to not only recognize specific biases but to bring them into the open and refute them. To help you with this, below are some of the more common myths about new mothers in the workplace along with the facts that debunk them.

Myth #1: Mothers put less effort into their jobs compared to fathers and non-parents due to the additional responsibilities they face at work and home.

Reality: The research shows that motherhood does not predict effort at work.[79] Even though women have more household duties than fathers and non-parents they are still very capable of effectively managing their time. In fact, some women say that they are even more organized at work because they have to pick up their children after school.

Myth #2: New mothers are less interested in career progression.

Reality: An interest in career progression depends more on personal career ambitions than on family responsibilities. A new mother's engagement depends more on the needs and desires of the individual woman. To make an assumption about every mother limits the woman and hurts the organization.

Myth #3: Creating work-life integration is not possible for mothers.

Reality: Commitment to work and family is not a trade-off. Many people working for an organization, not only mothers, have important responsibilities and commitments outside the office. Organizations that create a culture of care for all their employees, support them in their personal commitments, and acknowledge their outside responsibilities, will have employees that remain loyal and dedicated.

Myth #4: Family responsibilities motivate fathers but not mothers to work hard.

Reality: With the large number of mothers working today, many of them single mothers, it is clear that women are motivated to work hard to provide for their children. This incorrect bias fuels the wage bonus for fathers and the wage penalty for mothers.

While it's helpful to expose and debunk these myths if they exist in your organization, you shouldn't feel pressure to do so if you are not comfortable addressing them. Just being aware is a good first step. Use humour if you can: "Oh boy, is this one of those mommy traps?" Or "Wow! My husband just got super motivated at work after our baby was born and I have lost all desire to do anything at work! Ha-ha!" If you can call attention to the irrational nature of the assumption while showing that you can be lighthearted about it, perfect.

One thing often overlooked due to bias are the many benefits of maternity pauses to organizations. Some of the most commonly cited benefits include developing a culture of support, discovering new talent in a replacement employee, retaining the skills of the employee on maternity pause, and ensuring diversity.[80] If your organization does not value diversity or encourage a culture of support, you may feel a sense of discomfort or unease, and start questioning if the fit is right.

CAREER STAGE: FINDING THE RIGHT FIT

The impetus for a career shift after the initial years of developing skills and expertise often comes from a feeling that the fit is not right. Feelings of discontent can be demoralizing over time, so it is best to deal with these feelings in a constructive, creative, and timely way. It may be hard to admit when things are not working due to a fear of failure and what others might think. The tendency of women is to blame themselves for failure while men tend to blame others or the circumstances. So recognize that it takes great courage to admit when the fit is not right, identify the reason, and deal with it.

T&T: DETERMINE REASONS FOR UNEASE

Getting clear on the reason for your dissatisfaction is important as it helps you understand what you do want, determine what needs to change, and prevents you from doing anything (consciously or unconsciously) that might sabotage your career and reputation. It also allows you to find a more satisfying position, or to create your own where you can be successful.

There are many reasons why the fit might not feel quite right. To help you understand your discontent, start by asking yourself these questions. Have you developed expertise and relationships in a way and to the degree you want? Does the type and amount of work suit you? Are you challenged enough? If not, these can be reasons for frustration or dissatisfaction.

Feelings of unease or discontent can arise for reasons relating to workplace culture, gender bias, or limiting mindsets, among others.

Workplace culture: The culture of a workplace is an important factor in whether or not you feel valued and comfortable at work, so find out as much as you can before you start. The culture of an organization is determined by what the organization values, appreciates, and rewards. Four common workplace cultures are Control, Collaborative, Competence, and Cultivation.[81] In Control culture, rational decision-making is the focus. It tends to be impersonal and *either you fit or you don't*. In Collaborative culture, people-driven decision-making is the hallmark, where people work together. This culture can best be described as *you're a team player if you're with us*. In Competence culture the focus is reaching and going beyond high standards, so the work tends to be rigorous with a sense of urgency. The aim is excellence and, as a result, *you're either a winner or a loser*. Catalyzing and cultivating the growth of people is the aim of Cultivation culture, with a concern for fulfilling potential and inspiring success. It is described as *you are what you are becoming*. A disconnect between your personal values and those of your workplace can often be the reason for feeling the fit is not right. To discover your personal values, a questionnaire is provided in the chapter Politics.

Gender Bias: Workplace bias and GBS can cause you to feel uncomfortable and create hurdles for you. A lawyer confided in me at a networking event that a male colleague at her level had decided to go with her to meet with a high-profile potential client even though the contact, the CEO, had specifically approached her at a conference and asked her to meet with him. She was concerned that her colleague would take credit for the new business. She asked what she should do as she did not want to appear competitive or not to be a team player. Situations like this can wear you down. Perhaps like this young woman your discomfort comes from competitive behaviour you don't understand or from feeling tested and not measuring up. Maybe you feel uneasy because you recognize differences in standards used to assess men and women - performance for women and potential for men. As a senior woman, you might feel isolated; since success and likability are negatively correlated, many women at the top feel like they're on their own.

Belief in Meritocracy. A common belief held by many women, particularly younger women, is that organizations are meritocracies. It is believed that hard work, being perfect, and delivering results will be rewarded and that nothing else is required to succeed. When this does not turn out to be true, frustration and dissatisfaction often result. If you hold such beliefs, the chapter Politics will help you to better understand how organizations work and allow you to replace your current beliefs with more realistic and beneficial ones.

Uneasiness that comes from a change in the workplace is usually easier to identify than a shift in your own priorities and values. Perhaps you want to leave to find a more fulfilling job so your life can be more meaningful. Sometimes women recognize that a balanced life is of great importance. Women are known for pursuing passion and purpose in their work, so if you are feeling dissatisfaction, it might be because you are missing these elements.

Once you have a general idea of the reasons for your dissatisfaction, it is important to consider what you are eager to do. If you don't yet know what is causing your dissatisfaction, don't worry. The "Exercises" section below outlines a method my clients find helpful. It involves analyzing what you currently dislike to discover what you like. Once you have discovered what you want, you can begin planning how to attain it. This might include staying where you are, pivoting to another workplace, taking a new career direction, or starting your own business.

T&T: STAYING WHERE YOU ARE

If the source of discontent is something that can be changed without changing workplaces, such as by working with different people, moving to a different department, obtaining flex-time or requesting greater work responsibility, here are suggestions for action.

Gather the information — discreetly. Find out if it is possible to change the aspects of your work that are making you dissatisfied. The length of time you have been with the organization and your reputation are factors that will influence how receptive the organization might be. Look around for others who have done what you want to do. Has anyone changed areas recently? Has anyone negotiated flex-time? Make sure you talk only to trusted colleagues or indicate in your conversations with others that it is on a confidential basis. This will not guarantee that your questions will not be reported to others, but it is good to be clear with those you talk to that you don't want your inquiries to be made public.

Talk to your mentor or champion. Talking to a mentor can serve several purposes: you can gauge their reaction to your request in order to better assess how the organization will react; you might get information that you may not get from others; and your mentor will not be surprised by hearing from others that you are dissatisfied. If you have a champion who endorses you to others, talk with her or him once you are clear on what you want and what you are planning to negotiate for.

Set boundaries. If you want more personal and family time, you may find this is possible by learning to say "no" and changing expectations at work. The Thrive chapter outlines how to say no and build relationships. Often in our initial years of work we say "yes" to everything and everyone in order to build expertise and relationships. Learning to say "no" appropriately will increase resilience and allow you to manage your career more strategically.

Get help at home. This suggestion is also about reducing your work load by changing expectations at home. Think about what can be done by others and delegate those activities. Perhaps you can do what Tiffany Dufu did in Drop The Ball and negotiate with your partner for more shared responsibility at home.[82] Don't try to do it all on your own.

Negotiate for what you want. Once you are clear on what you want and know that it is possible based on the information you have gathered, think about how best to negotiate the change. If you want multiple changes, is there one that is most important? It might be more strategic to ask for just one change to begin with. If you want many changes, you may need to revisit whether you want to stay or change organizations. If you have a great reputation and are well regarded, this will greatly help. Organizations like to manage their talent and want to keep valuable employees.

If your unease is because of GBS, one way to bring these gender biases to light and to help change your workplace is to have a courageous conversation. Point out to leaders or mentors the blind spots that are holding women back. Start a conversation with a person in the organization you are comfortable with. The Conflict Conversation Process found in the Politics chapter and the Co-creating Questions in the Ask chapter are good approaches to use. The Expose chapter provides suggestions on ways to uncover and reduce gender bias. In having these conversations and shining a light, recognize your power. We hold more cards than ever before as women. Use your power to invite corporations to do the right thing. Invite them into the 21st century.

If you are able to bring about changes to make your current work situation a better fit and better workplace, wonderful. If not, pivoting may be the next option to consider.

T&T: PIVOT

If the cause of your dissatisfaction can only be solved by moving to a new job, changing career direction, or creating your own workplace, the next step involves pivoting. Women are starting to leverage their power in the workplace. Research shows that among young adults in their thirties, more women than men are leaving jobs for a higher salary – 65%

compared with 56%.[83] With greater salary transparency in organizations and the increasing number of apps providing salary information, this will only continue to increase.

Another growing area where women are flexing their power is business ownership. The global market forces are converging to produce a great era for women entrepreneurs; current research shows that women business owners are more ambitious and successful than their male counterparts.[84] So if the fit is not right or you are failing to thrive where you are, you may want to pivot.

Many women pivot naturally and often. Career pauses, which are more common for women than men, create the opportunity and the need to reinvent. Research shows that women around the age of thirty leave to find more interesting work while women in their fifties (at the peak of their careers) leave to find greater fulfillment. And leaving often requires reinvention.

To pivot, first you will want to gather information and discover options. Informational sources will be broader and more diverse than if you decide to stay where you are. Discreet information-gathering is still important, especially at the beginning of your search. In addition to trusted colleagues, use a broad range of external sources, including recruiters, contacts at organizations, family, friends, and social media. If including family and friends in the list of sources seems surprising to you, remember it is impossible to predict where important information or support will come from, so be as broad as possible.

Ensure that you match your priorities, strengths, and interests with the alternatives available to ensure you don't trade one unhappy situation for another. Another important aspect in this process is learning to negotiate for what is important to you. Read the Ask chapter before any salary negotiation. Negotiate for the items and benefits that are important to you and will ensure a good fit. Know that if you ask and don't get a certain benefit, at least the employer is aware of your interests and needs.

In her book *Pivot,* Jenny Blake, co-creator of Google's Guru Program, discusses a method for pivoting which includes Plant, Scan, Pilot, and Launch.[85] During the Plant stage, you identify what is working for you and where you want to end up, then start to bridge the gap between the two. In the Scan stage, you look for new opportunities and identify new skills you will need to move forward. In the third stage, Pilot, you run small experiments to determine next steps. This is of particular importance when starting a new business. The final stage, Launch, involves making the change.

When I started working, workplace choices were very limited. Fast forward forty years and we are into an era of women entrepreneurs. Economists and academics agree that women business owners are an under tapped force that can rekindle economic expansion globally. The stats are already impressive on the number of women-owned businesses and their economic contributions. In 2016 in the US alone, women owned 11.3 million businesses and employed 19 million people. Women owned 39% of all businesses in 2016, up from 29% in 2007.[86] From 2007 to 2016 the number of women-owned businesses increased by 45% compared to just a 9% increase among all businesses. More than 1100 businesses have been launched each day by women since 2007. Employment growth is even stronger with an increase of 18% in women's businesses since 2007 compared with a decline of 1% among all business employment. It is clear that starting your own business is not the only viable option for finding the right fit, but it is a popular one.

Having worked as a business owner since leaving law, I can attest that working on your own is well worth it when you have the requisite experience and are ready to do it. The ability to manage your own time and determine what you want to do is priceless. It does involve a lot of learning and hard work – I realized this with great frustration when I could no longer call someone in the IT department to quickly fix my computer glitches. However, the tools and support available now for starting your own business are amazing; from geek squads for solving your computer problems, to easy website creation for selling your services or product, to social media for quick and informative networking and connection. And technology is just one of the global external market forces converging to support women as business owners.

These statistics on women owning businesses and global market forces show that the future is favouring women by creating more opportunities to pivot. Furthermore, the key skills and attitudes needed in business owners are those most associated with women.[87] It is no surprise then that research conducted in 2016 found that women entrepreneurs are more ambitious and successful than men.[88] This has led some writers and commenters to suggest that that we are entering a great age of female entrepreneurialism.[89] And with that comes the power to plan and pivot.

EXERCISES

CAREER DEVELOPMENT PLAN

Part 1 — WHERE AM I NOW? (current operating level)

1. **Expertise:** Am I developing the expertise I need? (level of work, types of files, and independence).
2. **Relationships:** Am I developing the relationships I want? Am I working with the people I want to?
3. **Networks:** Am I meeting the people I should?

   Does this position fit my priorities, strengths, and interests?[90]

   Does the culture of this firm/corporation/department match my values?

How do I compare with others? Am I progressing like others at my level?

Part 2 — WHERE AM I GOING? (desired level and competency)

What is the next level?

What specific changes/improvements do I hope to achieve? What are my goals?

a.

b.

c.

Part 3 — HOW DO I GET THERE? (actions, tools, and resources)

Action Steps: **Status:** (start and complete dates)

a.

b.

c.

Which **resources** will help me get there?

Who will I enlist to help?

Part 4 – AM I THERE YET?

How will I know that I have succeeded? What performance measures can I use, if any? What feedback can I solicit?

DISCOVER YOUR IDEAL JOB

Use this exercise to become clear on the reasons for your dissatisfaction to help determine your ideal job.

List Your Priorities, Strengths and Interests: What is important to you? What are your interests and passions (activities that energize you and you are eager to do)? What appeals to you? Reflect on what you are eager to do and are passionate about in your workday. Often the most fulfilling and successful careers result from doing what you love.

If You Don't Know, Use Contrast: If you aren't clear on what you do want, start by listing in detail the parts of your current position you don't like. That will help you discover what you do want.

Your Ideal Job: Get detailed about this. Write out your perfect work day from when you arrive to when you leave, listing as many details as possible. Try to avoid evaluating your ideas as they are generated — just keep imagining. Your analytic, problem-solving side will want to get involved but try to set it aside until later. Stay positive to be creative. Also, resist trying to figure out how to make it work. Dream and create before critical evaluation.

Have fun with this process! It will lead you to a better future.

WHAT ORGANIZATIONS, LEADERS, AND MENTORS CAN DO

- Ensure flexible work arrangements for all employees, with a focus on productivity and results. Reduce the importance of face-time and time spent at the desk.
- Talk to managers and other employees who currently have flexible work to find out what works and what doesn't.
- Increase transparency about what success is and ensure that it is attainable. Make what is expected measurable so it is clear when it is attained.
- Ensure your go-to group is diverse and not a group that is only demographically similar to you.
- Sponsor a woman and advocate for them. Ensure their value is visible to others and that they work with influential others.

- Look broadly and deeply for talent and champion the development of such talent.
- Ensure that the women you work with are getting the work and support they need.
- Invite and encourage women to attend informal activities and socializing events that are important for advancement.
- Start a paid *returnship* program for women who have been out of the workplace.
- Ensure that your organization has good maternity and paternity pause policies, plans, and procedures. Make it easy for employees to take and return from such pauses.
- Provide career planning training and educational opportunities for skill building.

WANT TO READ MORE?

Blake, Jenny. *Pivot: The Only Move That Matters Is Your Next One.* New York: Penguin, 2017.

Downey, Allyson. *Here's the Plan: Your Practical, Tactical Guide to Advancing Your Career During Pregnancy and Parenthood.* New York: Seal Press, 2016.

Shipman, Claire and Katty Kay. *Womenomics: Write Your Own Rules for Success.* New York: HarperCollins, 2009.

Stromberg, Lisen. *Work PAUSE Thrive: How to Pause for Parenthood Without Killing Your Career.* Dallas: BenBella Books, 2017.

ASK

When I started as a psychologist at a large psychiatric hospital in the late 70's I was like most young women starting out – just happy to get the job. There were not a lot of positions for psychologists at the time, let alone in neuropsychology. So when I was offered a position in my field, I gratefully accepted it. I also took the low salary that was offered. I did not learn until decades later that accepting what is offered and being grateful is a common response for most women. This is not true for men.

Over the past decade there has been growing evidence of *specific and consistent gender differences in negotiation styles and outcome* shown by groups of business professionals, university students, and academics. These differences have nothing to do with intelligence, ability, or talent and everything to do with social conditioning, gender habits, and gendered expectations learned in childhood. These gender differences, which are triggered in specific situations by gender blind spots (GBS), have been labelled situational gender triggers.[91]

The research findings on gender and negotiation over the past decade are quite startling and make it clear that negotiation is an essential tool in managing your career and getting what you want. Here are some of the salient statistics from the book *Women Don't Ask:* men are four times more likely to initiate negotiations than women; an astonishing 20%

of women state that they never negotiate at all; most women recognize fewer situations as being ones in which negotiation is acceptable and accept what is offered; women set their expectations low – as much as 32% lower than men for the same job; 2.5 times more women than men feel "a great deal of apprehension" about negotiation, and 57% of men versus 7% of women negotiate their first employment package.[92]

But word is getting out. In a recent 2016 survey by Levo,[93] eighty-three percent of millennial women agree that it's important to negotiate their salary and/or benefit package and believe that they will earn less money over the course of their careers if they do not negotiate their initial job offers. However, results from this and other surveys of millennials reveal that only 41% of women had negotiated part of their salary or benefits package, and only 21% of women had negotiated any part of their first job offer.[94] So what is stopping women from negotiating?

Two major themes emerge from these findings. The first is a fear of relational, reputational, and social costs related to asking. Women intuitively know that there are costs associated with pursuing self-interests as this behaviour runs counter to gender stereotypes.[95] Findings show when men negotiate for themselves they are liked and respected but when women negotiate for themselves, the behaviour is not similarly rewarded. Instead, fewer men and women want to work with them. This shows women accurately intuit that advocating for higher pay will create a socially difficult situation for themselves.

The second theme coming out of these findings is women's lack of knowledge about what, how, and when to negotiate. Since women have been socialized to wait to be given something rather than ask for it, it is not surprising that most women don't know they can ask or how to ask. As I write this my husband tells me that a female family member took an accounting position after many years at home and did not ask what the salary was when she was hired.

This focus on women's skills and fears is in no way meant to ignore that women across professions and industries tend to get offered lower wages than men or to downplay the systemic bias that supports the gender wage gap. Unfortunately, changing societal attitudes is slow and difficult work. The information in this chapter is being provided to help you become a successful negotiator so you can mitigate this wage gap for yourself.

So how do you become a successful negotiator? Learning to negotiate for yourself in ways that are comfortable while at the same time reducing negative reactions from others is critical. Knowing when to initiate a negotiation, how to ask in ways that align with gendered expectations, how to use different negotiation strategies based on the situation, and how to harness the power of female gender culture are also important aspects. Research shows that just by recognizing when negotiation is possible, women negotiate similar salary outcomes to men.[96]

This chapter is divided into three sections: situational gender triggers; dealing with gender bias; and tips for negotiating salary. Situational gender triggers are covered in the first section together with questions for helping you identify your personal GBS. Since no one negotiates in a vacuum, tools and techniques (T&T) for dealing with gendered expectations and implicit gender biases are set out in the second section. Salary negotiation is such an important way for women to show gains and narrow the wage gap that tips and strategies specifically for negotiating salary are provided in the last section.

SITUATIONAL GENDER TRIGGERS

Certain situations consistently trigger differences in negotiated results for men and women and are referred to as situational gender triggers. Situations that reduce the chances for negotiation to occur or result in poorer negotiated outcomes for women are often related to self-limiting mindsets. However, not all gender triggers are disadvantageous for women. Under certain conditions, women achieve better negotiated outcomes than men. These situations debunk the notion that women are not good negotiators. The information in this section will help you understand gender triggers and the gender mindsets underlying them. It will also allow you to determine if you hold any common gender beliefs that are preventing you from being the best negotiator you can be. Using this information will enable you to harness your negotiation strengths and mitigate any negotiation challenges.

GBS: NOT ASKING

I did not negotiate my first salary.

I hate to ask as it may hurt the relationship and impact the way I am viewed.

When given a new assignment, I accept the terms offered rather than negotiate for other ones.

I don't want to make trouble so I accept files and clients even if they are not in my best interest.

I seldom ask for assignments or projects I want for fear I might be perceived badly.

If most or all of these statements sound like something you would say, you are like most women and are uncomfortable asking for *anything*. Asking can create embarrassment and might hurt the relationship. It may negatively impact reputation or brand. Consequently, women miss the opportunity to start a dialogue and let others know about their needs and interests. In contrast, men have been found to initiate four times the number of negotiations compared to women and push hard for results when they negotiate for themselves. As a result of this trigger, men negotiate and promote self-interests much more often than women do.

This tendency not to ask affects all women – even those at higher levels in organizations. I was approached by a CFO from a prominent real estate corporation after she heard me talk about this particular GBS. She was a fabulous negotiator but never asked or negotiated with her CEO; rather she waited and accepted what was given to her. She sought coaching lessons from me to learn more about this self-limiting mindset and her possible blind spot.

Not asking can have a significant economic impact on women and has been proposed as a substantial factor in the gender gap in wages. Over a lifetime, a small salary difference at the beginning of a career today can result in lost wages in excess of $1,500,000.[97] If you accept $100,000 and a colleague doing the same job negotiates for $107,000, are you okay with not having asked for more? With compound interest, increases, and raises, thirty-five years later you will have to work eight years longer than your colleague to have the same amount of money at retirement. So it is definitely worthwhile to ask, especially if you know how to ask in a way that is audience-focused and aligned with gender culture values.[98]

Failing to negotiate salary is not the only lost opportunity for women. Women also miss out on negotiating for projects, promotions, and other advancement opportunities that men commonly and aggressively pursue. The reluctance of women to advocate for themselves is often the difference between climbing the career ladder at a healthy pace and not climbing it at all.

T&T: LEARN TO ASK

The first step to becoming an excellent negotiator is deciding to negotiate in the first place. When you take the steps to negotiate in a way that makes you confident and the others around you comfortable, you increase your chances of success. Once you start asking for what you want you may be surprised at how easy it is, how it enables others to know what you want, and how it can enhance your reputation. The feedback from women who have asked at work for what they wanted after attending one of my seminars has been amazing.

- One young real estate agent told me her bosses were really pleased that she asked for a different portfolio – in leasing. If she hadn't asked, they never would have known she was dissatisfied and, most likely, this dissatisfaction would have caused her to leave rather than ask.
- Another woman told me that she went back to her office after a seminar on negotiation and applied for a position that she ordinarily would not have applied for. And she got it.
- One young high school student, who heard about asking from her boyfriend's mother, asked the manager at the fast food restaurant where she was hired if he could pay her more than minimum wage. He upped her salary by $1.00 per hour - more than a 10% increase!
- One young lawyer who was offered a position as a litigator used that offer to ask for a position at another law firm. She got it and was later told that they were very impressed with her asking. Interestingly her mother had advised her to accept what she had been offered and to not make waves.

Does this mean that every time you request something you will get what you ask for? Unfortunately not. However, if you don't ask you pass up the possibility of getting what you want, and others will not know you want it. Even if you don't get what you ask for now, you have started the process for getting what you want in the future.

GBS: NOT KNOWING IT'S POSSIBLE TO ASK

There are not many opportunities for negotiation.

It is best to take what is offered and fit in from the beginning.

I can't change the terms of a job offer unless I am told that I can.

Salaries are not negotiable but set on an objective grid.

I seldom suggest other options when presented with a decision.

It is hard to ask when you don't recognize that negotiation is a possibility. In ambiguous situations where the opportunities are unclear or the limits uncertain, most women will not initiate negotiations. This is a self-limiting mindset. Research shows that men initiate negotiations four times more frequently than women. Women tend to take what is offered. Recent research suggests that once women are told that salary or benefits are negotiable, they negotiate as well as men. Once you are aware of the items that can be negotiated, you will start to see more negotiating opportunities.

T&T: RECOGNIZE OPPORTUNITIES

There is uncertainty and ambiguity in all negotiations. Look for opportunities. Counter the self-limiting mindset that most things are not negotiable with the opposite belief – that most things are negotiable. Recognize when it is possible to negotiate the terms of an assignment, new responsibilities, or a new position. Learn to recognize and negotiate for resources that will make it easier for you at work. Once you start to become aware of opportunities, you will start to see them more readily.

Below is a list of different types of work opportunities – some of these may be relevant for you now or in a few years.

- Further Training
- Flexible Work Arrangements
- Raise in Salary or a Bonus
- Re-entry after a Maternity Pause
- Change in Area or Type of Work
- New Project
- Greater Client Responsibilities
- Stretch Assignments
- Committee Work
- Influential Mentor or Sponsor
- Informative Performance Review

Most of these are straight-forward and self-explanatory opportunities. Stretch assignments refer to those assignments that expand your current skills and experience while allowing you to make your value visible to others -- an important aspect of career advancement for women. A stretch assignment might involve working with people you don't currently work with or using skills you want to learn.

Is there an opportunity on the list you would like? If so, start planning who to ask and how to ask. If not, perhaps you can brainstorm other possibilities with a trusted colleague or friend. Or start watching at work for new opportunities that will make it easier for others to see your abilities and expertise. What resources would be helpful to make your work easier? And once you have identified what you want to ask for, think about how to ask.

GBS: NOT KNOWING HOW TO ASK

Recent studies show that there is good reason why women follow their intuition and don't ask: women may experience stereotype backlash when they ask. Studies have shown that women who are more direct and competitive (called disagreeable in the study) are paid less than men who exhibit the same traits. Men who were agreeable were also paid less than men who were direct and competitive. The researchers concluded that economic sanctions exist for both gender atypical men and women. These findings were a complete surprise to the managers at the corporations examined, providing evidence for unconscious gender bias. Interestingly the researchers did not point out that the group receiving the least pay was agreeable women – this is the group that most likely accepted what was offered to them. These findings show that women need to ask but in ways that are nuanced and align with gender stereotypes.

T&T: USE AUDIENCE-FOCUSED ASKS

It's unfortunate that women can't ask directly for what they want and deserve without being perceived as pushy and/or being penalized for violating gendered expectations. Hopefully this will someday change. Until then, it's best to be nuanced in your approach. Basing your type of ask on the person you are asking greatly increases the chance of a positive response while building or maintaining the relationship.

Several years ago, I had the privilege of teaching Afghan women who were brilliant negotiators. They confirmed the use of these nuanced approaches to negotiate in very tricky and difficult situations - first with their husbands to travel to dangerous provinces and then with the tribal chiefs in the provinces to set up schools for girls.

So before you ask for something, think about the grantor's characteristics and preferences. Often we frame our request based on our preferred way of asking or the style we would respond positively to if asked. It is important to think of your audience before selecting a type of ask. What do they prefer? How are they persuaded? What is important to them? Below is a list of the different types of asks and who responds best to them.

Direct Ask: This ask is simple in that you ask directly for what you want. It is best used with a person who is goal-oriented, speaks directly, and values assertiveness. Research has shown that direct people prefer direct requests and may interpret indirect requests as manipulative. If you notice that your manager or supervisor gets directly to the point and likes "straight-shooters," this style will be the best choice. Phrases you might use include: "I would like to attend/receive/be considered for/be given...," "I want you to...," "I need you to ...," "I would like you to ..." (You may wish to soften the direct request with a connecting question at the end, such as, "What do you think?" or "How does that sound?")

"Planting the Seed" Ask: This type of ask is meant to put an idea in the other person's mind and perhaps even allow them to see a situation differently. It is an indirect way of asking. It works well with managers who like to believe they came up with the idea on their own (I can see you smiling!). We have all used this technique with others, and sometimes ideas get planted even when we're not trying. With this type of ask, you allow the other person to take ownership of an idea; you are getting what you want so why correct the impression? Example phrases for beginning a conversation like this are: "Have you considered doing it this way?" "What do you think of...?" "Are there any alternatives?" "Have you thought of sending/ using/ hiring/ promoting...?"

Co-Creating Questions: The aim of these questions is to co-create with the other person. They allow both parties to find out what is important to the other and to come to an agreement based on those interests. The more you use this method, the easier and faster it is to use. It is a big plus if the other person has had training in collaborative negotiation. Collaboration is a natural fit for most women as we have been socialized to invite others to explain their perspective. Tiffany Dufu in her book *Drop the Ball* demonstrates the use of co-creating at home. She and her husband co-created a list of household tasks and then negotiated who would be responsible for each one. This allowed them to come away with a mutually beneficial agreement that satisfied their needs and interests. Example phrases for co-creating include: "Tell me what you think about this...," "Perhaps we can come up with a solution that works for both of us." "That is one option, what about some others?" "Why do you want that?" "Why not this option?" "What if we were to do this?" and "Let's review all of the options."

Positive Framing Ask: Use positive framing as often as possible, not only when asking, as it evokes positive emotions and allows you to be seen as keen and enthused. This type of ask allows you to phrase your request in a positive way.[99] For instance, instead of saying, "I am asking for this position as I'm the best person for the job and I've earned it," you might say, "I've learned so much in this job and I'd appreciate a chance to do more. I'm ready to move to the next level." Or instead of saying, "If we are going to get this project completed on time I cannot continue doing most of the work. You need to get others working as hard as I am," you might say, "We've accomplished a lot on this project. Let's assess what's left to do and decide who's going to do what."

Build a Golden Bridge Ask: The golden bridge enhances a relationship and is a comfortable way for most women to ask. The key feature is acknowledging the perspective of the other person before you make your ask. This communication technique is similar to positive framing in that the tone of the request is positive, however, with building a golden bridge the underlying intent is to connect with the person before making the request. Since this is about connection and relies on relationship, it is a comfortable way for most women to ask. Example phrases include: "I appreciate you taking this time to discuss this issue with me at such a busy time...," "I can see that you are in a tight spot with this file/ this client/ obtaining these resources," and "I really appreciate your concern for my family life in not asking me to travel more than once a month, however I would like to travel as much as my other colleagues and here's why..."

Collective Concern Ask: This type of ask is best for avoiding pushback as it aligns with feminine values and norms. It evokes communal concerns and thus harnesses the power of gender training. Using the feminine collective or group interests to further your own self-interests works well as it takes the focus off you – it is not about what you want but what you can do for others. Think about others who will also benefit from this ask and, where possible, include this information in your ask. It will show your concern for others. Use "we" instead of "me" whenever possible. Phrases that express collective concern include: "How can I help the organization?" "If allowed to go on this training course I will be able to assist others on the team in understanding this newly developing area," and "This is a great opportunity for the whole team."

One Step-Down Ask: Although this style aligns with masculine norms, it can be used with both men and women. It allows the grantor to feel comfortable as he or she is being acknowledged as one step-up. The most basic form of this is asking for help. This style works well in salary negotiations and works with both men and women but usually for different gender culture reasons. For men trained in masculine values it appeals to status and being one step-up in power, while for women trained in feminine values it appeals to the desire for relationship and helping others. One word of caution. I coach young women to use this type of ask sparingly as the asker may be viewed as helpless or lacking competence if always asking for help. Examples of one step-down phrases include: "Can you pay me more?" "I need your help getting on this committee." "Are you able to help me?" "Is there a way forward based on the information you have?" and "Can you help?"

Perhaps you already use some of these asks. You may have noticed that you already adjust your style to others. If you are feeling disingenuous or uncomfortable about using any of these asks, note the style. Don't use a style that is uncomfortable; however, it would be worthwhile to reflect on why you don't like it. If you understand why you are uncomfortable, the discomfort may lessen.

GBS: ASKING FOR OTHERS

I feel empowered when I negotiate for my organization, a client, or a family member.

I feel it is selfish to think only of myself when negotiating.

I like to achieve agreements that satisfy me and the other party.

I have been taught to put others first.

If you agree with all or most of these statements, this gender trigger of negotiating well for others most likely applies to you. This GBS creates a huge advantage for women and is evidenced by women getting better results than men when negotiating on behalf of others. For example, when negotiating as a mentor for another's salary, female executives negotiated 18% higher than when they negotiated for themselves. This increased performance was not shown by men who negotiated for others.[100] Most women in my negotiation seminars say they feel empowered and energized when they negotiate for family members, colleagues, and clients, and these findings support this. These findings directly contradict any notion that women are poor negotiators and confirm the power of gender culture training.

A university teaching colleague, after hearing me talk about this particular trigger, told me that he finally understood something that had puzzled him for years. At a large aeronautics company where he worked, the only female manager was paid the least of all the managers, but her team received the highest compensation of all the teams. And now he

finally knew the reason: she had negotiated the highest salaries for her team but not for herself.

This trigger also helps explain why, in 1988 when I started teaching negotiation to law students, I could not find any studies that showed gender differences in negotiated outcome for lawyers. As negotiators acting for clients, women and men show no differences.

Find ways to use this trigger to increase your negotiation outcome. One woman confessed she stayed in her office to negotiate work relating to her home because that is where she negotiated for clients and the space empowered her.

T&T: HARNESS THIS TRIGGER

Women are powerful representative negotiators – we negotiate hard for others. Harness the power of this trigger to up your negotiation success. Before you negotiate for your own self-interests (such as salary, benefits, or resources) think about who else will benefit from a great outcome. Focus not only on how to help those in your family with a great negotiated outcome but also, wherever possible, how to help your employer, manager, department, and organization. Due to the power of this gender trigger, it will allow you to push harder, hold firm longer, and set your expectations higher.

To reduce stereotype backlash in negotiation, go along with the gendered expectations of others. If you are able to help the other side satisfy their interests in the negotiation while ensuring that your interests are also being satisfied, point this out as a win/win. Using a strategy that allows everyone to achieve the best outcome while creating a good working relationship will make everyone more comfortable, reduce your own resistance to satisfying self-interests, and ensure people will want to deal with you again.

GBS: LOWERED ASPIRATIONS

Research has consistently found that women tend to have lower aspirations than men – we don't aim as high. This has also been offered as another factor in the gender wage gap. Some of the stories I have heard from women that illustrate this blind spot are summarized here.

- Five candidates were interviewed for a position in tech - four men and one woman. The woman was most qualified and was coming back from a maternity leave. When asked what their salary expectations were, the men all asked for salaries starting at $100,000. The women asked for $50,000 and added she was flexible on the amount.

- A woman was offered a position with a non-profit organization. When she was told the salary amount, she asked for slightly more. When the meeting was over and they were leaving, the female HR negotiator told her she could have asked for much more.

- An owner of a consulting company interviewed several men and women for a position. The men asked for a great deal more money than the women – although the women were the best candidates. The owner was aware that women tend to have lowered aspirations in negotiations (his wife was a coaching client of mine), so he offered the position to a woman and gave her what the men had asked for.

- A new MBA graduate was hired by a large accounting firm. When he was told the starting salary, he said he needed more and got it. All of the other starting graduates were women and took what was offered. His mother told me that she now finally understood why her son was the only one to ask.

T&T: KEEP ASPIRATIONS HIGH

Don't settle for "good enough." Research shows that women tend to set their salary goals as much as 30% lower than men. So set your value high, do your research, and know your worth in a salary negotiation. There is direct relationship between goals and end results. The higher your goal, the better the outcome. Ask for more and you'll likely get more.

Another way to keep your aspirations high is to make sure you don't give in too soon. One young female law student got a plum assignment to work with a professor on a case going to the Supreme Court of Canada. Many other students had wanted it. I asked her how she got it and she said she asked six times - more than any other student. Don't be discouraged by a "no." Find other ways to get what you want and know that by asking, others will know about your interests. Rather than giving up, engage in problem solving to look for another way to get what you want.

GENDERED EXPECTATIONS IN NEGOTIATION

On the other side of the negotiation table are men and women who have their own GBS. And these GBS not only affect their personal approach to negotiation but how they respond to you during the negotiation - including the expectations they hold, the assumptions they make, and the conclusions they reach. And our behaviour in turn is influenced by what we anticipate or fear may be their reactions, expectations, assumptions, and conclusions. And much, if not all of this, can play out unconsciously. Welcome to the world of unconscious gender bias. This shows how advantageous it is to become aware of what we anticipate and fear about gendered expectations in negotiation, what research shows is expected of women when negotiating, and how to deal with it. This section sets out common gendered expectations and specific techniques for dealing with them.

WOMEN WHO ASK ARE CONSIDERED PUSHY

Whether we are aware or not, women intuit that when they ask for what they want they will be perceived negatively - perhaps as too direct, selfish, or pushy. This is yet another factor in women not asking. And research proves them right. There are social, relationship, and economic costs to violating the expectation that women will wait for what is given and take what is offered.

So how does one navigate this thorny briar patch? Here are some suggestions.

- Be pleasant. Just because you are asking for more or holding firm at a certain amount does not mean that your demeanor has to be tough or aggressive. For details on this strategy see the section "Iron Fist in a Velvet Glove" below.
- Disagree or hold firm in an agreeable way. Point out all of the things that have been agreed to so far. List the many benefits of the negotiation overall. Stay positive and keep the negotiation on track with everyone seeing the end goal.
- Ask in a way that is gender typical. For examples see the section "Use Audience Focused Asks" above. Invoke the collective and use *we* instead of *me*. Wherever possible ask what you can do for them. Talk about your team or colleagues in ways to advance your negotiation goals.
- In a salary negotiation, to avoid looking adversarial and getting into a pure price negotiation, create a package of salary and benefits. This will allow you to trade-off using different items. Use collaborative strategy to co-create with the other side and expand the number of items in the negotiation. This strategy is a natural fit for women as we have been socialized to negotiate by inviting others to share their perspective.

- Develop a calm yet firm tone. You may be apprehensive or anxious but you want to give the impression that this is all in a day's work for you.
- Be warm but not flirtatious. As women we still unfortunately have to anticipate unwanted attention and incorrect assumptions about friendliness.
- Name gendered expectations. For example, you might make the following points: "You may think I am being direct with this ask but I think it is important for the team (the department, other women etc.) that this item be made available." "I hope you don't think I am being pushy but this is the salary being paid for this type of position at other companies." "I am very direct in my negotiation style, a style that has been very successful in negotiating great deals for my current company." By naming it you address the gender elephant in the room and make the unconscious conscious by using the *Shine a Light* career strategy. This exposure reduces the effect of the gendered expectation.

MASCULINE STYLE AND STEREOTYPE BACKLASH

Some women think that being tough is effective in negotiation. However, tough and competitive behaviour from a woman will tend to elicit backlash. There are two GBS in operation when this happens. Due to gender stereotypes and expectations, masculine behaviour displayed by a woman can create negative responses and be viewed as more extreme than it is. In addition, based on how power is displayed by male gender culture, by pushing hard you will have put yourself in a one-up position and thus the reaction (unconscious or conscious) will be to take you down a peg. The resultant backlash may include holding firm to an unreasonable position, making no concessions, giving no information, and attempting to reduce your expectations about the outcome. Given the significant risk of an impasse where neither party will compromise in a competitive negotiation, acting tough usually leads to no agreement rather than to success.

T&T: IRON FIST IN A VELVET GLOVE APPROACH

Women who are skilled in negotiation often use an approach in which they get what they want or what the client wants while still being pleasant and agreeable. This tactic, called the *iron fist in a velvet glove*, works well and involves being pleasant in demeanor but competitive and inflexible in substance. By separating demeanor from substance, the other side will have a hard time figuring out your strategy. You don't have to be tough or push hard for what you want to be competitive in substance. You can be very pleasant and congenial as you take the biggest piece of the pie. You can appear friendly and cooperative as you hold firm on those items that are important to you. This approach works well with competitive players on the other side of the table who won't or can't use a different strategy.

Another advantage of this approach is that it plays into feminine stereotypes. The same feminine traits of warmth, friendliness, empathy, and concern for others could be a major disadvantage in competitive negotiation if used unconsciously, but can offer an advantage when used consciously. This strategy is called "Use It" and is discussed in the Expose chapter. It works by allowing you to outwit and outplay others that misjudge your skills and abilities due to gender bias. Annie Duke, a famous poker player, calls it "stereotype tax."

WOMEN GIVE-IN

Research shows that both men and women push a woman harder in negotiation than a man. This is due to gendered expectations that women will give in and fold their tents sooner than men. Most women are not comfortable in a competitive situation as it feels hostile. And this feeling is not surprising as the psychology of competitive strategy is to move against the other side to get the outcome you want.

T&T: HOLD FIRM

To counter the tendency to give in due to pressure during a competitive negotiation, here are tips for holding firm.

- Appreciate competitive strategy for the game that it is. Understand the tactics, psychology, and rules of competitive negotiation. Never take it personally. Instead realize that the moves are based on the goal of getting the best outcome.
- Research shows that most women are more risk averse than men. It often seems safer to give in and take the lesser deal than to hold out for more and lose it all. Also, women tend to have lower expectations then men. Use this information to hold firm longer.
- In any negotiation over price, do your research and be confident about the price you want to get (your target price).
- Preparation will allow you to set a reservation or walk-away price. You would not accept a lower salary or fewer benefits than you are getting in your current job unless there was a good reason.
- Knowing your alternatives or having other options also helps you hold firm. If you are negotiating a job offer, having another interested employer allows you to use that information to increase a low offer. As a seller, having multiple interested buyers will allow you to negotiate a good price for a product.
- Harness the power of negotiating for others to hold firm. Think about who else will be benefiting from you getting a good salary or a good result in the negotiation.
- If you intuit they are not going to compromise, think about other ways to get what you want. Can any items be added to the negotiation? Be creative. Rather than just giving in on price, look for items that are easy for the other side to give but are valuable

to you or your company. That way you can compromise on price but still have a good negotiated outcome.

· Take a break if you are being pushed hard to agree. Especially if you are feeling uncomfortable and pressured. Go get a coffee or use the washroom. You may even stay where you are and take a mental break by saying, "Let me think about that." A break will allow you to refocus on your negotiation goals and walk-away amount. It will give you a chance to reflect on why the pressure tactics are being used. You will be able to clear your head, refocus, and go in stronger.

T&T: USE POWERFUL NON-VERBAL TOOLS

Most women have habits that signal a soft approach and allow them to connect with others. These habits include filling the silence, smiling at others, and nodding when listening. Opposite behaviours can thus be used with striking effect to signal power, detachment, and cool resolve when used consciously and strategically in a negotiation.

· Don't be afraid of the pause. Use silence – it is a powerful tool. Women report this works remarkably well and causes others to jump in to fill the void by either agreeing to your position or offering compromises. Silence also gives you time to centre yourself and gather your resolve.

· In addition to filling silence, women tend to smile more than men. Learn to strategically use your poker face. You might confuse the other side with a smile when a shocked, disappointed, or neutral face would work better.

· Use expansive postures to increase your confidence. Take up space. As discussed in the Presence chapter, the body leads the mind due to the powerful mind/body connection.

· Use body scans during the negotiation – it will tell you how you are feeling.[101] Do you have tension in your neck and shoulders?

Is your stomach feeling queasy? Are your knees hurting from muscle tension? This information will tell you how you are reacting to the negotiation. Discover what emotions are present. If needed, ask for a short break. This will allow you time to refocus on your negotiation goal, recall your reservation point and think of all the people who benefit from a successful negotiation outcome.

· Avoid nodding your head to indicate you have heard the other side. Also avoid saying "uh-huh" as you hear each item. The other side will think you are agreeing when you are only indicating you have heard what they said. They will feel deceived when they discover they don't have your agreement on all of those items or issues.

SALARY NEGOTIATION TIPS

To be clear, there is not just one factor that contributes to pay inequity. Whether it is due to women being offered less than men, hiring managers wanting the best employee for the least amount of money, or men negotiating aggressively for more, many external factors support and maintain the gender wage gap. To totally reform this situation, change is required at the macro levels of society. However, you can make your individual contribution to closing the gender wage gap by using this information and self-awareness about GBS to negotiate a higher salary and better benefits package for yourself.

Tools and techniques previously discussed in this chapter are included here again for those reading this as a stand-alone section. Negotiation is a dynamic interaction so it is not possible to provide a script. However, there are best practices as set out in this section. So read the following tips, take what you want from them, and know that you will do a great job! These tips and tools are set out according to a time line with the process starting immediately after a job offer has been made.

IMMEDIATELY AFTER A JOB OFFER

When you get a job offer it is best to take the time to objectively assess it and prepare. You don't want to immediately accept what is offered or start to negotiate right away. The salary may be three times what you expected but you still want to think about it. Thank them profusely for the offer, say you will get back to them, and leave the room or hang up the phone. Don't believe it when you are told that there is no room to negotiate. Apparently 84% of hiring managers expect some sort of negotiation.[102] So if you don't ask, you are leaving money on the table. If at the time the offer is made you are prepared to negotiate for more, you know your worth, you have done your research and practiced how to ask, then ignore this advice, seize the moment, and go for it!

BEFORE THE NEGOTIATION

Determine Your Worth

Be prepared by knowing what you are worth. Be aware of the skill set, knowledge, and experience you bring to the job. Do your research so you know what others in similar positions are making.

- Find similar companies geographically close to where you're interviewing and research those salaries.
- If possible, find out about the salary structure at your prospective workplace. What is the salary range for the position you are seeking? What about raises? Are there incentives such as bonuses and profit sharing? You want to be as prepared as you be can be going in.

- If you are part of a profession, find out the salary information provided by professional societies or associations. Often such information is published in trade magazines.
- Use your network: talk to your friends, family, acquaintances, recruiters or anyone you know who can give a helpful perspective on what to ask for.
- Search the internet to get insights and information. There are now numerous apps and websites that provide market information on salaries.
- Keep looking until you get the same approximate salary amount or range from multiple sources. Once you know the salary range and compensation packages, aim high. Set the target amount. That target will be psychologically powerful in the negotiation.
- Don't settle for "good enough" but do consider in advance your lowest acceptable salary.

Once you have a salary range in mind, think of reasons to justify your ask such as your experience and credentials. If you are pushing the salary range envelope, be prepared to talk about your worth. Anticipate that you may need to make assurances about what you will accomplish in the job. Prime your fast processing system with words about your competence and experience. Have phrases you can use during the interview to make your value visible and obvious.

Prepare – Interests and Items

- In any negotiation you want to know the terrain not just the trail. So in addition to knowing your worth, you want to prepare more broadly. Here are some suggestions for doing that. Prepare from two perspectives – **yours and theirs.** What do you want and what are their interests? What do you have that they need? What about you is unique? We frequently discount our abilities and skills and instead focus on our needs. How can you help them? List the ways. It will provide you with confidence to go into the interview. Remember – they would not be interviewing you if they did not have an interest you can satisfy.

- Think about **the other items you want to negotiate.** Are the benefits standard? What about vacation time? Flex time? Training and professional development? Add them to the mix so the negotiation is about multiple items and not just one – salary. As discussed in this chapter, price negotiations – those just about money – can become competitive quickly.

- Be prepared for the question **"what are you making now?"** It will be used as a starting place for salary so think about whether you want to reveal it. To deflect the question, you might talk about how this position involves greater responsibilities and different skills. In other words, you may want to argue that the two positions are like apples and oranges: they can't be compared.

- Prepare for the negotiation by knowing when you plan to hold firm and when you will compromise. Knowing your walk-away amount and your options outside of this negotiation will help with that.

Assess Your Options

Another way to gain confidence for a salary negotiation is to assess your options or alternatives. The more options you have, the more in demand you are going to be. The more sought after you are, the more valuable people think you are. If you are interviewing at one company or firm, consider if there is another organization that would be interested. The ideal situation is being able to leverage one offer against another. For example, if you want to stay at your current workplace but want a raise or better benefits, getting an offer from another company can help in your negotiation with your current employer (i.e., by requesting that they match the other deal or starting a bidding war). Assessing your options also helps determine your reservation or walk away point. You would rarely take a new position that offered less than your current one unless there were other great incentives.

Get Comfortable with the Ask

Before the salary negotiation you want to be comfortable with the ask. So start preparing before the job interview. You may want to start practicing now even if there is no job interview on the horizon. Get comfortable with asks generally. Start with small asks at work, such as for a project that is easily obtained or for a day off that you know you are going to get in order to get comfortable with the act of asking.

Avoid demanding or asking in an aggressive manner. This approach does not work well due to gendered expectations, and it might not feel good doing it that way. Look at the various ways to make requests set out in this chapter. Think about how you might ask. It is always advisable to have some familiar phrases to use that feel comfortable. Although these audience focused asks are also discussed elsewhere in this chapter, the example below are specifically for use in a salary negotiation.

- "Are there alternatives to this salary package? Might it be possible to increase the salary through other incentives? Have you ever paid more money to someone with similar experience and background? On what basis was that possible?" (**Planting the Seed**)
- "How can we work this out so it is a good outcome for both of us? Tell me what you think about this …? What are some other options? What is important to the company? What is important to you? These are my interests and needs. Can we figure out how to come up with a great agreement for both of us?" (**Co-Creative**)
- "I am delighted to be offered this job and know I will enjoy working here. This company's reputation is stellar and I am sure that I can contribute a lot. With regard to salary, I was wondering

if this is the highest you can go? My research shows that the salary for this position is more than what you are offering." (**Positive Framing**)

- "I anticipate that you must get a lot of questions about salary packages and I appreciate your patience. I am puzzled by the amount you are offering as my research shows that a salary amount of $XXXX would be more reasonable and fair. Could you help me understand the difference?" (**Build a Golden Bridge**)

- "How can I help you with this issue? Is there a way we can work together on this? How can I help you to help me? It is important to me that everyone is satisfied with this agreement. How can we come up with a win/win solution?" (**Collective Concern**)

- "Can you pay me more? What would you advise me to do? If your daughter or sister were in my situation what would you advise her to do?" (**One Step-Down**)

- "I would like to be paid what I am worth. Is this the starting salary of everyone working here with my experience and credentials? This salary amount is not in line with market rates – can you raise it to make it more consistent?" (**Direct Ask** is not recommended in a salary negotiation as you may appear too direct and perhaps even hostile to people who don't know you and you don't yet know their style. It's better to use this in asking for a raise with a manager who has a direct style).

There are advantages and disadvantages to each of these types of asks and they are dependent on the characteristics of the person you are asking. For a fuller discussion about these types of asks, see the section above on audience-focused asks.

DURING THE NEGOTIATION

Breathe

Take a deep breath and relax. If you negotiate in a relaxed way you will appear confident, make others around you comfortable, and greatly increase your chances of success. Being relaxed will also allow you to be open, flexible, and more observant.

Establish Credibility/ Exude Confidence

Understand that it is important to establish credibility early on in the encounter, especially with highly competitive players. Research shows that women will assume you have the credentials to be at the table but men will not. If you are negotiating for work, weave in your experience and credentials. "This is an issue I have dealt with before on a similar project, although it was much larger in scope." By weaving it in rather than stating it bluntly at the beginning of the negotiation you reduce the chance of backlash.

It is also important to make sure they know you have done your homework. For instance, if you are negotiating the price of a car, let them know you have researched the dealership's costs and associated expenses. Also, if you've equipped yourself with background research you will be able to enter into the negotiation with confidence and optimism.

Harness the Power of the Feminine

Salary negotiations involve negotiating for self-interests. As previously discussed, this skill runs counter to traditional feminine values. To align with gendered expectations and harness the power of gender training, use the collective. This can be done in several ways.

- Use a cooperative approach during negotiations. Framing negotiations as beneficial opportunities for all parties instead of approaching negotiations in a competitive manner often results in more acceptance and less backlash. Use compromise and problem solving to reach agreement.

- Focus on how you can help the employer and organization with your skills and experience.
- Show respect for organizational relationships by acknowledging that this is the only time you will be across the table from each other. Also point out that the negotiation skills you are using now will be a great advantage when you use them to negotiate on behalf of the organization.
- Talk about the gender wage gap. Mention that women who ask for better compensation violate gender norms and often experience economic sanctions as a result. Bring the GBS into the light.[103]
- To bolster your negotiation prowess, evoke the collective by remembering all the people who will benefit from you getting a higher salary and better benefits. Negotiate for them.

Use a Velvet Glove Approach

Women can be just as tough as men when it comes to staying firm on positions in negotiations. However, women who ask for what they want in gentler, more socially acceptable and friendlier ways, and who hold firm while still being pleasant have a better chance of being successful in the negotiation than those who adopt an in-your-face, no-nonsense approach. Velvet glove women lawyers are the best negotiators I have seen and are in great demand by their clients. A woman described two women lawyers that her organization had on retainer. They preferred the one who was very friendly with the other side, picked her battles, and ultimately got what the client wanted. The other, described as a barracuda, was disagreeable, fought everything and, as a result, often did not get what mattered most to the client.

Set High Goals

Don't settle for "good enough." If you go into salary negotiations with anxiety or feel pessimistic about the outcome, you'll most likely ask for - and get - less than you deserve. There is a direct relationship in negotiation between goals and end result - the higher your goals, the better the outcome. Ask for more and you'll get more. It's that simple. Don't be like the many women who are the best candidates for the position but who ask for much less than their male counterparts. Do your research and don't sell yourself short. Set your expectations high.

Shine a Light on the Gap

You may wish to raise the gender gap directly, especially if the amount offered is below what your salary research revealed. Use humour about what it would mean for you to get more – "one small step for woman, one giant leap for womankind." Ask sincerely if they are aware of the gender gap and express your desire to help narrow the gap. By raising it you shine a light on the bias – and bias does not do well in the light. By raising the gender wage gap you also harness the power of the collective. Your higher salary will help narrow the gap and make you realize you are not alone in negotiating for what you are worth.

AFTER THE NEGOTIATION

It might be the case that some of the items you thought of while preparing for this salary negotiation were not appropriate to negotiate right now, although they would make this position ideal. For instance, what about resources to make you more efficient? Will you have an assistant? What is the budget you are being allocated? Perhaps these are not even possible at your current age and stage – but it is good to think this way strategically.

What if you ask but don't get an item that is important to you at the salary negotiation? Add it to your wish list. Create a calendar reminder so you don't forget. If it involves a raise, find out when salaries are reviewed. Ensure you understand what success is and what is rewarded in your organization. Revisit the items you did not get with your boss or with someone in HR when a sufficient amount of time has passed and you understand the organizational culture better. Be aware that gender is a significant factor not only in salary negotiation but also in asking for a raise. Research has shown that men are more comfortable asking for a raise, they are more likely to have asked for one during their careers, and they ask for more money than women.[104]

Know that you can always make small asks at another time. For example, you may ask for a project that fits your skills and will show your value to others you don't normally work with. Or ask for a committee position that will allow you to meet the people in the organization you want to meet. Once you ask and are rewarded for asking, you will start seeing opportunities everywhere.

With more women understanding their own GBS and the GBS of others, and with the use of these tips and tools, I am confident the wage gap will eventually be reduced. Of course these small steps won't completely solve the larger problem. It is important that men and women join together to advocate for transparency in organizational compensation, audits to identify and close gender gaps in pay, legislation to support fairness, and awareness and training to illuminate and reduce GBS. By working together, the gap will close in time.

WHAT ORGANIZATIONS, LEADERS, AND MENTORS CAN DO

- Support pay transparency for both salary and bonuses. This is now law in Iceland and the UK.
- Ensure everyone involved with salary negotiations is made aware of the gender wage gap.

- Do a wage audit to determine if there are any gender gaps in your organization.
- Implement standardized pay grades at entrance level positions.
- Implement a "no negotiation" policy for salaries or increase transparency about what is negotiable in salary negotiations – for both first time positions and subsequent wage increases.
- Ensure that previous salary histories are not used as anchors for setting starting salaries.
- Invite and encourage people to speak up or initiate negotiations.
- Provide training in collaborative negotiation and model its use.

WANT TO READ MORE?

Babcock, Linda and Sara Laschever. *Women Don't Ask: Negotiation and the Gender Divide.* Princeton: Princeton University Press, 2003.

Babcock, Linda and Sara Laschever. Ask *for It: How Women Can Use the Power of Negotiation to Get What They Really Want.* New York: Bantam, 2009.

Brzezinski, Mika. *Knowing Your Value: Women, Money, and Getting What You're Worth.* Reprint edition. New York: Weinstein Books, 2012.

Fisher, Roger and William Ury. *Getting to Yes: Negotiating Agreement Without Giving In.* Rev. ed. Middlesex, England: Penguin Books, 2011.

Kolb, Deborah and Judith Williams. *Everyday Negotiation: Navigating the Hidden Agendas in Bargaining.* New York: Jossey-Bass, 2003.

Kolb, Deborah, Judith Williams, and Carol Frohlinger. *Her Place at the Table: A Women's Guide to Negotiating Five Key Challenges to Leadership Success.* Rev. ed. New York: Jossey-Bass, 2010.

COMMUNICATE

To make your value visible and to advance in the workplace it is essential to use clear, effective, and confident communication. When communication is clear, fewer misinterpretations occur and there is a greater chance that you will be understood and succeed. Effective communication in the workplace allows your ideas to be heard and makes your contributions obvious. If you are not able to communicate well, others may not see your abilities and value. And for advancement, this is key.

In addition to clear and effective communication, it is important for women to learn how to express the language of confidence, influence, and authority. Boys learn early in life to express these characteristics through communication due to the masculine hierarchical view of power (being one-up or one-down) and the emphasis on status. Deborah Tannen who has studied gender communication differences for decades concludes that as a result of this world view, masculine communication patterns revolve around independence, orders, advice, and information as well as negotiation of status in the group. In direct contrast, feminine communication patterns revolve around relationship, with a focus on equality, connection, support, intimacy, feelings, and rapport.[105]

Feminine communication styles and habits when viewed through masculine lenses can, and often are, misread. Women and men who use a tentative style are often viewed as lacking confidence or even competence. On the other hand, women who only use a direct masculine style may gain a reputation for being bossy or arrogant. And those are the polite descriptors. The way around this gender blind spot (GBS) is to become a skillful communicator who is able to select the style that best fits the circumstance and appear confident, competent, and professional.

Language styles and verbal habits arise from personal factors in addition to gender, including national culture, age, geographical area, profession, and personality. All styles or language patterns are valid and work well when used with people who have the same style. They act as a shortcut to understanding and make communication faster. However, differences in style can cause problems in interactions. When men and women communicate without appreciating gender differences in communication or use gender communication habits and rituals unconsciously, miscommunication, misinterpretation, and even conflict can arise. To understand your gender style of communication, a questionnaire is provided at the end of this chapter.

Communication rituals and habits that distract from your ideas and make you appear less competent and confident are examined in this chapter. The career strategy promoted in this chapter is *Go Along to Get Along*. The focus is on managing impressions by managing automatic gender habits and approaches. Tools and techniques (T&T) for speaking clearly, for reducing tentative and uncertain language styles, and for standing firm when challenged or interrupted are provided. Since the goal is not to abandon a feminine style of communication but rather to expand communication skills, the appropriate times to use feminine language patterns are also discussed.

DEALING WITH COMMUNICATION BLIND SPOTS

GBS: RAPPORT NOT REPORT

For women using a feminine style, conversations are a way to build relationships and enhance intimacy. For men, they are a way to solve problems, give information, and establish status. Thus men tend to be direct, voicing their ideas and opinions boldly and concisely. Women, who like to solicit perspectives from others, tend to use a conversational style that invites comment and discussion *even when they have already made a decision.* Women have been found to provide a lot of detail to show that we have done the work. They use preamble as a way to connect with the listener before providing information.

Feminine language styles or habits can be misread as tentative and uncertain rather than what they really are - connective. Through a masculine lens it can appear that an idea, opinion, or plan is being sought. By being direct and concise with others who value and use this communication style, you will be seen as confident, competent, and certain.

Speaking in this way also allows your ideas and opinions to be heard. A clear speaking structure makes it easy for your audience. Listening is difficult because our capacity for processing words far exceeds the rate at which words are spoken. As a result, our minds tend to wander and we lose focus.

In the following section, I include a simple and standard communication guide that may be used in a variety of situations. The description of the elements explains how to use the guide and how these elements, both the order and type, make it easy for the audience to listen and follow your ideas.

T&T: COMMUNICATION GUIDE

In workplace meetings where time is often of the essence, it is important to be able to express ideas with brevity and precision. Due to the importance of connection in female gender culture, however, women tend to use more words to appear to be friendlier. Brief and curt emails, for instance, are often interpreted by women as uncaring and rude. However, communication is all about the audience. For men, being wordy is a signal of uncertainty and even defensiveness. Through a male lens, conciseness communicates competence.

To help you expand your communication skills and become a clear and concise communicator, a communication guide template is included here. This guide may be used in a variety of situations including face-to-face interactions, voice messages, speeches, and written communications, such as emails or memos.

COMMUNICATION GUIDE

The Opening:

The Subject:

Main Point:

The Body — statement about structure:

(*e.g.*, reasons, ways, chronological order, data, results, location)

1.

2.

3.

4.

Main Point (repeated):

Requested Response:

COMMUNICATION GUIDE ELEMENTS

The Opening

Begin with an opener or grabber, even if it's a simple "hello." Openings are opportunities to catch the audience's attention, build connection, establish your credibility, and get people thinking in the direction you want them to go. Don't fill this opportunity with words lacking intent or focus. Openers should be aligned in content and tone with the rest of your remarks. Examples include, "I am pleased we are meeting to discuss this important issue," and "We can get agreement on how to solve this problem." The opening allows acknowledgement of and connection with the audience before the message is stated.

The Subject

The subject provides a context for the information you are about to share and tells your audience what you will be talking about. For instance, you might say, "I want to focus on ...," "this is about why I think XX...," or "I have called you together for..." This helps the person you are addressing to mentally switch from the work they are doing and more easily follow what you are about to tell them.

The Main Point

The main point tells the listener the essence of your point. Think of it as a headline. To make it more memorable, try to create a main point that is short and concise. Putting the main point up front allows those with a preference for the big-picture and those who are impatient listeners to get your message quickly. Have you ever been frustrated by a voice message or an email because the main point did not occur until the very end? This structure prevents that problem.

The Body

After the main point, state the structure of your supporting points. Structures are varied and can include reasons, ways, chronological order, research results, statistical data, geographical location, and procedure. For example, you could say, "Here are three reasons..." or "Here are five ways we could deal with this issue." Explaining the structure gives the audience a roadmap. You support the main point you are making with ideas, reasons, details, evidence, proof, illustrations, facts, research data, or stories. This structure allows your listener to hear the material in a mentally coherent pattern, making it easier to understand.

Restated Main Point

You may wish, depending on the context, to tell them your main point again to focus the conversation that follows. Repetition makes it easier to listen, comprehend, and remember.

Requested Response

If appropriate, tell them what you want them to do based on what you've said. Perhaps it is a discussion you want to have. Perhaps you would like an indication from them that they agree with your argument or proposal. Making clear what you need from them allows them to more easily respond to your request and to the information you have provided.

Below is an example using the Communication Guide in a face-to-face meeting.

The Opening: "Good morning."

The Subject: "Is now a good time to discuss the legal issues raised in the report?"

Main Point: "Several aspects of the project need to be reviewed by outside legal counsel."

The Body: "They include:

1. Privacy concerns re: the data being collected from our shareholders and clients.
2. The required legal notice period appears longer than anticipated by the closing date.
3. Competition Act issues arising from the acquisition."

Main Point again: "Several aspects of the project need review by outside counsel."

Requested Response: "Do you want me to start the review process with outside counsel?"

GBS: ALWAYS BE AGREEABLE AND SUPPORTIVE

This GBS is both a help and a hindrance in the workplace. Being agreeable and supportive makes you a team player and others will like working with you. It is obviously a great strength. However, this feminine ideal becomes a hindrance when competitive verbal tactics are used to undermine your authority, impugn your credibility, and decrease your influence. Such competitive challenges are seldom about the substance of the discussion and are usually about power dynamics. These tactics influence which ideas are heard, how ideas are received, and who gets the credit. In order to manage impressions, claim and maintain legitimacy, assert power and influence, and shape perceptions, it is best to deal with competitive tactics quickly and effectively.

Unfortunately the feminine rules of *always be nice and never fight back* and *always smile and be sweet* do not serve us well in dealing with competitive verbal tactics. They hinder our ability to manage the power dynamic and to look confident and competent. To more fully understand how these feminine rules impact behaviour at work, here are some examples.

- Giving in too easily in negotiation or when asking for what you want
- Backing off when faced with opposition or sharp criticism of ideas
- Not dealing with interruptions or stolen ideas
- Ignoring challenges to authority and even sexist remarks
- Avoiding giving a controversial opinion only to have someone applauded for voicing it

So what can we do? How do we navigate our internalized gender rules and others' gendered expectations in a way that allows us to appear confident and authoritative without appearing aggressive? Below are some tools and techniques (T&T) that will allow you to stand firm.

T&T: STAND FIRM

What does it mean to stand firm? Being on the receiving end of a verbal tactic can be uncomfortable and unsettling. And that is what is intended by the tactic – to throw you off your game and show power. How can you respond? If you ignore it you remain at a disadvantage. If you confront it, you risk escalating the situation. The objective is to find tools that allow you to calmly and confidently stand up for yourself and your ideas. It can be done very quietly and quickly by knowing the right tools to use. Stopping it quickly is very important where the comment or the repeated pattern of comments have the potential to damage your reputation or challenge your credibility. You shouldn't need to challenge these competitive tactics alone. Others are complicit if they don't speak up. Enlist the help of colleagues or even supervisors.

Here are some common workplace situations that require standing firm instead of being agreeable and supportive.

Interruptions: Men interrupting women is very common so you are not alone if it is happening to you. If it makes you feel better, men also interrupt other men. Here are some suggested communication tools for dealing with this situation.

- Preface your comments with a road-map so others will know where you are going with your point and when they can jump in. For instance, you could say, "I would like your views on this but let me give you the background on this issue first." Or, "I would appreciate your opinion on this matter but first I would like to describe the situation as I see it."
- Here are some responses when you are interrupted.
  - "Let me finish my thought," or "Let me complete my sentence."
  - "I would like to finish."
  - "I have another point to make."
  - Keep talking over the interruption firmly and calmly without speeding up or going higher in tone.
  - Hold your hand up and reinforce it by saying, "Hold on I am not finished." Look the interrupter in the eye until you have taken back the floor.
- Avoid asking for permission by saying things like, "Please let me finish," or "I would appreciate if you would let me complete my sentence."
- Enlist a colleague to build an alliance. Having someone else say, "Let Jess finish. Let's hear what she has to say," makes it clear that others don't support interruptions. It also takes the heat off you in having to deal with it each time and makes you feel good knowing you have support.

Stolen Ideas: Another common workplace situation is having your ideas stolen or having others take credit for what you have done. This behaviour makes sense in light of the masculine mindset where status and achievement are paramount, however, there is no excuse for taking credit for someone else's idea. This behaviour needs to be dealt with. Here are some tools for responding in this situation.

- Ensure that you state your idea clearly and confidently. Avoid using tentative language patterns such as, "I was wondering if it might not be a good idea.... Would that be OK?" Instead take yourself out of the statement. You might say, "the software has not performed as expected. I propose ..." If you wish to soften the statement you may encourage others to add their thoughts and opinions by adding at the end, "Does anyone have other ideas?"
- Employ a tactic called "Thank'N'Yank."[106] This response involves thanking the person and taking back ownership of the idea. For instance, you could say, "Exactly. So glad you like the idea. Now let's talk next steps." Or, "Thanks for building on my idea. Glad we agree. What are some other ways we could approach this?"
- Enlist a colleague to acknowledge that the idea was yours. Have them repeat the idea and your name. They don't have to agree with it (although that helps) but rather they are ensuring the credit is not lost. Do the same thing for them if interruptions and stealing ideas is common.

If you know such behaviour is about power dynamics and gender culture, then you will more likely be able to stand by your ideas and opinions to make your value visible. And others will start to recognize your ideas as well. A friend who worked in the very masculine world of mining told me she knew she had made it when junior males started acknowledging her contributions and ideas overtly in meetings.

Undermining Comments: Remarks meant to undermine you can run the gamut from sexist comments to sharp criticism. In calling you *kiddo, honey, sweetie,* or *young lady,* for instance, the speaker aims to get you off your game. Holding firm under these circumstances can often be very difficult. These comments almost always involve competitive tactics used consciously and they are aimed at reducing your status and negatively impacting your professional image. Here are some tools that may be used on their own or in combination for dealing with these tactics.

Don't take it personally and stay focused. Often competitive tactics are just that – a game to get you to do or say things you wouldn't normally do. They are meant to throw you off and reduce your credibility, power, and legitimacy. By responding calmly and rationally, you have won.

Use the power of the pause. One of the easiest ways to show that a line has been crossed is to become silent. Women often try to smooth things over or make them better by talking. So silence is a very potent tool. Early in my career as a psychologist I was asked out for dinner while attending a conference. The waiter approached our table of seven men and me, the lone woman, and while looking at me said, "Those are great odds." No one spoke as we did not know each other well and our only connection was the conference. The silence told the waiter he had been inappropriate and he immediately apologized. I did not need to say or do anything. After you have used the power of the pause, just continue as if nothing has happened. The message has been sent.

Go to the balcony. This is a negotiation term that refers to becoming detached and viewing the situation from a distance. If possible, remove yourself from the situation or take a break. Even the shortest break can disrupt the tactic. Or take a mental break to the balcony by saying, "Let me think about that." Or use the power of the pause. It will make the commenter think about what he or she just said.

Analyze the use. While away from the situation think about why this tactic was used. Analyze if this is a habitual style or if it is being purposely used to reduce your power and create a negative impression. It is important to know if you are a casual target like everyone else or a threat to this person. This determination will help you assess how to deal with it over the longer term.

Use the power of alliances. In meetings or in front of others, let others deal with the person. This is a very powerful and effective way to stop the behaviour. When I was a junior lawyer, a client in a meeting kept calling me "Blondie" and then asked me to get him coffee using this name. It was this request that caused the lawyer for the other side to speak up and say it was not appropriate. It stopped the behaviour immediately and made my senior colleague rather embarrassed that he had not called it earlier. If you are the subject of sexist comments, bullying or harassment, talk to your mentor. Depending upon the type of comment you may even seek the support of HR. Know that there are others there to help you – enlist them.

Call it. This can be more difficult. Confront the comments directly only if you feel comfortable doing so. Perhaps use humour, such as, "I only let my parents call me young lady." You may want to wait until after the meeting to pull the person aside and talk to them about their comments. However, it should not be on you to have to deal with this behaviour – especially when you are junior and when the person involved can influence your career. Talk to your mentor, supervisor, or colleagues and use the power of alliances to deal with this inappropriate behaviour. By calling out such comments you are ensuring that the culture of your organization is a respectful, healthy, and safe place to work. You will also gain respect by holding firm.

GBS: EQUALIZING POWER

The previous section deals with making your value visible through clear communication. This section looks at making your value visible by moderating language styles and verbal habits that can affect your image negatively if they are misinterpreted. It is important to note that these styles are only detrimental if used habitually without awareness; there is no absolute right or wrong style or habit. Rather, it is important to select the appropriate style based on the situation and the audience instead of using the same default style each time. Conscious selection allows for appropriate, contextual, and strategic use of language, which will enhance your image.

An important factor in conscious selection is being aware of the misunderstandings that may occur when styles differ. If the style you employ differs from the norm at your workplace, inaccurate impressions about abilities, character, confidence and intention may be created. Consequently, it is important to be aware of the style you use habitually and how that style may differ from others. In communication, it is all about your audience.

The key to becoming a skillful communicator is being aware of your preferred language style so you can become fluent and versatile in other styles. Being able to use other styles allows you to select the best style for the circumstance and to always appear professional. This versatility also allows you to be authoritative and assertive without appearing aggressive, and deferential without being self-deprecating.

Feminine language habits and patterns that try to equalize power tend to weaken the image and message. They include tentative speech patterns, the use of "I" inappropriately, indirect style, and the passive voice. Each of these undermining speech habits is discussed below together with tips and tools for minimizing or changing them.

TENTATIVE SPEECH PATTERNS

Hesitant speech is a verbal habit that suggests the speaker lacks confidence. This weakens the impact of her ideas, assertions, and messages. Speaking tentatively is not wrong in all circumstances and may be used strategically to show deference or deflect aggressive stances. However, these advantages tend to be limited when compared with the image created by their habitual and consistent use. If you want to create an image of confidence and certainty, be aware of these tentative speech patterns and limit their use to appropriate situations.

Undermining Starts

Undermining starts are phrases added at the beginning of sentences to signal uncertainty. When used automatically and frequently, they reflect uncertainty where none exists. When you have an idea or opinion that you want others to know about, it is important to stand out. Some common examples include: "Maybe it's just me but...," "This may be a dumb question...," "I feel this is about...," "I may not be right but...," "I don't have all the answers but...," "I guess my question is...," "I'm not an expert on that but...," "I kind of think that...," and "I may be the only one that feels this way..."

Weakening Modifiers

Using certain modifiers also weakens the impact of your message. These modifiers have the same effect as undermining starts. I have had more than one woman describe men they work with who are completely wrong on an issue but sound totally certain about their assertion. This is the reverse; there may be total certainty on the speaker's part, but the insertion of these habitual modifiers signals otherwise. Here are some common examples: "**Hopefully** we will be able to deal with this," "I **just** want to explain that...," "It's **kind** of normal for this...," and "**Basically** the main issue is..." Keep in mind that if you need to communicate actual uncertainty, use these modifiers. Again, the key point is to use them consciously rather than habitually.

Diminishing Endings

Diminishing endings are words added to the ends of sentences that signal uncertainty. They are the equivalent of verbal "up-speak" — the tonal upswing at the end of a sentence that makes it sound like a question. When every sentence that is spoken has a tonal lift at the end, the pattern becomes obvious and distracting. I hear it more and more in seminars and individual coaching. Psychologically, it is used to connect with the other person — to signal that you want the other person to share in the conversation. Unfortunately, up-speak and undermining endings minimize the message and reduce the person's authority. To be clear, there is nothing wrong with these endings or with up-speak, and the use is entirely appropriate with friends or others who speak in this manner. However, for a listener with a different, more authoritative style, it will often be viewed as indicating a lack of certainty, knowledge, and ability. Here are some common examples: "How does that sound?" "Isn't it?" "Right?" "Okay?" "Does that make sense?" and "If it's okay with you."

Stories from clients reveal that we often use these as verbal ticks when we are under stress. They are insidious and unconscious speech patterns that can slip in under the radar. Become aware by listening to yourself or asking trusted colleagues if they have noticed any particular speech pattern you use.

Misplaced Focus — "I" as Subject

Research analyzing approximately 400,000 computerized texts suggests that people who often use the pronoun "I" come across as more personal, warm, and honest, while people who use fewer "I"s come across as more self-confident. This research also reveals that the person with the highest status tends to use "I" the least, while the person with the lowest status tends to use "I" the most. Thus, if you want to convey confidence, check your use, and possible overuse, of the word "I".[107]

Another inadvertent consequence of overusing "I" is becoming the inappropriate subject of a sentence; this minimizes the strength of the message and focuses a misplaced spotlight on the writer. Some experts suggest never starting a sentence with the word "I" unless you are specifically talking about yourself.[108] Consequently, use "I" only if you intentionally want to be more personal, and convey warmth and honesty. Below are examples of phrases to use instead of "I" phrases.

Instead of These "I" Phrases	Try These
"I feel the research is complete."	"The research is complete."
"I have a problem with my assistant - she is always late."	"My assistant is frequently late for work."
"I am pretty sure that this project deadline is problematic."	"The project deadline will not be met."
"I love this file."	"This file is interesting and challenging."
"I don't have enough time to complete the work."	"The work cannot be completed on time."
"I estimate this to be a 50-minute presentation."	"It's approximately a 50-minute presentation."

DIRECT/INDIRECT COMMUNICATION

Direct communication is straight forward, with the purpose of giving and getting information clearly and efficiently. In contrast, indirect communication can convey multiple meanings and the aim is diplomacy and saving face. Since clarity is important with a direct style of communication, the speaker is responsible for the listener's understanding. With an indirect style, the listener is responsible. An indirect style is therefore of great benefit when dealing with sensitive matters. However, what indirect style gains in diplomacy it loses in clarity. When a listener is required to determine which of the multiple meanings the indirect speaker may have intended, misinterpretation and miscommunication often result.

In his book *Outliers*, Malcolm Gladwell describes the difference between direct and indirect communication using a dramatic example.[109] He explains that in South Korea, as in many cultures, individuals who are subordinate in status employ an indirect style with those of higher status, while those of higher status employ a direct style. Gladwell looks at South Korean Air where pilots spoke directly and navigators spoke indirectly and examines various plane crashes that resulted from the dramatic clashing of these two styles. In one case, the navigator said, "we have a fuel issue," as an indirect way of saying, "there is no fuel left." Unfortunately, his statement was not interpreted by the pilot, a direct speaker, as an emergency. As a result of this miscommunication, the plane crashed.

To understand the differences, here are some examples of each style.

Indirect Style	Direct Style
"The letter has not been sent."	"Please get this letter out."
"It would be good for you to see John about this matter while I am out."	"Please see John today about this matter."
"We have an issue with the opinion."	"The third paragraph of the opinion is wrong."
"Would you like some coffee?"	"I am going to get some coffee, would you like some?"

There are advantages and disadvantages to each style. A huge advantage of direct communication is that it reduces confusion. The indirect approach is often less clear, especially when the receiver is a direct speaker.

After a discussion on these two types of communication, a woman left my seminar at the break to email her assistant. The night before, she had left a message for him which said, "It would be good if you see X about the Y issue." Based on this discussion about the two styles, she realized he would interpret this indirect communication as a choice and would most likely not do what she had asked. Her message, although diplomatic, was not clear.

One disadvantage of the direct style of communication is that it can evoke stereotype backlash. So when used by a woman this approach may be judged as bossy or even hostile, especially when used with an indirect speaker. In contrast, indirect communication can reduce contention, smooth over conflict, and save face for others.

In the business world, direct speaking is valued and is the approach most often used. However, where diplomacy and face-saving is required, especially with clients, bosses, and colleagues, indirect communication works best.

PASSIVE, ASSERTIVE, AND AGGRESSIVE VOICE

It is important for everyone to have a full range of voices in order to use the right one at the right time. As you will see as we go through the three voices - passive, aggressive, and assertive - the voice of choice in most situations will be assertive.

The *passive voice*, like the indirect approach, backs down from the encounter and allows the other person to save face. It can be used to soften a request, to reduce the aggression in the encounter, and to lessen tension. It is self-effacing, and typically a person who uses it will be viewed as subordinate. It is associated with feminine style and tends to be used more by women than men. In a masculine workplace, this voice can easily be misinterpreted as reflecting a lack of confidence.

The *aggressive voice* asserts dominance over the other. When used in day-to-day communication it can significantly damage relationships. It is the approach of choice when meeting aggressive opponents who are unwilling to change their approach. This stance indicates that you will not back down from the position you are advocating.

The *assertive voice* reflects the most balanced stance, and as such is an excellent default approach. This voice allows you to stand your ground while respecting the boundaries of others.

Below are some examples of each of the three approaches.

Missing Documents

Passive: "I may have missed them and I will look through the file you gave me again, but I can't locate some important documents. I am sorry to interrupt, but could you tell me the place you typically put them?"

Aggressive: "I can't believe this! I have wasted two hours trying to find documents that don't exist. Next time you give me a file make sure all of the documents are in it."

Assertive: "The documents you asked me to review are not in this file. Is it possible that they are elsewhere?"

Problematic Clauses in a Report

Passive: "It may just be me, but it seems that some of the charts I have marked in red are not as clear as they could be. If you could get those changed, that would be great."

Aggressive: "What were you thinking? These charts are a disaster!"

Assertive: "There were a few charts at the beginning of the report that are not clear. I have marked the ones that require changes. Please make the necessary corrections and get the report back to me this afternoon."

It is advantageous not only to be able to use all three voices but to use them consciously and purposefully. If you use one voice habitually, it will reduce your ability to communicate clearly and will affect the perception others have of you.

WHEN TO USE SUBORDINATE LANGUAGE

After a seminar on confident communication, I was approached by a participant who was trying to understand this information in light of her very powerful boss who typically used tentative and passive language patterns. The participant further described her boss as being carefully listened to by others and well respected for her ideas and expertise. This story makes clear that using the language of subordination alone will not prevent your value from being made visible. However, when you are starting out in a profession, the image you project should be one of confidence and competence.

Once you have attained a certain level of power and influence, you may wish to intentionally use minimizing language patterns to soften your image and signal connection with others. Using diminishing endings in particular allows for greater connection and makes you more approachable. Such endings encourage others to disagree and respond, so if you want a discussion about the point you are making, use them. Research even suggests that superfluous apologies (saying sorry when you are not responsible such as, "sorry about the rain") builds trust and liking.[110] The key, therefore, is not to completely drop feminine habits but rather to use language skills and patterns consciously to align with your communication goals.

GBS: AVOIDING CONFLICT

Feminine culture teaches girls to avoid conflict and confrontation due to the importance of relationships and harmony. Thus, most women avoid confrontation and conflict by agreeing, supporting, or avoiding.

Masculine culture, in contrast, teaches boys to be comfortable with confrontation and competition as part of status and power display. Neither approach encourages a positive and constructive way to deal with conflict. Learning how to respond well to conflict is a tool that everyone should have. It maintains relationships, resolves issues and, if handled appropriately, enhances your brand.

T&T: THE CONFLICT COMMUNICATION PROCESS

It is never easy to have conflict conversations due to the high stakes that are often involved and the conflicting views. By using and mastering the skills of conflict communication and developing the attitudes suggested in this section, such conversations become less difficult and the opportunities more obvious. The conflict communication process, outlined below, allows you to better understand the other person's perspective, recognize your possible contribution to the conflict, and come to a satisfactory resolution. Putting it all together may seem daunting at times, but having a process to follow makes it easier.

The various stages in the conflict communication process are described below in chronological order. Using these stages in the order provided allows the conversation to continue and the dialogue to stay open. Often in conflict where judgements are rampant and accusations numerous, the conversation stops and the parties shut down. Through the use of these communication tools and techniques you will have an opportunity to communicate and come to a resolution, or at least a better understanding of the conflict, from both sides.

Make your opening objective. Avoid the *why* and focus on what happened. Start the conversation with the facts. Describe it as a third party observing the situation would. This allows you to be more objective and prevents shutting down the conversation before it can get started. Avoid any opinions or judgements. Appearing to be in the right in a situation and acting superior is the default approach of many people but it is not an attitude that helps resolve disputes. Rather, be curious and respectful.

Introduce your view. This is the stage where you start to include your point of view and conclusions. Continue to be honest and respectful, while being observant. Try not to make your view or conclusions sound like they are written in stone and are absolutely correct. Instead, talk tentatively, keeping the purpose of the conversation in sight. You may introduce your view and conclusions by saying, "it makes me wonder if..." "I am thinking that..." "It makes me feel...," etc. Make it clear that it is you who is thinking, wondering, or feeling, and that your view is not the absolute truth of the situation. You want to ensure the other person knows that you are open to changing your view once you are aware of all the facts and circumstances.

Invite their view. Showing that you are open to hearing from the other side allows you to naturally invite them to tell their view of the circumstances. You might do this by asking: "What's going on?" "I'd really like to hear your view on this," or "How are you seeing things?" Know that there will be information you don't currently have — information that may totally change your view of the situation. Use the listening techniques set out in the Politics chapter to listen carefully and fully.

Collaborate. Tell the other party your needs and interests — what was important to you in the situation? What were you hoping for? What happened that upset you, and why? Perhaps this is the reason that the conflict arose and created the problem. Find out their needs and interests. Generate solutions to the issue that fit your needs and theirs. This conversation can be initiated with prompts such as: "What is important to you?" "What would you like to see happen?" and "Help me to understand..."

The following are optional steps that may be used in a more formal process.

Document the agreement. You may wish to document the resolution in detail, including who will do what based on this resolution, what will be done, when it will be done and finally, how it will be done.

Decide on follow-up actions. The resolution may also involve follow-up actions, with details such as who will be involved, what they will do to follow up, when this will take place and what the consequences will be depending on what has occurred. This type of follow-up is more common in corporate settings or large organizations with formal reporting structures. To assist you in working through a conflict communication process, the worksheet below shows the various stages as well as point-form reminders for each.

Conflict Communication Process Worksheet

Stages/Notes	Description
1. The Objective Opening	The facts only; the *what* not the *why*
2. My View	Your point of view, including both facts and your conclusions · be honest but respectful · talk tentatively · soften the message · invite opposing views · keep sight of your goal of wanting resolution · be observant
3. Their View	Invite them to share and be curious "Help me to understand what's going on." "I'd really like to hear your opinion on this." "Please let me know if you see it differently." "I'd really like to hear your thoughts on this."

4. Collaborate	Tell them your needs and interests. Find out their needs and interests. Generate solutions that fit both of your needs.
5. Agreement	Who What When Document the details
6. Follow-up	Who What When

EXERCISES

QUESTIONNAIRE : M/F COMMUNICATION STYLES

Read each statement carefully. If the statement describes you, circle T and if it does not, circle F. As you respond, your frame of reference should be communication at work. The purpose of this questionnaire is to create awareness of your use of masculine and feminine communication styles and your ability to use both flexibly. If you are uncertain as to your use, ask a trusted work colleague.

1. I can leave out details and get to the point. **T F**
2. I can say no to requests. **T F**
3. I can change my communication style to flex to the other person's style. **T F**
4. I use minimizing openings such as "maybe it's just me" or "I guess my question is..." **T F**
5. I am comfortable questioning or debating my colleague during a conversation. **T F**
6. I often use minimizing endings such as "OK?" **T F**
7. When I speak it sounds authoritative and factual. **T F**

8. My communication shows that I value and support others. T F
9. I am not offended or hurt when someone does not agree with my ideas. **T F**
10. I watch non-verbal cues during conversations. **T F**
11. I use greetings in most of my emails such as "dear" or "hello." **TF**
12. I don't use emoticons in business emails. **T F**
13. I ask questions to gather information <u>and</u> to enhance the relationship. **T F**
14. I talk with others primarily to provide facts and information. **T F**
15. If interrupted in a meeting, I actively seek to take the floor back. **T F**
16. I have no problems making demands. **T F**
17. I wait my turn to talk. **T F**
18. I speak indirectly to allow others to save face. **T F**
19. I speak in an assertive manner most of the time at work. **T F**
20. When listening I use head nodding and make sounds like "uh-huh" and "yes." **T F**
21. I tend not to deal with others when they interrupt or take my ideas. **T F**
22. I can deal with sharp criticism of my ideas and don't take it personally. **T F**

To score the questionnaire, circle the questions below to which you responded true (only T answers are scored), then add them up to determine which style you favour, if any.

Masculine Style   **Total Score**

Question # 1, 2, 5, 7, 9, 12, 14, 15, 16, 19 and 22   = _____

Feminine Approach

Question # 3, 4, 6, 8, 10, 11, 13, 17, 18, 20, and 21   = _____

Difference between the scores   = _____

KEY TO SCORING

A difference of four points or greater for either the masculine or feminine style indicates a predominate style. If you are using one style more than the other, you will benefit from trying out the other approach. Equal or almost equal scores indicate the use of both styles, which is the goal. Please note that no one style is better, however, in business the masculine style is most often used and valued. As with any skill, the ability to use both styles based on the situation is important.

TRY IT OUT!

Diminishing Endings:

Next time you want to use this phrase:

"Have you got a couple of seconds, I won't take much of your time, I just thought we might take a look at this. Okay?"

Try this one instead:

"I would like to discuss the opinion you asked me to draft. Is now a good time?"

Passive, Assertive, and Aggressive Voice:

Using any **one of the following fact situations,** write out a response in each of the three voices.

1. A colleague always involves you in projects at the last minute and typically past the deadline.
2. The person in the next office likes to come and chat at least four to five times a day, typically when you are working on rush projects.
3. You are in a meeting and a person starts to demean your ideas in front of your boss or client.

Which voice would be most appropriate in each situation?

Direct/Indirect Communication:

Here is a simple exercise to help you become more fluent in both direct and indirect styles.

Direct: "Write the report."

Indirect: "It is important that this report be written by the person who knows the subject area best and the client well."

Fill in at least three more statements in the range between direct and indirect. For example, in the exercise above, after direct, you might write, "Please write the report." Under that and more indirect might be, "You have the most knowledge about this particular area so please write the report." Next might be, "Knowledge and experience in this area is important in writing the report and you have the most of any person on the file."

Here is another example.

Direct: "I need the merger file."

Indirect: "I was looking in my office for the white merger file and recalled that you had taken it a few weeks ago to look at one of the reports as a precedent. Am I recalling that correctly? Do you have it?"

Now imagine appropriate situations for the use of the two different approaches at work. What would be your impression of the person who used the direct response above? The indirect approach? If the direct approach is common where you work, you are in an environment that values direct style. You may find that those who have more influence and are more senior use direct style while others use variations of indirect style. What is important is that you are now aware of the styles used and valued. If you use a different one, be aware of how you are being viewed.

WHAT ORGANIZATIONS, LEADERS, AND MENTORS CAN DO

- As a leader ask yourself – "Am I a good communicator? Am I setting a good example for others on my team?" If the answer is no, get training or coaching.
- Are you seeing people you supervise who are not expressing themselves clearly and confidently? If not, coach them in the fundamentals or hire a professional coach.
- Make the workplace safer and healthier for everyone. Ensure that any behaviour that involves interruptions, sexism, stealing ideas, undermining, harassment, or bullying will not be tolerated.
- Help out those who are interrupted, have their ideas stolen, are bullied or harassed. When someone is interrupted, pointing out that the person has not finished works well. In meetings where sexist remarks or bullying occurs, asking for everyone to be respectful is an appropriate response.
- When an idea is stolen, comment that the person is agreeing with the originator's idea. Or perhaps use the amplification technique – repeat the idea and the person's name.
- For repeat offenders you may wish to speak to them privately or address it more formally with a policy. Make it clear that such tactics will not be tolerated.
- Organizations can ensure that the workplace culture is one of respect and inclusiveness.

WANT TO READ MORE?

Kramer, Andrea S. and Alton B. Harris. *Breaking Through Bias: Communication Techniques for Women to Succeed at Work.* New York: Bibliomotion Inc., 2016.

Mindell, Phyllis. *How to Say It for Women: Communicating with Confidence and Power Using the Language of Success.* New York: Prentice Hall Press, 2001.

Patterson, Kerry, Joseph Grenny, Ron McMillan and Al Switzler. *Crucial Conversations: Tools for Talking When Stakes Are High,* 2nd ed. New York: McGraw Hill Education, 2011.

Tannen, Deborah. *Talking From 9 to 5: Women and Men in the Workplace: Language, Sex, and Power.* New York: Quill, 2001.

Stone, Douglas, Bruce Patton and Shelia Heen. *Difficult Conversations: How to Discuss What Matters Most,* updated ed. New York: Penguin Books, 2010.

PRESENCE

There has been an increased focus on personal presence recently. *Confident presence. Executive presence. Authoritative presence. Authentic presence. Leadership presence.* So why all the attention? The importance of personal presence is two-fold: your non-verbal behaviour significantly affects how others perceive you, and your body position influences what you think and feel. Judgements of competence are made in less than 100 milliseconds, which shows the importance of the fast processing system in our quick judgements and its reliance on visual data. And these first impressions, regardless of accuracy, are hard to change.

So what is presence? It is like great art — hard to define but obvious when we see it. Think of people who exude confidence. How do they sit? How do they stand? What is their voice like? Their energy? Now think of people who are folded in on themselves at meetings. Do they look engaged? Ready to respond? Or do they look withdrawn and perhaps even apprehensive? Although hard to capture in words, *presence is an energy and attitude we display that commands the respectful attention of others.* What we convey is mostly through non-verbal language. Presence is something that can be learned and enhanced - often with minor tweaks.

Gender culture does play a role in how we present ourselves. Gender habits and mindsets reveal themselves in body language. Think about a meeting you've attended and how people were sitting. Were some taking up only part of the chair? Were their arms and legs crossed? Perhaps they looked like they were hugging themselves. Most likely the people you are thinking of are women. Now think of the people in the meeting who were sitting expansively. Perhaps they were even taking up three chairs – with arms draped over the adjacent chairs. Chest forward, shoulders back and, perhaps, legs spread. Would anyone guess this is a description of women in a meeting? Not very likely.

GBS: REDUCING TO FIT IN

You might recall from the first chapter that an important gender rule for females is to fit in while for males it is to stand out. This instinct to fit in influences many different skill areas, not just presence. It affects self-promotion, leadership, communication patterns, and asking. The physical expression of fitting in is to minimize or constrict one's body. And this physical reduction is often misinterpreted through masculine lenses as a lack of confidence.

At the same time this lack of confidence and authority is being conveyed to others through your body language, your body posture is informing your mind. What you tell others you are telling yourself. When a person assumes a constricted posture, it is harder for that person to feel confident, self-assured, and authoritative. That is the incredible power of the mind-body connection – the body leads the mind. It makes sense that when you assume constricted postures it is not only harder for you to feel confident, you are less likely to engage and participate.

Non-verbal language is one of the most influential and powerful communication tools you can use to enhance your brand and image. Yet most of the women I teach agree that it is not something they consciously think about; they are not aware of their non-verbal habits nor what they may be signalling to others. Since these habits are not innate but are developed, usually in early childhood, what has been learned can be re-learned. And from my experience with coaching women, it takes only minor tweaks to make huge changes in your body language. And these tiny adjustments have the power to change thoughts and summon a feeling of confidence.

Everyone can learn this and should. Men don't have the edge when it comes to confident presence. Although expansive postures are more typical of men than women, too much of a good thing can be bad. Men in meetings who spread out too much can appear overly dominant, perhaps even threatening to others. Finding balance in the amount of space you physically take up is important.

The goal of this increased awareness about presence is to allow you to better manage impressions and be more aware of what you may be signalling to others nonverbally. A word of caution about the use of any of the techniques in this book; it is always best to make these changes gradually. Wait until you are comfortable with them and try them out slowly. Of course, verbal communication — the language you use, the verbal habits you display, and the opinions you express — is also very important in making your presence authoritative. These topics and more are covered in the Communicate chapter.

HARNESSING BODY LANGUAGE

Using only body language, we speak to others about our inner lives and they speak to us. Since a large component of all communication is non-verbal (up to 93% according to some estimates), if you want to be perceived as persuasive, authoritative, confident, and in control — *body awareness is paramount*. To create favourable impressions, it is essential to show that you are relaxed, open, and engaged. Why relaxed? Very simply, people who are confident and in control are relaxed. They know they can deal with whatever comes their way.

Being relaxed also allows you to be present; it helps to dissipate anxious or frenzied thoughts that can form a barrier to listening and responding to others. When you are relaxed you can more readily make your value visible and see others and the situation more clearly.

So how does one use body language to signal power and confidence in order to counter early gender training? Four simple and powerful ways are discussed in this chapter, including using open and expansive postures, decreasing distractive movements, shunning subordinate signals, and being both physically and mentally centred.

If you are unsure of the feminine habits you are displaying at work, a questionnaire is provided at the end of this chapter. You may want to fill it in with a trusted colleague or friend since others often know our nonverbal habits better than we do.

T&T: DISPLAY EXPANSIVE POSTURES

What actors have known for centuries is now being supported by science. The most powerful and confident postures are open, expansive, and take up space. To convey power, a character walks with a swagger, chest out, and relaxed arms. To convey the opposite – powerlessness - actors crouch, fold in on themselves, and make themselves small. You know very quickly who is showing power on stage by watching the body language of the actors.

To take up space and show an open, expansive posture when sitting or standing, pull your shoulders back. You can do this when sitting by resting your arms on the armrests of the chair and placing your spine and shoulders fully against the back of the chair. Your mother was right – no slouching! Fill the chair to prevent any of the chair back from being seen. These tiny tweaks make such a big difference in how you feel, think, and are viewed. In the "Try it Out!" and "Using It At Work" sections below, detailed suggestions are given for how to sit, stand, and present in a confident and authoritative way.

Research on the effects of constricted posture (CP) and expansive posture (EP) was first undertaken by Professor Amy Cuddy at Harvard to increase the class participation of female MBA students. She describes this research in an entertaining talk for TEDGlobal.[111]

Using EPs to convey confidence works. A coaching client who is a VP at a major US Bank told me that when she started taking up more space sitting across from her boss, he started approving all of her requests. Sound amazing? Not according to some research. Studying CP and EP poses, researchers at Harvard University and Columbia University suggest that not only does a woman look more confident, her EP also creates feelings of confidence, self-assuredness, and power that in turn allow her to act in a more confident way.[112]

TIPS FOR CONFIDENT PRESENCE

- Start your day with an EP. Stretch like a star fish or sit expansively in a chair with your hands behind your head. You might even want to sit with your feet on your desk or stand over your desk with your feet shoulder width apart and your hands on the desk supporting you.
- Use an EP in a private area such as a washroom before an important meeting, presentation, pitch, or other event where you need to appear confident.
- Use an EP before meetings with people who can influence your career so that you will appear confident, enthusiastic, and engaged.
- If you generally feel cold in the office, make sure you are warm in meetings. Keep a suit jacket in your office or perhaps layer up. It is hard to look relaxed and expansive when you're freezing!

- When waiting in reception areas, don't sit down. This may entice you to crunch up and check your smart phone. Instead, wait standing up. This will give you significantly more energy and allow you to immediately engage with the other person or people when they arrive.
- While sitting in a challenging situation, open your shoulders by ensuring your entire back is touching the chair back. Place your arms on the armrests of the chair or your hands far apart resting on the table. Be aware of your shoulders - no scrunching!

T&T: DECREASE DISTRACTIVE MOVEMENTS

In addition to EPs, there are other ways to strengthen your body language. Form a mental image of a person who commands great authority and respect. Does this person fidget or display jerky movements? Do they avoid eye contact or touch their face, neck, hair, or clothing often? Do they have another physical habit that distracts from what they are saying? Probably not. These unconscious movements allow us to discharge excess anxious energy and comfort us. They also reveal our nervousness. Stillness conveys confidence and power. To appear open, relaxed, and confident, it is important to limit, as much as possible, any distracting movements or gestures.

T&T: SHUN SUBORDINATE SIGNALS

Subordinate signals are types of non-verbal behaviour that make us look less confident. Descriptions of a number of these, such as nodding and smiling excessively, are included below. Although one of these habits used in isolation or consciously will not affect impressions, when used habitually or excessively they signal subservience. These habits are not right or wrong *per se* and may be used consciously in a very effective way. For example, they can be used to soften an approach and show that you are open and listening since they tend to signal receptiveness and connection with others.

Nodding and Assenting Noises

Nodding your head and making noises to show you agree are related habits – one non-verbal and one verbal. They indicate that the listener has heard what is being said. This gender habit can get you into trouble if you don't realize you are doing it because others will assume you are agreeing. I learned early in my legal career to avoid assenting noises in any circumstance where they could be misinterpreted as agreement — particularly when this worked to the other side's advantage. Again these are helpful behaviours to use consciously when listening to others and encouraging them to talk. It shows that you are following the conversation and are being attentive to that person. When used consciously they are valuable tools.

Smiling Excessively

We all like to smile spontaneously when we feel happy and when a situation is funny. However, it is important to be aware when we use smiling to deflect or appease rather than display true inner emotion. We are socialized as girls to look happy for others from a young age. Girls learn as early as age five to mask feelings of discomfort with a smile. Smiling excessively can signal subordination, appeasement, and discomfort rather than happiness and elevated mood. It also sends mixed messages. Others will not know when you are genuinely upset.

A female lawyer told me she had become aware that she always smiled when offers to settle a law suit were proposed by the other side — and the worse the offer the bigger the smile. She meant it as a smirk but instead the other side interpreted it as her being pleased with the offer. Once aware of this habit, she learned to use a poker face and the power of the pause to achieve much better results.[113] As with all non-verbal signals, it is best to use smiling appropriately or strategically, and never habitually or excessively.

Touching Your Hair or Neck

This is a distractive and subordinate habit that I used to display at the start of presentations. I would touch my bangs. It took me a few times in front of audiences to notice and then get rid of the habit. I can tell you from experience that a habit like this does not disappear the moment you become aware of it but does decrease with time once you consciously avoid doing it. Awareness and intent are key to eliminating a habit.

Another subordinate habit is touching your neck in the front – either at the top of the collarbone or just above the Adam's apple. If you do touch your neck when nervous, note when you do it. As with any of these distracting movements or subordinate signals, it may reveal that you are tense in situations that might surprise you. The body is a great truth teller and will give you information that your rational mind won't or can't.

Vocal Level

Talking loudly takes up social space. When we feel confident, powerful, or enthused we get loud. In contrast, nervous individuals often minimize vocal presence, and for women who have been socialized to reduce their vocal level, this can be a double whammy. For vocal presence there must be enough volume to fill the room. Otherwise others may assume you doubt the substance of your assertion, comment, or question. And the level needed may be more than you think. When I coach women on filling a room with their voice they often think they are shouting when they get to a level that is barely filling the space. To help with projection, I tell them to speak to the far wall, especially in large spaces.

T&T: BE CENTRED

Due to the powerful mind/body connection, an EP will likely make you feel confident and powerful. The flip side of this, of course, is that when you are feeling stressed, frantic, distracted, or highly emotional, your body will reveal this and betray you. Thus a calm and confident presence needs to be supported by a calm and confident interior. Women consistently report higher stress levels than men, so staying centred both physically and mentally can be a challenge.[114]

Physically Centred

To maintain a confident presence, you want to stay physically centred and appear visually balanced. When sitting, position your shoulders squarely in your chair and avoid slumping. Crossing legs or ankles is not advised as it affects how you appear above the table and it is a constricting posture.

Any dipping of the body takes away from looking centred. A dipped head, if maintained, is particularly distracting and can even look like avoidance.

When standing, stand tall and securely on both feet (you would be surprised how many of us cross our legs even when standing). Ensure that your feet are about shoulder-width apart or at a width that is comfortable and stable. This will also make you feel more solid and in control. Since tight dresses and skirts can prevent this, be aware of this when dressing for a presentation.

Mentally and Emotionally Centred

Just as an EP can make a person feel confident and energized, remaining mentally balanced and centred works to promote and sustain a relaxed, confident, and authoritative exterior. There are many things that can destroy mental balance, but extreme emotion is one of the worst culprits.

Stress and frustration at work can evoke strong emotions - particularly when we are physically tired or hungry. If you find yourself going ballistic over something minor, assess if you are tired or hungry and, if possible, deal with it. If you are unable to deal with it immediately, such as when you have to pull an all-nighter to get work done, often just the recognition of the source of the frustration will help to reduce the intensity of the emotion.

It is important to realize that emotions in and of themselves are not the enemy. Emotions help to motivate and provide us with information. Neurons exist in the gut as well as in the brain, so often our gut reaction or emotional response can add valuable information to what we know through our analytical and cognitive functions. Such information may be telling us that a personal boundary has been violated by behaviour we find unacceptable. So appreciating, recognizing, and dealing with emotion allows us to remain mentally centred while getting information about ourselves and others that we might otherwise miss.

USING IT AT WORK

Power posing, in the privacy of your office or a washroom, allows you to prepare for a challenging event. But what about during the event? What other factors can be harnessed to promote a confident and engaged presence? Below are ideas for displaying a confident presence in some common work situations. And since what you wear is an important factor in nonverbal communication, a section on how to dress for work is also included.

T&T: IN MEETINGS

A lot of time at work is typically spent in meetings. This is where you are seen by others. To make a favourable and confident impression, you want to use an expansive posture that is relaxed, open, and engaged. This body language communicates not only ease but also readiness for whatever is coming your way. Try to avoid distracting gestures, nervous habits, and adjustments to hair or clothing, especially as you are entering the room.

Chair Height. Make sure you are comfortable and that your chair height is appropriate. As a rule you should be at the same height as others in the room. One six-foot-tall litigator told me she uses height depending on what she wants from the meeting. If she wants to signal that she is one of the group, she keeps her chair at a level that is the same as others. If she wants to signal dominance or authority, she ensures she is taller than others in the room. If you are petite, crank the height to maximum, even if your feet don't touch the ground. Many petite women in seminars have told me this is how they feel comfortable – when they are at an equal height at the table with others. It is also important from a psychological perspective; when a person is lower in height than others they can tend to feel less confident and competent than others.

Don't Let the Chair Back Show. If you are petite, avoid sitting in one corner of a chair with lots of chair back showing. Centre yourself, with your spine against the back of the chair to take up the full chair. Take up space and don't minimize your presence.

Arms On and Out. There are many reasons for crossed arms. Boardrooms are often cold so we cross our arms to conserve heat. Or it might feel comfortable to sit this way. Whatever the reason, crossed arms can minimize our physical appearance and make us appear withdrawn and less engaged. Place your arms on the armrests of the chair or on the table. One woman I taught really liked resting her arms on the table with her elbows out to take up space. With a big smile she told me it was like playing hockey - her elbows stopped others from knocking her out of the game. So have some fun and find a comfortable position that expands your personal space at the table.

How You Sit. Try to sit in an open, relaxed, and confident way to make the best impression. Ensure that you don't come across as too timid or lacking in confidence (folding in on yourself), but don't go to the other extreme by sprawling on the furniture with your hands behind your head. This can be intimidating and also makes you appear too dominant. Such poses are fine to use before a meeting in a private area to ramp up your energy, however, in the presence of others you want to have a posture that is not too big or too small. Be like Goldilocks - the happy medium is always best.

Where You Sit. It is important to take your seat at the table. It is generally accepted that the closer you sit to the leader, the more powerful and credible you are perceived to be. However, you want to show that you are aware of your age and stage while at the same time not appearing subordinate. As a junior don't sit too close to the leader, but if you wish to be taken seriously and be seen as having confidence, you want to be at the table.

T&T: WHEN PRESENTING

Presenting is a wonderful way to build credibility, gain visibility, and make your value known to others. It is also the time to show confidence and self-assuredness. However, according to survey data, most people rate public speaking as scarier than death! And for women who have been taught to fit in rather than stand out, it can be very stressful. One important way to reduce the stress and to appear more relaxed while speaking is to prepare.

Preparation

Paradoxically, the best way to appear natural is to prepare, prepare, prepare. Here are some easy-to-use tips. Write your own introduction – it sounds more natural than having others read your bio out loud. It also makes it easier for the person who introduces you and is a wonderful way to connect with the audience. Memorize the first few minutes of your speech – this will greatly help with the surge of performance anxiety that typically hits at the very beginning. Use words that are easy to say and simple sentences, especially at the start. Arrive early so you can get comfortable with the room. For maximum connection with your audience, and where possible, speak without a podium.

Ensuring Vocal Presence

Often when we are nervous we reduce volume and withdraw our energy. Make sure that you don't reduce volume at the end of sentences as you think of what comes next. To increase voice projection, try to speak to the back wall. If you are wearing a microphone, check the volume before the audience arrives and then again when you start speaking. With the room filled with people the acoustics can change. Display a relaxed, open posture. Being relaxed allows your voice to project.

Non-Verbal Communication

Display confident body language when you present. To look relaxed and assured it is important to have a comfortable and expansive posture (EP). An EP opens up the chest area and allows for better breathing - a must when presenting. Limit, as much as possible, any distracting movements or gestures.

To maintain an assured presence, stay centred and appear visually balanced to your audience. This means sitting squarely in your chair when being a part of a panel. When standing to present, stand tall and securely on both feet as it is common for female presenters to cross their legs even when standing. Ensure that your feet are about shoulder width apart or at a width that is comfortable and stable. Narrow skirts or dresses can restrict standing this way so be aware of this when dressing for a presentation.

It is common for people with excess nervous energy to discharge it by moving. There are several ways to avoid this, or at least minimize it. If you can, exercise on the day of the presentation so that some of the excess energy will be discharged before you arrive. Use the podium to anchor yourself if one is available. If you tend to walk, stop for important points or stop to look at the PowerPoint slide you are talking about. Doing this will also help reduce your overall movement.

Remember that verbal and nonverbal communication work together to convey a message. Use body language that reinforces and supports what you are saying. Hand gestures that are natural and large (in contrast with small nervous ones) tend to work well unless you are using a podium. Large gestures may cause you to hit the microphone on the podium and significantly detract from your presentation. Use vocal tone and speed of speaking instead of physical movements at the podium to reinforce what you are saying. Watch recordings of yourself to ensure that you are enhancing and not detracting from your presentation.

Performance Anxiety

If you experience anxiety before presenting, you are not alone. As previously mentioned, more people are afraid of speaking in public than dying. Performance anxiety is normal and the more familiar you are with your material, the less stress you will experience. Also as you become more experienced in presenting in public, the lower your stress will be. Performance anxiety can work for us or against us. Research shows that if you rename the feelings of anxiety as excitement, you will do better. This allows you to use anxious energy to achieve peak performance with increased focus, perception, and attention.

Stillness signals power and slow speech indicates confidence. It is important to slow down when presenting. Rapid speech is often a physical response to increased anxiety. Practice your opening until it is memorized and use words that are easy to say. Use phrases that come naturally to you. You may also want to remind yourself to breathe in your opening – this will slow you down and ensure you get enough air. Try counting "one-two" after important points or phrases.

DRESSING FOR WORK

Professionalism, confidence and competence are judged by the clothing we wear. And given the power of images and nonverbal communication, our clothing can speak volumes about us. Consequently, we want our clothes to say the right things. Here are some guidelines for dressing at work generally and for special situations, such as job interviews and casual days. Keep in mind that there are many factors in how we dress and none of these guidelines are set in stone. Use your best judgement and be aware of the impression you are making.

Dress Like Others. It is best to dress like others at work — either at your level or one level up. Use that as a benchmark. It is unusual to have a formal dress code at work but often there is an informal one. Try to learn what it is. If you want to wear a really trendy outfit, make sure that it is very good quality. Keep in mind that although you want to dress to fit in (yes that gender rule helps rather than hinders in this context), you also want to stand out from the crowd a bit so others will know who you are. Jewelry and shoes are two good ways to express yourself.

Avoid Sexy. Your clothing and jewelry make a statement about you to others, whether accurate or not. I have heard of qualified candidates being passed over due to clothing that was too sexy and provocative. Sexy clothes distract from the skills and abilities you want others to notice and value about you.

Dress for Your Age and Stage. A woman who owned her own company challenged the first guideline above, dress like others, at a seminar. She was elegantly and femininely dressed in a tailored outfit that was very good quality. She said that she wore what she wanted and she stood out in the boardrooms of her clients. I assured her that that was fine – for her. She could stand out - she had the experience to pull it off and her own company. I wear large necklaces and dress with more variety then I did when I first started working in the corporate world. However, for meetings with new clients, especially law firms and banks, I still dress conservatively to fit in.

For Job Interviews. Dress conservatively for interviews. If you are not sure of the company's dress code, check out their website to see how people are dressed in the images. Women have many choices — pants, skirts or dress suits. If you are uncomfortable in dresses or skirts, wear pants. The most important thing in an interview is to be yourself, and you can only be yourself if you are comfortable.

On Casual Days. Be aware that clothing says a lot about your values, background, and outlook. If you are petite and young, casual clothing can make you seem more junior and younger. Another tip is to always dress as if you could be called into a client meeting, even on casual days. Always make sure that your clothing is clean and well kept; regardless of the style, shoddy is never well received. If you are unsure, dress like your colleagues on casual day.

EXERCISE

QUESTIONNAIRE: PRESENCE

Read each statement carefully. If the statement describes you, circle T and if it does not, circle F. The purpose of this questionnaire is to create awareness of any personal GBS or habits that are getting in the way of a confident and engaging presence. If you are uncertain, ask a trusted work colleague or friend to answer them with you.

1.   I feel comfortable taking the spotlight.   **T F**

2. In a group I prefer to fit in and not stand out. **T F**

3. I notice that I constantly look at my phone for messages, even in meetings. **T F**

4. When stressed I will touch my hair or neck. **T F**

5. When standing I try to stand tall and securely on both feet. **T F**

6. I like to take up space when sitting in a chair. **T F**

7. I make a point of not crossing my legs when sitting. **T F**

8. In a meeting I ensure that my chair is at the same height as others. **T F**

9. I have been told that I can appear scattered when I get stressed. **T F**

10. I like to keep my hands on the table or on the armrests of chairs in meetings. **T F**

11. I feel more comfortable crossing my arms and legs when sitting in a chair. **T F**

12. I often nod or say "uh huh" when listening to others. **T F**

13. When in a group I try to stand out and be noticed. **T F**

14. I have been told by others that I am always smiling. **T F**

15. I often have to repeat what I say in meetings as others can't hear me. **T F**

16. I have been told that I am very calm, cool, and collected at work. **T F**

17. I tend to get cold in meetings so I cross my arms to stay warm. **T F**

18. I use my voice on conference calls to ensure I am heard and have presence. **T F**

19. When I present I try to have the audience focus on the slides and not me. **T F**

20. I wear trendy clothes at work unless I am meeting with conservative clients. **T F**

21. My hands seem to have a will of their own and I fidget in meetings. **T F**

22. I do expansive poses in private before important meetings. **T F**

23.   I have been told I have wonderful focus and great presence. **T F**

24.   When stressed, I often slump over my computer.   **T F**

To score the questionnaire, circle the questions below to which you responded true (only T answers are scored), then add them to determine whether you have more habits that help or that hinder you in making your value visible.

Habits That Help   **Total Score**

Question # 1, 5, 6, 7, 8, 10, 13, 16, 18, 20, 22 and 23   = _____

Habits that Hinder

Question # 2, 3, 4, 9, 11, 12, 14, 15, 17, 19, 21 and 24   = _____

KEY TO SCORING

This questionnaire promotes self-awareness that will allow you to increase body language habits that help you exude confidence, and decrease those that hinder. With this increased awareness, you can begin to use them consciously and contextually. This will greatly enhance your presence and ensure that your value is made visible.

WHAT ORGANIZATIONS, LEADERS, AND MENTORS CAN DO

- Provide opportunities for women to develop and show powerful presence.
- Display powerful presence as a role model for others.
- As a woman leader note that your confident presence will inspire others.
- Assess your team's presence and talk to them one-on-one with your observations.

- Emphasize the importance of this skill and how small changes can make big differences.
- If appropriate, provide a coach and training on presence.

WANT TO READ MORE?

Cuddy, Amy. *Presence: Bringing Your Boldest Self to Your Biggest Challenges.* New York: Little, Brown and Company, 2015.

Heim, Pat and Tammy Hughes with Susan K. Golant, 3rd ed. *Hardball for Women: Winning at the Game of Business* New York: Plume, 2015.

Humphrey, Judith. *Taking the Stage: How Women Can Speak Up, Stand Out, and Succeed.* San Francisco: Jossey-Bass, 2014.

PROMOTE

Self-promotion is a skill that is often underused or completely neglected by women due to early gender training. Having been taught the value of fitting in and not standing out, most women find self-promotion uncomfortable and thus difficult. And this can be a major gender blind spot (GBS). Self-promoting while being held back by this GBS is like driving a car with one foot on the brake. How comfortable or smooth is that? To be truly comfortable and authentic in promoting yourself, it is important to be aware of any unconscious beliefs that may be holding you back.

If you are comfortable with self-promotion, it's worthwhile to consider if you are doing it in the best possible way. Are you using your credentials, experience, and unique strengths to maximum effect? Do you stand out in situations where others have similar skills and experience? Do you know and understand your audience? Many people, especially men, promote themselves in a way that is more like a monologue than a dialogue. This can create hurdles to getting new business, increasing professional alliances, and getting others to view them as accomplished. In short, self-promotion is about making your value visible and doing it in a way that is conversational and connective.

Individuals who are conscious of the image they present, know the value of networking, and are skillful at self-promotion, tend to be very successful. They show both competence and connection, providing a balance between fitting in and standing out. They are considerate and show great social intelligence while ensuring that others know their value. They are aware of what is important to others – that is part of their likeability. They understand how others will react and respond to events because they are aware of the interests and goals of their audience.

If you are one of the lucky women who has a champion —someone influential who endorses you to others -- then you may not need to do as much self-promotion in the first few years. Your value is made visible by that influential person. However, it's still important to develop your own ways to self-promote because you can't count on that person forever, and nor would you want to. Furthermore, self-promotion is a valuable skill for getting interesting work, connecting with others, and building strong networks. If you do not start developing this essential skill in the initial years, it will not suddenly appear fully formed when you need it later.

This chapter describes the many GBS that can hinder and prevent self-promotion by women, including self-limiting mindsets and gendered expectations. Also provided are practical tools and techniques (T&T) so that when you self-promote and network you are able to talk about yourself in an authentic, professional, and knowledgeable way. This is achieved by knowing yourself, knowing your value, and knowing your audience. Questions to discover your skills and strengths are provided at the end of the chapter. Knowing your audience and being able to engage them in a positive and memorable way is essential for successful self-promotion and for making your value visible. And once you know the sound bites you want to use, you can use them skillfully and confidently in a variety of situations and events.

Since many women dislike networking, this chapter also provides information and advice for this skill. Networking is one of the most effective ways to make your value visible and build relationships. It is cited by women as the number one unwritten rule for success in business.[115] Through networking you can learn about opportunities and meet decision makers. It ensures that your connections are broad and your contacts robust. Whether you need information or introductions, you will have people in your network who can help you. The two career strategies that are featured are *Go Along to Get Along* and *Shine a Light*.

COMMON GBS IN SELF-PROMOTION

GBS: FEAR OF STANDING OUT

Many of us don't like to talk about ourselves and our achievements. As girls, most of us learned it is best to get along, fit in, and not stand out. Perhaps you were told by a parent not to *toot your own horn* when you had done well and were enthusiastically telling others about it. Or you learned the hard way by bragging to other playmates and were then excluded from games and parties. Whatever the experience, many of us don't like to talk about our accomplishments and credentials, or even mention our positions.

Women I coach tell me that it seems distasteful and they feel arrogant even when they just recite the facts of their accomplishments. Does that sound like you? Here are some of the most common reasons women give that prevent them from self-promoting.

- it is distasteful
- don't want to appear arrogant or egocentric
- don't want to stand out
- a fear of rejection
- a fear of failure

- it is unprofessional
- expertise should be enough
- it is boring
- don't want to oversell yourself

Women generally don't want to be seen as setting expectations that can't be met — they fear overselling themselves. This is why most women do not set their aspirations high in ambiguous negotiation situations. The self-promotion guide set out in this chapter uses self-description: who you are, your unique abilities, and the pattern of your successes. With this method, the risk of overstating or misstating your abilities or skills is greatly reduced, if not eliminated.

National culture can also play a large role in your level of comfort in telling others about yourself. If you are Canadian, you may fear the *tall poppy syndrome* — the tendency to resent those who stand out above the crowd in terms of their success. An Asian client told me that the Japanese have a saying that *the tallest nail gets the biggest whack*. That image alone is enough to stop anyone from talking about their well-earned accomplishments!

A fear of standing out affects women regardless of their experience or seniority. One senior litigator described a learning experience she had after a huge win at court. She had returned to the office after hearing the decision and quietly started working her way through the many emails and files that had accumulated while she was at the trial. Her assistant, who had previously worked for a very successful and senior male lawyer, came in and asked what she was doing. The assistant described how a previous boss would have responded to a big win by walking the halls proudly telling others about the court decision. It was a good lesson. The senior litigator made her value visible that day and learned that *tooting your own horn* was a lot of fun as well.

Gendered expectations also play a huge role in women's ambivalence in self-promoting. Standing out violates the gender stereotype of the feminine ideal and we know that we may pay social penalties for talking proudly about ourselves. Female lawyers tell me when they are out socializing they tell others they work at law firms and let the listener make assumptions about the positions they hold. It is often assumed they are secretaries, assistants, or paralegals. Women intuit that to make a favourable impression they need to align with traditional female roles.

I think there is a better way for women than failing to promote themselves or promoting themselves in a limited, traditional way. Women can learn to be androgynous by adopting aspects of both feminine and masculine styles. Be connective while showing your competence. Be interested in others while ensuring they know what you do. This is an approach that works well for both women and men. Suggestions are offered in the T&T sections below for how to develop this type of promotional approach.

GBS: WORK IS A MERITOCRACY

Many women believe that organizations are fair, that advancement is based solely on talent and ability, and that men and women's career opportunities are the same. This belief is especially prevalent among young women coming out of high school and university since the ways to advance and do well are more transparent in educational institutions. Unfortunately this is not the situation in most workplaces and such a belief discourages self-promotion.

The inaccurate assumptions that fuel this belief are if you work hard enough, perform well, and become technically proficient, you will achieve career success. Although this may be the recipe for success at junior levels (although even at those levels more is usually required), it does not guarantee advancement at senior levels. Instead, career success also requires being proficient at the interpersonal skills featured in this book and seeing GBS with clear eyes.

GBS: OTHERS WILL DO IT FOR ME

If you have others that endorse you or make your value visible, that's wonderful. If you have an agreement with others that you will promote them and they will promote you, that's also great. Promoting each other is one way around gendered expectations. However, if you don't self-promote because you believe others will or should do it for you, this can be a GBS that comes with several significant limitations. One is that you don't know exactly how others are promoting you. Also, at a certain level this begins to work against you. The workplace can be competitive and as you advance, your champion may be less inclined to provide a good word or endorse you. And your champion may have had the advantage of self-promoting for years.

A related belief is that if you have to talk about what you are good at, then you aren't good. This can be a very self-defeating and self-sabotaging belief. If you are not making your value visible while others are talking about what they do well, you will be at a disadvantage. So the question is not whether you should self-promote but how to do it in a way that is connective, comfortable, and effective.

GBS: IT'S ALL ABOUT THE TEAM

It's a commonly held belief that success is not about personal expertise or talent but about team effort. Its origins are widespread and include gender socialization, generational differences, and national cultural norms. Although there are situations that involve a team effort where the praise should be extended to all team members, many people habitually defer to others. In response to a comment like, "great job!" the automatic response is, "it was nothing, it was the team." I have heard many stories from women who believe they are self-promoting when they are just talking about their team. This is appropriate where it is true or where it is used to avoid stereotype backlash. However, if this is a habit that you use consistently and unconsciously, the moment to make your value visible may be lost time and time again.

T&T: KNOW YOURSELF

Do you know what you are telling your colleagues and clients about yourself? What messages are you sending both verbally and non-verbally about yourself? Do you appear authoritative and exude confidence? Or do you unconsciously signal discomfort or even fear? If you're not sure, refer to the Presence chapter. Non-verbal behaviour plays a large role in signalling whether or not you are relaxed and self-assured. It's important that your non-verbal and verbal messages are consistent. Confident non-verbal behaviour together with a persuasive promotional verbal message will ensure successful and authentic branding.

Brand as used here includes those abilities and skills you are known for (reputation) as well as the talents, abilities, interests, and skills you want others to know about. Brand and reputation go together, and the more self-aware you are, the more the two will overlap. Branding is the conscious and pro-active building of reputation. I have found that strategic branding by women is rare, whether in the day-to-day with colleagues, with senior colleagues, or with clients in meetings. In fact, most women think very little about what they tell others about themselves. Often at formal networking events only the basic facts are revealed — name, position, and organization. This type of information is fine for census-taking or filling in a name tag at an event, but is forget-table if you are at a large event. Most likely you are bored telling others about yourself in this way, and the energy and non-verbal behaviour that accompany such a recitation will not help in making you memorable. The main goal with self-promotion is to come across as likable, positive, and worth remembering.

T&T: KNOW YOUR VALUE

To achieve authentic self-promotion, you need to know your strengths and successes. This self-awareness will allow you to create a brand statement. Start by thinking about your greatest successes. What do others think is exceptional about you? What are your best skills, abilities, and traits? What energizes you — what are you passionate about? This will give your self-promotion contagious energy. It is important that you know and feel your value. To convince others, you must first be convinced yourself. This is the beginning of a confident and memorable brand statement.

Below is a list of skills and abilities to mentally prime the pump and get you thinking about what you are good at. Consider which skills, abilities, talents, strengths, and successes separate you from others.

Types of Skills and Abilities

Organizational Skills

- Categorize large amounts of information
- Prioritize and manage projects
- Keep and manage records
- Manage documents

Analytical Skills

- Deal with complex situations and information
- Display excellent reasoning using logic and thinking
- Separate elements of complex systems

Communication Skills

- Explain thoughts and ideas with clarity
- Listen attentively and respond appropriately
- Ask questions to obtain pertinent information

- Express information clearly in writing

Leadership Skills

- Develop a vision for the team and commit to it
- Support and coach others
- Coordinate resources to reach objectives
- Cope with stressful situations and help others do the same

Planning Skills

- Plan tasks effectively to complete requirements efficiently
- Prioritize demands and multi-task when needed
- Organize activities to be completed within a set timeframe
- Prepare for change

Problem-Solving Skills

- Seek out likely causes of problems
- Determine an effective course of action
- Generate possible solutions
- Predict potential future problems

Teamwork Skills

- Collaborate to reach common goals
- Accept individual differences and honour diversity
- Cooperate with others to complete tasks
- Provide feedback to others in a positive and constructive way

There are two sets of questions found in the Exercises section at the end of this chapter called My Accomplishments and Promotion Foundations. By answering these questions, you will become more aware of your uniqueness. What do you do well? What do you do better than most? If you have difficulty answering them, ask yourself if it is due to deep-seated beliefs or a lack of information. If it's the latter, ask trusted colleagues at work. At one seminar when a participant said she did not have anything to start with, the women in the room started texting her with information about her unique skills and what she does well. Start collecting emails and texts containing good feedback. Start a binder of positive comments from others about what you have done really well. Jot down the verbal praise you get and put it in the binder. Often when something is easy for us, we assume that it is as easy for others. So ask and get the feedback. If you are like my clients, you will be delighted and surprised by the responses.

At one seminar a woman admitted she kept a binder of negative comments to spur her on. This might – and I emphasis the word might – help if she were impulsive and made a lot of careless errors. Even in this limited circumstance, though, fear and negative thoughts are counter-productive. In the Thrive chapter the importance of positive intelligence and the problem of self-sabotage with negative thoughts are discussed. As research on negative stereotype threats show, pessimistic thoughts about your abilities result in a decreased ability to think, reduced cognitive performance, and increased stress levels. Instead of being creative and bold, you become cautious and conservative. If this is the state you work in, you are greatly handicapped and are not expressing your natural talents, ability, and skills.

Answering the questions set out in the Exercises section below is also a way to determine if you have deep self-limiting beliefs. Some women in my seminars are totally unable to answer these questions due to the active nature of their self-limiting belief that standing out is wrong. If it feels wrong to be thinking about what you do well, take some time to think about why that is. By becoming conscious of this belief you shine a light on it, allowing you to deal with it rationally and constructively.

T&T: KNOW YOUR AUDIENCE

Make it Easy for Them

Successful self-promotion starts with knowing your value, understanding your audience, and being able to engage them in a memorable and comfortable way. Once you are clear on what you do well and what gives you energy, the next step is being able to talk about yourself in a conversational way. Being able to weave in your credentials, achievements, and successes will make your self-promotion sound authentic and natural. Canned and fast is not best. Instead it will leave a less than favourable impression, or, worse still, no impression at all. It does not matter how well you think you self-promote — it is ultimately about what the listener thinks. Think about your audience. How can you best tell them about yourself? Information in and of itself is not persuasive. It's what you do with that information that counts. Make your message easy for them to follow. Remember, it's all about your audience.

Your goal should be to get the listener interested in you and engaged in the conversation. You must also be as curious about them as you'd like them to be about you. Research shows that when we listen to others, our brain waves and regions of activation synchronize with the other person's brain waves — we really do have a mind-meld.[116] So if you think of self-promotion as less of a monologue and more of a mind-meld you will be off to a very good start.

There is no one right-way to self-promote. The promotion guide below is provided as a suggestion. It is designed to make it easy for the listener and is based on the Communication Guide in the Communicate chapter. Get comfortable with it and feel free to adapt it to suit you.

MEEE Promotion Guide

Them: Acknowledge your audience
M (Main Point)
E (Elaborate)
E (Give a concrete example)
E (Extend a question to your audience to include them and/or ask for what you want)

Note: How do I get them curious about what I do? How do I help them? How do I pay it forward?

The first element (Them) allows you to create a bridge to the listener, and this is of particular importance for individuals who value relationship. One of the easiest ways to connect and acknowledge the listener is to say "thanks for asking what I do."

The next element — the Main Point — is most effective when it is concise. This is a sound bite to garner interest and get them curious about you. This element of the promotion guide is especially appreciated by people who are big picture thinkers. Knowing where the discussion is going allows them to relax and to listen more fully to the details. You may want to try using only the Main Point as a conversation grabber and allow them to ask you questions about it. Getting them engaged and interested is a major goal. So if you get them asking questions right away, you have achieved the goal.

The Elaboration step further helps the listener understand the Main Point by providing information about it. The Example is particularly helpful for detail-oriented individuals. The combination of the Elaboration and the Example steps allow the listener two different ways to more fully understand the Main Point.

The Extend allows you to pass it back to the listener, avoiding a mono-logue. The listener may then either answer the question posed, or may be eager to ask you more questions. If the latter happens, you have hit the self-promotion equivalent of a home run. You have made the listener curious and he or she will remember you. Here are examples using the MEEE Guide.

MEEE Guide Examples

Them: "That's interesting."

Main Point: "I am a locator."

Elaborate: "As a real estate broker I help clients find houses they might otherwise miss."

Example: "Just last month..."

Extend: "How about you? What fills your day?"

Them: "That's an interesting business focus."

Main Point: "My focus is getting women what they want."

Elaborate: "I teach women how to negotiate."

Example: "It's interesting that most women negotiate very well for others but have difficulty negotiating for themselves."

Extend: "Do you like negotiating?"

KNOW THEIR VALUES AND NEEDS

You want to be as audience focused as possible in your self-promotion to put them at ease, know what they value, and make them feel respected. To achieve this you may wish to balance your questions with informa-tion sharing. The optimum ratio is around 60% questions with 40% sharing. This allows you to find out about the other person's personal interests and share your own. Some women have told me that they only ask questions, so although they may appear interested and curious, they will not be memorable. It is important to have a balance so the other person understands what you do and a connection is made.

The self-promotion guide set out above is based on networking and self-promotion in North America. Networking in another cultural context will require a different guide. For example, at Chinese networking events there is very little small talk. Instead, business cards are immediately presented and the conversation is focused on how each party may assist the other. This is incredibly efficient from a business development perspective but quite different from networking in North America. Thus, if you are going to an event involving people from another culture, find out as much as you can.

T&T: PROMOTE IN DIFFERENT SITUATIONS

In the Office

In large organizations, the persons who influence your career may not know you or know your work; only those people who work directly with you or who supervise you will. As a result, it is often important to be able to promote yourself in a natural and conversational way to those you don't work with directly. Any interaction, conversation, or observation in the workplace can be an opportunity to be seen as someone who is keen, knowledgeable, and easy to work with.

So how do you promote yourself at work naturally? The next time you are asked "what's new?" or "what's up?" try not to respond with a standard phrase such as "not much" or "same-old-same-old." Instead, tell them succinctly about an interesting issue that has arisen on a file you are working on, an interesting research memo you have written or read, or an unusual aspect of a project. Divulge your successes. Tell them about some goals you are working on. Business development goals are good to discuss if business development is valued. If the organization values creativity, mention a recent success with a new idea. You will be seen as keen and interesting.

Be prepared and get into the habit of telling influential others about yourself. Some of my clients prepare a talking point on Monday before they start their work week. It is then top-of-mind and current when they later bump into someone to whom they want to appear engaged and informed.

Keep in mind that sometimes you may wish to give just a simple friendly response, especially when it's clear that this is all the other person wants or expects. However, be alert for those times when you can go deeper and build your brand with others, especially those people in your workplace who are influential and who don't work directly with you.

Often the best self-promotion is in showing rather than talking. A great way to let others see your abilities and make your value visible is by working with them on non-client projects such as committees and events. Join committees or activities to ensure that you are meeting others from outside your immediate circle of work.

Be careful about reporting to others about your performance in a way that detracts from your competence and abilities. If you report only on what you could have done better, the entire focus of the reporting becomes the small thing that went wrong rather than what went well. Remember, there are others who will report back about all the great things they did and perhaps even exaggerate a bit about their great performance. You will be compared with them and if you have been too self-critical it will be to your detriment.

A story that illustrates the gender differences in reporting about performance comes from a colleague of mine. She and another senior lawyer had successfully obtained 19 out of 20 of the requests for their developer client in a board decision. When she got the decision, she was in a quandary about how to tell the client about the one they did not get. When her male counterpart returned to the office he was surprised that she had not yet called the client. He immediately got on the phone to tell the client about their huge win. The client was so pleased with the overall results that the one they did not get was not even discussed. It was a huge lesson for my colleague on reporting to clients. So always think about how you frame your report in a positive light and don't lead with the negative.

Client Meetings

Informal networking in large organizations is a key skill in getting others to know you. For conference calls that involve others in your organization, go to the office of another person on the call instead of staying in your office, especially if they can influence your career or are influential in the organization. Go to internal meetings a bit early so you can chat with others and get to know each other.

Do you promote yourself at meetings with executives, senior people, or clients? Do you even speak? Often this depends on the senior person you are with. They may wish to always take centre stage. However, when you are able to speak, ensure that the executives or clients know who you are. Often you get the chance when talking about the work you have done on the project, particularly on an aspect you have worked on alone. Try to say at least one thing per meeting so that others know who you are.

Be conscious of your brand — do and say things consistent with it. Building and maintaining good relations with those who can influence your career is a soft skill that is essential when you are junior. For more discussion on how to manage relationships at work see the chapter Politics.

Out and About

Do you anticipate what you might say if you bump into a client when you are out and about? Often these meetings are ideal for creating and maintaining a brand. You may wish to compliment them or ask about their current projects. This shows your interest in their business. Ask their view on something current. You may wish to talk about a recent personal success that you know will be of interest to them. Remember, the aim is to have them remember you in a positive and comfortable way.

T&T: NETWORKING

Networking is one of the most common and effective ways to make your value visible, build relationships, and provide benefits to others. So why don't women like to network? There are many reasons. One is a lack of time. Despite the great benefits of a strong network, most women are pressed for time due to family commitments. Networking can seem like a waste of time when you have many other things to do. However, when I speak to senior people from different types of organizations, they all tell me that getting to know people outside your immediate sphere of work is the best way to be more effective at work.

Another common reason women give for why they dislike networking is its strong association with selling. One woman described it as having a hidden agenda that made her feel inauthentic. However, the true goal of networking is to develop relationships by getting to know others and finding ways to provide mutual benefits. If you focus on the goal of being of value to others, there is less pressure to get immediate results.

Another reason networking events are disliked is that they are often held at the end of the work day when most people are tired and hungry. This can ramp up social anxiety which is already high when meeting new people, especially people who can influence career advancement. This anxiety can in turn ramp up any existing social awkwardness and negativity, neither of which is conducive to connecting with others in a positive and comfortable way.

It is especially important to be aware of your energy level before going to an event if you find being with people draining and you prefer to recharge alone. Take 15 to 20 minutes in recharging mode before going to an event, especially if you have spent the day in meetings with others. One of my clients puts on her make-up slowly in the bathroom before going out to network. This gives her a chance to recharge alone and she comes out feeling more energized and looking great. If you are exhausted and don't want to go, don't go. You want the energy and presence you display to be conducive to forming good impressions, showing interest in others, getting to know them better, and making your value visible.

Networking Steps

There are various steps that can help make the process of networking easier and more skillful. They include steps that can be taken before, during, and after the event.

Before the Networking Event: In coaching sessions, clients are typically surprised by the idea of preparing but quickly concede it makes sense. Networking is similar to interviewing for a job where it is standard practice to research the workplace and the interviewers and prepare for questions such as "tell us more about yourself."

To network effectively it is important to know your target audience. These are primarily others who give you work or can influence your career. So they may be individuals within your organization if you are junior and clients or potential clients if you are more senior or run your own business. It is key to figure out where you should be networking; you don't want to be spending time at events that don't have your target audience. Perhaps you will find them at industry conferences, client events, professional societies, networking groups, cultural events, or charitable events.

At the Event: Go with deliberate intent — whom do you want to meet? If stressed, lower your threshold and don't try to meet everyone. If you connect well with one or two people, that is sufficient. Always leave feeling good and having energy. The typical stages at networking events include introducing yourself, listening and sharing, determining if you can help others by sharing information or contracts, and leaving graciously. You will want to ensure that small talk is light; strong views and opinions are generally not appropriate. By focusing on the goal of helping you will avoid any need to market or sell. And when you leave a conversation, don't just walk away, compliment them or thank them. Make them feel comfortable with you – people remember how you made them feel far longer than what you said.

After the Event: Many women and men who are good at preparing for and networking at an event stumble with follow-up. Technology can help with quick follow-ups: send an email to check-in or introduce someone; provide a link to an article they might be interested in; or thank them with an Ecard. It does not have to take a lot of time and, with a little thought, can keep your networks strong. Think of your network as a communication structure with information as a resource. Networking and networks viewed this way are about providing value as well as getting and sharing information.

Having a strong network ensures that you don't have to build one when you need one. I found when I quit law to start my consulting business, my first clients were people in my network. Having had a good relationship with them as a lawyer allowed me to reach out and let them know about my career change. If I would have needed to start building a network at that point to get work, the time lag would have been substantial.

Start with manageable goals and try to achieve one per month, such as: meet one new person from your industry or deepen an existing relationship; join a formal network with members who share your interests, industries, or profession; or join a committee that seems interesting and has influential members. Remember that what you do frequently and consistently is far better than what you do a lot of only occasionally.

EXERCISES

1. **Shine a Light on Personal Beliefs:** Go through the GBS in this chapter to determine if any of these blind spots form part of your belief system. If they do, they may be inhibiting you from fully self-promoting and connecting with others. An awareness of why you feel uncomfortable doing this will help you objectively evaluate what's holding you back and whether it is valid. Often GBS provide false navigational guides. When you realize the discomfort is based on inaccurate childhood rules and beliefs, you can re-evaluate these rules for yourself and learn new patterns of behaviour. Ideally, you will be able to more fully express yourself and tell others about what you do, the unique skills you possess, and the passion you bring to your work.

2. **My Accomplishments:** Below are questions to help you focus on what you are good at and determine which skills, abilities, talents, strengths, and successes separate you from others. Think about what others have told you about your strengths, your unique skills, and how you stand out from the crowd. If you don't know, ask some trusted colleagues and find out.

    ° Describe a situation in which you were complimented for good judgement.

    ° Describe an instance in which you managed a project or assignment really well from beginning to end.

- ° Describe an instance where you went beyond what was expected on a file or project. Where have you made your value and special skills visible? It may have involved finding an issue that was missed or correcting an error.
- ° What actions have you taken recently to support and/or promote your work place?
- ° What success at work are you most proud of? Be specific.
- ° What activities outside of work (e.g., volunteering for committees, non-profit organizations, alumni associations) energize you? Help others? Have made your value visible?
- ° What kudos, praise, or positive comments have you recently received? What were they for?
- ° What do you do better than your peers?
- ° What have you done to help others reach their goals?

3. **Promotion Foundations:** These questions allow you to summarize your experience and credentials.
   - ° What do you think your strengths are? Your best characteristics?
   - ° What do others at work say are your strengths?
   - ° What is the pattern that runs through the successes you have achieved? How are they similar?
   - ° What work energizes you? What do you have a passion for? What do you find easiest to do?

WHAT ORGANIZATIONS, LEADERS, AND MENTORS CAN DO

- As a leader or mentor ask yourself, "Am I good at self-promotion? Do I show others the importance of networking?" If the answers are no, you may wish to seek training or coaching.

- Encourage your team to network informally. Provide opportunities for them to get to know each other outside of work and make events easy for women to attend.
- Introduce your women colleagues to clients and influential people in the organization.
- Acknowledge to others the skills and talents of female team members.
- Extend invites to both men and women colleagues for networking events regardless of the activity. Don't assume the women won't come or don't want to come.
- Ensure that women don't feel dismissed or excluded from opportunities to promote and network.
- Examine networking opportunities where women don't show up and assess the factors preventing them. Add new social activities and get feedback from women about them. Find activities that everyone can enjoy together.
- If you are a man, promote women. Research shows that your reputation will be enhanced when you do.
- If you are a woman, promote other women. You may want to tell others that helping other women has been found to weaken a woman's reputation. Calling a bias reduces its effect.
- Allow time in meetings to praise your team and let them divulge successes. This will ensure that women will get practice promoting themselves where self-promotion is encouraged and accepted.

WANT TO READ MORE?

Heim, Pat and Tammy Hughes with Susan K. Golant. *Hardball for Women: Winning at the Game of Business*, 3rd ed. New York: Plume, 2015.

Klaus, Peggy. *Brag! The Art of Tooting Your Own Horn Without Blowing It*. New York: Warner Business Books, 2004.

LEAD

We need more women leaders. Leaders provide organizations with strategic vision. By setting goals, recruiting personnel, and harnessing skills, leaders move organizations forward. The gender gap in senior leadership has been ongoing for decades as findings mount for the many benefits of diversity at senior levels. One often cited reason for this gap is implicit bias. Unconscious stereotypes hinder women leaders from attaining leadership positions as easily as men and make it harder for them to be perceived as effective leaders. At the heart of these significant gender blind spots (GBS) is an unconscious association of leadership with men. And with the majority of leaders in business still being male, it is difficult to change this association to include women.

As a result of this GBS, women leaders are expected to adapt to traditionally male-oriented models of leadership. However, when they do, they risk being judged as hostile, aggressive, strident, masculine, demanding, or domineering, not to mention unlikeable. And women who use feminine styles don't fare much better. They may be seen as more likeable but are judged as not tough enough, too accommodating, and not competent.

What is amazing about these negative biases and tests that disadvantage women leaders is that the underlying assumptions are so inaccurate. Current research on leadership finds no significant differences in how men and women lead, there is no single best style as it depends on the situation, and the most effective leadership styles are those associated with feminine approaches.[117] These findings highlight how outdated the leader stereotype is and that feminine styles can and should be employed.

Future trends tell us that leaders can no longer tell or demand but need to collaborate and cooperate due to team-based, consensually driven organizational structures that are becoming more prevalent. The ability to influence others comes not from commanding but from listening. A different skill set is required to harness the knowledge and talent of others – and most of these skills are those associated with women.

Implicit bias is not the only significant hurdle for women attaining leadership positions. Another comes from within; we tend to have a self-limiting mindset that says "I am not a leader. I don't have the skills - I can't lead others." Due to childhood training, we often don't see ourselves as leaders, even as we influence and lead others. We buy into the notion that men are the leaders and the only way to lead is through command and control. We discount our own abilities, credentials, and approaches. We think we don't have the skills to lead, ignore the evidence, and decline opportunities. We hold the same image of leadership that society has shown us for decades and it is not an image of women. McKinsey, a leading global management firm, suggests that organizations learn to hunt, fish, and trawl for the best hidden leaders. Why are they hidden? Often it is due to gender, racial, or other biases.[118] Let's endeavour to stay hidden no longer.

BREAKING THROUGH LEADERSHIP BIAS

It's time to bring all of the implicit gender stereotypes and beliefs about leadership into the open and replace them with accurate ones. So how can we start? Building on the methods for exposing and reducing GBS set out in the chapter Expose, here are some suggestions.

- *Drag gender stereotypes, beliefs, and biases into the light.* Be able to recognize them so you can say something. Is a double standard being applied? Question it. Is the assessment of a leader an objective evaluation or distorted by GBS? Correct it. Does the conclusion align with evidence or facts? Talk to others about what you see. Build alliances with others to have courageous conversations about gender bias. Use humour like the woman in one of my seminars who said in response to a sexist comment: "do we have to call in the diversity police?"[119]

- *Identify any self-limiting mindsets you may have about women and leadership.* Being raised with images and messages about what leadership looks and sounds like, we are all susceptible to gender bias. Recognize and replace any incorrect beliefs you may hold about women and leadership with new ones that are beneficial and accurate. See the Expose chapter for details.

- *Become androgynous.* Be able to use both masculine and feminine leadership styles. Research shows that women who are androgynous have the same chance as men to be identified as leaders.[120] Many studies have shown that the most effective leaders are versatile and flexible, being able to switch fluidly and seamlessly among different leadership styles as required by the situation. Learning to use different leadership styles contextually is key to being an effective leader, and being seen as one.

- *Develop your social intelligence.* All leaders are tested but some tests are reserved just for women. To be able to navigate tests and key challenges as a leader it is imperative to receive accurate information, ensure you have powerful allies, and negotiate the conditions for success.

Various aspects of breaking through leadership bias are discussed in this chapter, starting with the various leadership tests reserved for women. By understanding what they are you will better be able to recognize and expose them. Leadership styles based on emotional intelligence put forward by Daniel Goleman are discussed and a questionnaire to help you identify your preferred style is provided. Leadership challenges often require advanced political and social intelligence skills, including getting reliable information, building an alliance of powerful backers, and negotiating conditions for success. All of these key skills are discussed in this chapter.

By being able to recognize leadership tests, flexibly use leadership styles, and employ advanced political skills to deal with leadership challenges, you will be well on your way to becoming an authentic, effective, and versatile leader.

GBS: LEADERSHIP TESTS

All new leaders are tested to some degree. However, research has consistently shown that a woman lacks the presumption of credibility and competence when she takes a leadership role. There are still tests that women have to navigate that males often bypass. They are triggered by gender, based on gender bias, and reserved especially for women. They undercut a new leader's authority with others and undermine her self-confidence. Understanding what they are allows us to expose and correct them. Here are some of the most common ones.

Token Test. This test is rooted in the suspicion that a woman has not really earned the appointment. There is an assumption that she landed a prized job because she is a woman, she worked hard, or she is just lucky. One senior woman in financial services told me that this was stated by a male on her team at the lunch celebrating her senior appointment when he thought she could not hear. To pass this test it is important to be clear on why you were selected and what you bring to the table. This will allow you to be confident in the position and not buy into incorrect assumptions.

The Double-Bind Test. The underlying question with this test is whether a woman can be both a leader and a woman. The implicit stereotype of a leader is that of a man with masculine traits. Women are consistently rated as less effective leaders when they adopt authoritative, take-charge stances. And if they adopt warmth? Then they are seen as office facilitators and not as tough-minded risk takers.[121] Regardless of a woman's choice she will be judged harshly – a perfect storm of the *Tightrope* and *Double Standard Biases* applied to leadership.

The Fitness Test. This test questions whether the woman has the right experience for the job. It suggests that she may not be a seasoned professional or have the line experience required of leaders. A result of this test is that appointing women is seen as risky, so they are less likely to be promoted.[122] Although this is a valid concern for all leadership candidates, the standards for suitability tend to be higher for women. Consequently, it takes them longer to be deemed ready. Recognition of this bias and the fact that no one is a perfect match in the rapidly changing global economy help reduce the effect of this test on promotion.

Behind each of these tests for women leaders is gender bias. Whether unconscious or conscious, these biases and tests need to be called out, corrected, or questioned so that the true nature of effective leadership can be brought forward. This is crucial so that diverse leadership with all of its economic, social, and psychological benefits, can be achieved.

T&T: RECOGNIZE SELF-LIMITING MINDSETS

Everyone is vulnerable to unconscious gender bias. Women as well as men subscribe to the stereotype of leadership as masculine. Due to early socialization girls learn that power is equal, bossy is bad and fitting in is good. They also learn that leading means controlling and commanding others. As a result, women often pass up leadership opportunities as they don't see themselves as leaders. McKinsey's recent article about hunting for leaders illustrates the need for more women to step forward when they feel comfortable.[123] This waiting to be comfortable may sound contradictory since self-limiting mindsets often make us feel uncomfortable to act even with great leadership skills. So how do we get out of this catch-22 situation? Start thinking of yourself as a leader and look for the evidence.

The evidence will become apparent when you broaden your view of leadership. Look at how you lead others in ways that are not typically thought of as leadership. Do you mentor others? Check. Do you coach others to help them develop and grow in their careers? Check. Do you motivate others by aligning their personal goals to those of the organization, set an example as a role model, and tap into the wisdom of your colleagues to help everyone move forward? Check, check, check. If you answered just one of these questions in the affirmative, you are a leader.

The section below includes a questionnaire that will help you confirm your preferred leadership style or styles. And if you think command and control is evidence of being a leader, be prepared to replace that belief.

T&T: USING LEADERSHIP STYLES

There are many ways of describing and categorizing gender leadership styles to reflect masculine and feminine traits including, agentic and communal, transactional and transformational, and task oriented and relationship oriented. The styles I have found most helpful for understanding and developing effective leadership are associated with emotional intelligence.[124] They were identified empirically by studying business leaders and reflect both feminine and masculine approaches.

To understand which style or styles you prefer, a short questionnaire is included below. By knowing the style you prefer and use most often you will be better able to find opportunities for using and developing the other styles.

EXERCISE

QUESTIONNAIRE: LEADERSHIP STYLES

Read each statement carefully. If the statement describes you, circle T and if the statement does not, circle F. As you respond, your frame of reference should be leadership at work. The purpose of this questionnaire is to create awareness of different leadership styles and your ability to use them flexibly. If you are uncertain as to your use, ask a trusted work colleague.

1. I lead by motivating others to work towards a shared ideal. **T F**
2. I am good at connecting individuals' needs with organizational goals. **T F**
3. I often motivate others by listening and letting them figure out the answers. **T F**
4. I enjoy creating harmony in work teams to allow for greater connection. **T F**
5. At work I value people's input and get commitment through participation and discussion. **T F**
6. I set high standards for myself and I like others to follow my lead. **T F**
7. I give clear instructions on what needs to be done, how it should be done, and by when. **T F**
8. I value the independence of others and prefer to inspire others to achieve group goals. **T F**
9. I enjoy mentoring and developing juniors at work to improve their performance. **T F**
10. I prefer to lead by getting others' input and building consensus through participation. **T F**
11. I highly value compliance and expect others to do what I tell them. **T F**

12. I believe that to lead well and get results you have to put people first. **T F**
13. I like to lead by example. **T F**
14. I like to use the experience and skill of the group to encourage creativity, consensus, and engagement. **T F**
15. I value a cohesive and connective environment where positive feedback is commonplace. **TF**
16. I like to set the pace for others to follow. **T F**
17. I like to tell others how to determine goals and how to achieve them. **T F**
18. I like to share a clear vision and then allow others to work towards it in their own way. **T F**
19. I lead others by listening and questioning, allowing them to discover the answers. **T F**
20. I like to lead by getting consensus through discussion and participation. **T F**
21. I like to achieve and expect those around me to follow my directions. **T F**
22. I like to ask what others need to motivate them and strengthen connections with them. **T F**
23. I like to do things better and faster and often expect others around me to do the same. **T F**
24. I like to motivate others by making clear how their work fits into the larger vision of the organization. **T F**

To score the questionnaire and determine your preferred style or styles, circle the question numbers below that you answered true (only T answers are scored), then add them to determine which style you prefer. A high score is three or four "T"s per box. High scores for more than one style is common and indicates flexibility and versatility in their use. To be an effective leader and avoid the Double Bind test as a woman leader, this is what you are aiming for. The six styles are categorized below according to whether they are primarily relationship or task oriented as these categorizations reflect masculine and feminine styles.

Relationship Oriented Styles
Coaching 2T 3T 9T 19T
Democratic 5T 10T 14T 20T
Affiliative 4T 12T 15T 22T
Task Oriented Styles
Pacesetting 6T 13T 16T 23T
Commanding 7T 11T 17T 21T
Task and Relationship Oriented Style
Visionary 1T 8T 18T 24T

DESCRIPTION OF LEADERSHIP STYLES

As you read each description, think of how you lead and influence others. When you delegate work or provide feedback, how do you do it? Often this will reflect your preferred leadership style.[125]

- *Pacesetting style* (Watch me!) This task oriented style is focused on excellence. The leader is the role model for the group and sets high standards of performance for both themselves and others. This type of leadership results in a culture where competence is highly valued and the aim is excellence. This style is most associated with a masculine approach and promotes the type of workplace culture found in many masculine professions and industries.

- *Coaching style* (You tell me.) This relationship oriented style is focused on the development of junior professionals by helping them improve their performance. It helps employees to grow by facilitating learning through discovery rather than by directing (Commanding) or by example (Pacesetting). This style is most often associated with a feminine approach.

- *Commanding style* (Listen up!) This task oriented style is most often used and associated with leadership. The leader tells the group not only how to complete the goals but also determines the goals. Compliance is highly valued. This style is most associated with a masculine approach.

- *Affiliative style* (What do you need?) This is a relationship oriented style. The use of this approach builds strong teams by focusing on each person's personal and professional needs. It connects people with each other. With its emphasis on the needs of others, this style creates a very cohesive, connective environment where positive feedback is common. This style is most associated with a feminine approach.

- *Democratic style* (What do you think?) This relationship oriented style allows the leader to tap into the wisdom of the group while encouraging creativity, consensus, and engagement. The entire group's skills and experience are made available with the use of this style. The focus is on decision-making by the group and is most associated with a feminine approach.

- *Visionary style* (Come with me.) This task and relationship oriented style allows others to act independently while in alignment with group goals. It motivates people to work towards a goal or vision. Leaders use this style to provide a clear vision and direction for others to follow. This style involves elements of both masculine and feminine approaches.

If you are still not sure about your preferred leadership style, ask a trusted colleague or junior - they will most likely know. Perhaps you have more than one style. A study of law firm partners found that among outstanding partners, 70% used four or more leadership styles compared to the average partners in which only 40% used four or more styles. Stronger professional performance and higher firm revenues were associated with the partners' ability to utilize a variety of leadership styles.[126]

And what are the styles used by leaders who were judged the best? Visionary, Affiliative, and Coaching styles were found to be employed by the most effective leaders -- all of which encourage group involvement and are more associated with feminine approaches. In contrast, the masculine style of Pacesetting was far less likely to be used, while Commanding style was employed but in combination with other styles.[127]

Results collected from responses to the questionnaire set out above from 300 senior business women revealed similar findings.[128] Commanding style was the least used of all six styles and only in combination with other styles. Only 1-2% of women in the sample used this style. Pacesetting came in a close second as the least used style with approximately 5% of women reporting they used it.

The most popular style in this group of women was Democratic; this is in keeping with feminine norms where power is viewed as equal. The vast majority of women who took the questionnaire used a total of four styles routinely. The main styles used were three relationship oriented ones – Affiliative, Democratic, and Coaching styles – plus

Visionary style. This sample provides clear evidence that women tend to use relationship oriented styles more than task oriented styles, with many women using multiple styles.

When to Use Them

Being adaptable and versatile is key to using leadership styles effectively. Research shows that the best leaders know when to use each style appropriately by matching the style to the situation. This means being skilled in the use of different styles as well as knowing which one works best in a given situation. Think of them as tools in a toolbox. If you have only one style it might be like having only a hammer – everything starts looking like a nail.

By increasing the number of leadership styles you are able to use, you can start to be selective and strategic in their use. By being able to use both feminine and masculine approaches, you will more easily be able to pass the Double Bind test faced by most women leaders. Key factors for the best use of each style are listed below.[129]

- *Pacesetting style*
  - Works best for getting quick results from a highly competent and motivated group
  - Use with groups that want challenging goals and high levels of achievement
  - The goal is high-quality performance and excellent results
  - The leader is a good role model with high standards for excellence
- *Commanding style*
  - Works best in a crisis or emergency situation that needs quick turnaround
  - The goal is immediate compliance

- The goals typically are performance based and outcome driven
- To attenuate and manage group tension through clear direction from the top
- *Coaching style*
  - Works best with juniors who need mentoring and professional development
  - Focus is less on achieving performance goals and more on personal development
  - Learning through discovery is valued
  - Works especially well with millennials -- individuals born after 1981
- *Visionary style*
  - Works best where a change is needed and past practices are no longer succeeding
  - The group needs to work together and not be directed from the top
  - The leader is able to motivate the group to work towards a common goal
- *Affiliative style*
  - Works best where conflict and stressful situations exist
  - Use to build trust, create morale, and improve communication
  - Group morale, relationships, and harmony are primary
  - Can be combined with other styles such as Coaching, Visionary, and Democratic for best results
- *Democratic style*
  - Works best in a situation where group buy-in and consensus are important
  - Forges agreement and commitment through participation
  - Any new direction is determined by the group
  - The group's experience, competence, and knowledge is high

To be an effective leader it is important to be able to switch styles and use them in sequence. By recognizing situations that call for a particular style and practicing different styles of leadership you will be able to greatly expand your leadership skill set. If you are currently using one style predominately, look for opportunities to practice others. You might start by looking for ways to address the professional needs of those you lead.

NAVIGATING KEY CHALLENGES

There are many challenges for leaders, especially for new women leaders. Being able to navigate key challenges requires advanced political skills associated with social intelligence. The ones discussed below include gathering reliable information, having the backing of influential others, and negotiating conditions for success.

GATHERING RELIABLE INFORMATION

Accurate information is a prized asset in today's complex and multi-layered organizations. This is the reason solid and broad networks are so valuable. Reliable information allows you to be confident about a position even before taking it and allows you to negotiate the conditions that will ensure your success in the new position. It helps you determine expectations and quantify how your success will be measured. Knowing what you are working towards and when you have achieved success is important for all women in new roles.[130]

This intelligence allows you to understand what is expected from you in the position and to determine the unspoken codes of behaviour. In particular, it helps you understand where resistance to what you are doing may come from. Good intelligence allows you to anticipate the pot holes and steer clear of them.

Knowing who the key decision makers are in your organization is essential for gathering reliable information. In addition to being in the information loop, both observing and listening are effective ways to gather information and understand the perspectives of others.

Do you ask a lot of questions about others' perspectives? People enjoy being listened to – especially in today's world where the pace is so quick. When you listen, are you open to new information or do you judge and infer? If it's the latter, you are like most people. Due to the ability to control the flow of information, it is often thought that speaking is power. However, listening has more power. It allows you to fully understand the other person's perspective and gain important information.

Below is a detailed discussion of the challenges of listening well together with some listening checks and techniques for improving this skill. The benefits are very worthwhile– not only for gathering important information but also increasing resilience.

T&T: Listening Skills

Listening is one of the most underrated and underdeveloped skills in communication. Although it is a skill more associated with women than men, given the nonstop nature of today's workplace with the strong emphasis on productivity, listening is difficult for most people. One of the biggest obstacles to good listening is multi-tasking – trying to do many things at the same time. This notion that we can multi-task and listen relates to excess processing capacity. Each of us can process 500 words per minute while most people speak at a rate of only 150 words per minute. That means we have excess processing capacity of around 350 words.[131] This is why our mind naturally wanders. As we listen, we check our devices for new messages; think about and decide what we will have for dinner; and remind ourselves where we parked the car. As a result, we usually don't fully listen. Below are tips to help you improve your listening skills and situational awareness.

To keep the conversation flowing, use listening skills that allow the other person to open up. Move from certainty to curiosity. Avoid being judgemental and critical. Listen empathetically, even if you don't agree. What perceptions and information does the other person have that you don't? Ask others for their views and mean it. Acknowledge the feelings of others as they express them. Draw the other person out with questions. Use checks not only for clarifying the facts and your understanding of them, but also for a better understanding of the speaker's feelings. Below are five basic ways to enhance active listening.

THE FIVE LISTENING CHECKS

Type of Check	Purpose	Method	Examples
Gather	You want facts. You want to explore and discuss more fully.	Use a what, how, when question to get the facts clearly and correctly.	Is this a problem for you? What did you say then? So how did you respond?
Clarify	To ensure you have heard accurately and to let the other person know you grasp the facts.	Paraphrase what you have heard. Restate the person's basic ideas.	As I understand it, the problem is ... Am I hearing you correctly? To clarify, you said .... What I understand you to say is ... is that right?
Acknowledge	To show you are listening and interested.	Use non-committal words with a positive tone of voice.	I see. Tell me more. I get the idea. Please go on.

Empathize	To show you are listening and empathize.	Reflect or restate the other person's feelings. It does not mean that you agree with them.	You feel that you didn't get proper treatment. It was unjust as you perceive it. It's annoying to have this happen to you. I sense that you like doing this job, but you are uneasy about making mistakes.
Summarize	To focus the discussion and move to a new level of discussion. To pull important ideas or facts together.	Summarize, restate, and reflect major facts, ideas, and feelings.	These are the key elements of the problem. Let's see now, we've examined these four factors .... These seem to be the key ideas you expressed ....To summarize — the main points are ....

Listening well can slow or stop the constant mental stream of thoughts that often create anxiety and stress. When we listen fully we become present, and that allows us to relax. Time may even expand and slow down. This allows us to refresh and recharge so we are more resilient. This is a great bonus to the listener while also allowing the other person to feel heard.

T&T: Listen with Your Eyes

Paying attention to someone's body language as we listen to them uses up the excess mental processing capacity previously mentioned. It also provides us with important information. You may see big shifts in a speaker's posture or position, or smaller movements that indicate nervousness. Watch for behaviour that contradicts what the person is saying. Recently, I watched two separate televised interviews where the people speaking shook their heads side-to-side, clearly indicating disagreement with their own words. Important meaning can be obtained and the truth revealed when you listen with your eyes.

You will want to demonstrate attentive non-verbal behaviour as you listen. To appear receptive and curious, open your posture, lean toward the speaker, and relax. Try not to multi-task as you listen. If this is a habit, try not to read emails or check the time. Monitor your non-verbal behaviour to help ensure that you are not becoming defensive or dominant in the exchange. One of the key aspects of conflict communication is keeping it safe for the other person.

Listening to what others say with their body is an art; there are no hard and fast rules that apply to all people across all situations. To understand it accurately, non-verbal language needs to be observed in the larger context of the situation and what is being said. The reason it is so important is that the body seldom lies and emotional reactions are hard to hide.

Body language is conveyed by various body parts. We tend to focus most on the face and eyes as that is how we connect when we talk. Eyes can tell us if the person is concentrating on what we're saying or focusing on a report on the desk. They can also show subtle shifts in emotion and tell us if the person is comfortable. Watch for subtle shifts in expression and for tension in the mouth. Does the person refuse to make eye contact?

Generally receptive facial clues are shown through smiling and lots of eye contact. The opposite - unreceptive clues – include little or no eye contact or squinted eyes, tension in the jaw muscles, and head turned slightly away. There are gender differences in facial expression clues: women tend to smile more, make more eye contact, and tilt the head either to one side or slightly away; men tend to make less eye contact and smile less. However, it's important to remember that a person's baseline behaviour and deviations from it are very important in reading body language while gender tendencies can be variable. For more information about non-verbal language see the Presence chapter.

BUILD AN ALLIANCE

As a leader, it is important to recognize and mobilize backers in the organization to provide you with critical support. Scrutiny of women leaders can be intense and in any competitive environment there will be skeptics. Most senior women believe their success is not presumed when they take prominent roles, although they do not anticipate the scrutiny.[132] With key backers you have individuals you can trust who will provide you with early and accurate intelligence and help you deal with resistance and skepticism. This support will allow you to focus on your goals and achieve results.

With relationships that go back a long time, a new leader can usually count on the support of senior people. If you are less known or new to the organization, then establishing this support will be key to your success. Relying on the faulty notion that the appointment will speak for itself is risky because you may not negotiate for conditions that ensure your success. It may also make you think that you don't need to be political or gather powerful allies to support you. This is similar to the myth that if you work hard and get results you will advance and be given credibility and authority. Organizations are not meritocracies and politics operate everywhere.

Many leaders fall into the trap of working hard for results without prioritizing relationships or recognizing politics at play. However, results take time and impressions are made quickly. As you are grinding away, you may be perceived as aloof, disinterested, or missing the big picture. Combine this with the tendency to avoid self-promotion and talking about successes and you could easily be perceived as someone who is not producing results.

T&T: Use a Collaborative Mindset

Asking for support may feel weak. You may think that strong leaders go it alone and don't ask for help. However, the individuals who hired you will want to ensure your success. By building alliances you are paving the way for mutual assistance. Use a collaborative mindset to determine the interests of important and strategic backers and then identify mutual interests. How do your interests align? Step into their shoes – what is important to them? What interests do they have and which interests do you share? By ensuring your work relationship is mutually beneficial, you will not look weak but will come across as a powerful ally.

A collaborative mindset underlies Principled Negotiation.[133] This mindset is described in the Politics chapter as one of five strategies to deal with conflict. It is also the basis of the Co-Creating approach to asking in the Ask chapter. A collaborative approach appreciates the perspectives of others, understands their interests and needs, and looks for options that encourage joint gains. It is creative and seeks to create value for all parties. This mindset recognizes that social intelligence is important and solid working relationships pave the way for career success. With this mindset, others will want to work with you and your reputation will be enhanced.

To contrast a competitive mindset with a collaborative mindset, the hallmarks of each are shown in the chart below.

	Competitive Mindset	Collaborative Mindset
Attitude	win-lose	win-win
Priority	outcome	outcome/relationship
Interests	self-interests	identifies interests of all parties to find mutual interests
Goal	get what you want	a mutually beneficial agreement
Exchange	withholds information	shares information appropriately
Ethical	no; seeks advantage	yes; is trusting, but verifies
Psychology	seeks to reduce expectations --convinces other person that their case or position is weak in order to win	Seeks to understand interests and uses problem solving to arrive at a fair arrangement for all parties involved
Value	claims value	creates value

A collaborative mindset allows you to be socially intelligent while maximizing your results and building good working relationships. Using this mindset builds trust and a good reputation, allowing you to become influential in your organization. This mindset is the foundation of Democratic and Affiliative leadership styles which allow the needs and interests of others to set the goals and direction of the organization.

NEGOTIATE CONDITIONS FOR SUCCESS

There are no absolute guarantees for success when you become a leader. However there are certain conditions that can be negotiated to greatly increase the probability that you will achieve your goals. The two conditions of great importance for new leaders include quantifying what success means before you take the position, and negotiating for the resources you need to do the job successfully.

T&T: Quantify Success

Making sure success is well defined before you start a leadership position matters.[134] When success is quantifiable you know when you are on track. A clear mandate helps you avoid moving targets as issues and problems change the goal. Failing to get clarity on what success looks like is a common mistake. So no matter what profession or industry you work in, when you are asked to step into a leadership position identify the markers of success and ensure these markers are within reach. If you have taken on an expanded role, find out what others define as success in quantifiable terms. Also be clear at the start about the expectations of those who support your leadership and are influential in the organization. Needing to change your goals and priorities mid-course to align with such expectations will make you appear uncertain and cause others to question your commitment.

Understanding what success means to the people selecting you also helps determine fit. If you have worked there a long time then the fit is likely good and the corporate values likely align with yours. If you are new, knowing how the organization measures success will help you see if your goals and values are aligned. It is a big red flag if they are not. Having alignment in your goals and values is important for helping you lead with passion and purpose.

T&T: Negotiate for Resources

Once you have determined how success will be measured you will need to identify and negotiate for financial, human, and time resources. It would be great if the necessary allocations of resources were automatic, but they are not. They need to be identified and negotiated for, especially in organizations where the bottom line is paramount. You may be expected to do more with less. Not having sufficient resources to do the job can result in frustration and failure to deliver. If the necessary resources are not available, then set priorities for the use of those which are available. Making use of existing resources will ensure that your perception as a leader remains strong.

Some of the ways to get the necessary resources include aligning requests to the organization's strategic objectives, appealing to key players who have a vested interest in your success, calling on supporters with common interests, and using small successes to garner more resources.[135]

In addition to their practical uses, resources also have symbolic value. The amount and extent of resources are an early indicator of the power and influence of a new leader. And these early impressions are important. Judgements are made by others based on what they think a new leader can deliver and what interests they expect the newcomer to satisfy. Support will be provided to someone who has the ability to deliver, and the most obvious indicator of that is resources. Without sufficient resources, the organization may appear to lack commitment to the job you have taken on. This may bleed into perceptions of your ability to act on your agenda or lead at all. This makes the need to negotiate for the necessary resources all the more important. Before taking on a leadership position always ensure you have the resources you need to get the job done.

WHAT ORGANIZATIONS, LEADERS, AND MENTORS CAN DO

- Model for others how to use a variety of leadership styles.
- Implement training programs on leadership.
- Recognize true leadership and hunt, fish, and trawl for hidden leaders that may have been overlooked due to bias and stereotypes.

- Broaden criteria for leadership positions and emphasize cognitive skills over specific types of experience. Recognize that women will typically not apply for a position if they do not satisfy all of the requirements.
- Set clear numerical goals for the number of women leaders.
- Show your commitment to women's advancement through actions, not words. If leaders are not visibly committed, it's not going to happen.
- Build a culture of diversity, inclusion, and innovation.

WANT TO READ MORE?

Abbott, Ida. *Law Firm Management and Economics: Women on Top – The Woman's Guide to Leadership and Power in Law Firms.* West Publishing, 2010.

Eagly, Alice H. and Linda L. Carli. *Through the Labyrinth: The Truth About How Women Become Leaders.* Boston: Harvard Business Review Press, 2007.

Goleman, Daniel, Richard Boyatzis, and Annie McKee. *Primal Leadership.* Boston: Harvard Business School Press, 2013.

Krawcheck, Sallie. *Own it: The Power of Women at Work.* New York: Crown Business, 2017.

Lublin, Joann S. *Earning It: Hard-Won Lessons from Trailblazing Women at the Top of the Business World.* New York: HarperCollins, 2017.

POLITICS

If you feel aversion to this topic, you are not alone. Most women dislike and avoid office politics, associating them with gossiping, meddling, lying, sucking up, and manipulating – in short, being Machiavellian. However, none of these negative behaviours help career advancement. And avoiding politics does not make negative office politics go away nor decrease the value of smart political behaviors in helping you advance and succeed.

An executive from the banking industry told me that when people called her political she vehemently denied the label and took offence at being viewed that way. Now she takes it as a compliment. Her insight came during a performance review when she was told that no one in her large organization knew who she was. She realized that to be an effective and influential leader she needed to become political. In other words, working in her office quietly and efficiently was not enough.

Women's reluctance to embrace politics in the workplace may be due to the hierarchical power structure women are taught as children. For women who learn that power is shared and equal, figuring out an organizational chart or determining who is influential in an organization is not automatic. Instead the opposite instinct tends to kick in with women shying away from understanding who holds power in the organization. Where everyone is equal and the group is important, women generally think that doing their job and doing it well is all that counts.

Unfortunately, working hard and doing an outstanding job might still cause you to lag behind political individuals who, in addition to having technical expertise, manage important relationships with people who can reward them. Politically savvy individuals tend to be both connected and competent. One senior lawyer defined being political as being sensitive to others' needs, ambitions, and ideas - in other words, being connected. She told me this helped her have credibility with her team and to lead effectively and competently.

To avoid negative associations with the word politics, I have chosen to use the term *social intelligence* (SI) in this chapter. Being socially intelligent will not only help you to be more successful, it will also protect you from being blindsided by negative office politics. The social skills discussed in this chapter, unlike negative office politics, work as a shield and not a sword. They won't hurt others, but they will help you to advance, help your team and the people you supervise, and help you anticipate changes that can have negative effects.

GBS: AVOIDING OFFICE POLITICS

Avoiding office politics is the significant gender blind spot (GBS) addressed in this chapter. Most of the skills linked to SI are those associated more with women than men due to gender training. To help you become politically savvy and more aware of your SI strengths and challenges, a questionnaire is provided at the end of the chapter.

USING SOCIAL INTELLIGENCE

The chart below sets out five SI dimensions and the relevant skills relating to each. The highlighted skills are discussed in detail in this chapter while many of the other skills are discussed in other chapters. There is overlap of skills across dimensions so, for example, understanding the culture and values of the organization relates to both Situational Awareness and Organizational Awareness.

SI Dimensions and Relevant Skills

Social Intelligence Dimensions	Description	Relevant Skills
Situational Awareness	· Reading social situations well and being able to accurately interpret people's motivations, intentions, emotion, and actions · A respectful interest in people and an understanding of social dynamics and codes of conduct	· Reading Social Situations · Listening Skills · Non-Verbal Communication · Knowing Codes of Conduct · **Business Etiquette**
Organizational Awareness	· Understanding the culture and values of the workplace to know what is important · Being able to find the inside track by accessing information from those up the ladder · Getting connected to those who know how things work	Information Gathering: · How Are Things Done? · Who's in The Loop? · **Who's Essential to your Success?** · What is Rewarded?
Influence and Authenticity	· Being credible and speaking with conviction · Knowing your personal values and letting others know your voice, how you think, and where you are coming from · Being able to gain others' trust and cooperation · Creating alliances and a circle of influence	· **Your Personal Values** · Informal Networking · Being Persuasive · Being Audience-Focused · Creating Alliances · Informal Networking

Relationship Management	• Building and maintaining connections with others both internally and externally • Responding well in conflict situations and with difficult people • Recognizing that both connectedness and competence are needed for success	• **Using Conflict Modes** • Mind Mapping • Setting Priorities • Conflict Steps and Strategies
Communication	• Being able to express positions and ideas in a favourable and compelling way • Delivering confident and clear messages that are easy to listen to • Dealing with conflicts constructively • Using communication techniques to support and empower others	• **Conflict Communication** • Listening Skills • Clear Communication • Empowering Others • Stopping Interruptions • Preventing Idea Theft • **Being Agreeable While Disagreeing**

SITUATIONAL AWARENESS

Situational awareness is the ability to read people and the context quickly by interpreting patterns, social cues, and circumstances. This often involves recognizing when there is a disconnect between what is being said and non-verbal behaviour. A recent study reveals that inter-personal space can accurately predict unconscious bias, with the larger the space the bigger the bias.[136] Something as simple as distance between people can provide important information about unconscious attitudes. The chapter Lead offers information and advice on listening fully and interpreting non-verbal communication.

One of the most important things to learn in any new workplace or profession is what is considered acceptable behaviour. To learn this for each of my professions I watched what other professionals did and listened to what they said. What was the social code of conduct? What was the culture of the workplace? This information helped me to understand not only how I should act, but also how my behaviour would be interpreted. This information was as important to know as becoming technically proficient. It allowed me to show good judgement and fit in well with the group and the organization. Another way to appear situationally aware is to know business etiquette.

T&T: Business Etiquette

Knowing what is appropriate in the workplace and in business generally is key to enhancing your image as someone who is knowledgeable, sophisticated, and respectful. Actions, even small ones, tell others how you operate in the world and have a huge impact on overall impressions. They indicate your respect for others and interest in them. They allow you to appear confident and knowledgeable while establishing connections and earning trust. To enhance and reinforce your brand of competence and expertise, make business etiquette habitual – a part of you and your personal style.

Etiquette Mindset

Underlying all proper protocols and rules of etiquette is a mindset that, if adopted, will allow you to appear professional and polite even when you don't know the specific rules. The fundamental characteristics of the mindset relating to business etiquette include

- Being respectful
- Being considerate
- Being other-focused
- Making others comfortable
- Making others feel included and important
- Being mindful of differences

If you keep these goals in mind, people will forgive a misstep and appreciate that you are trying. If you observe the protocols and rules impeccably, but embarrass or annoy someone due to arrogance or lack of consideration, your image will be tarnished nevertheless. The rules come from being focused on others and making it socially easy for them. In making it socially easy for others, you make it socially easy for yourself. As these are fundamental attitudes, approaches and norms of female gender training, this mindset comes naturally for most women.

Below are descriptions of common situations where business etiquette is of particular importance. All of this etiquette is from a North American perspective. There are of course geographic and cultural differences in what is considered socially appropriate. If you are dealing with clients from a different culture or doing business in another country, there are many good books on business etiquette in different cultural contexts that can help.[137]

Hand Shakes and Hugs

The fundamentals of a good hand shake include extending the right hand with the thumb up and palm down. Use a medium firm grasp, avoiding the extremes of a grasp that is too hard or too soft. Maintain eye contact as you shake hands and smile. Two up-and-down pumps will do, lasting about three to four seconds in total. Longer than that becomes awkward. As a woman – to avoid confusion – be the first to hold out your hand.

What about hugs? Are they appropriate in professional settings? A hug indicates that the relationship is more than just business, so shaking hands, which is the conventional business greeting, should be your default greeting in conservative industries and professions. However, sometimes it is appropriate to hug the other person. Circumstances where you might consider a hug are where: you know the other person well; you have a relationship that goes beyond work; the situation is less formal and less business-focused; and/or you know the other person will be comfortable with it.

It is more common and acceptable for women to hug other women in business settings. Men hugging women can be interpreted in other ways, so err on the side of convention and shake hands with men.

Introducing Others

As the business world becomes increasingly casual, the ability to introduce others with elegance and style will set you apart as being etiquette savvy. Don't worry about making mistakes – people will appreciate that you made the effort. It is far worse not to make an introduction when you should and could have than to make a mistake.

The fundamentals of a business introduction are:

- Say the name of the more senior person first;
- Introduce the junior person to them, and
- Provide some information about one or both to facilitate discussion.

The general rule is to say the name of the more experienced or more senior person first and then to introduce the more junior person. For example, if introducing a more junior person, Sara Bolton, to a more senior person, Joanne Smith, you would say, "Joanne Smith may I introduce you to Sara Bolton." The introduction formula may vary widely from basic to formal, however, the general rule is always to introduce the senior person first. Here are some introduction variations.

- "Joanne Smith, Sara Bolton" (bare bones intro)
- "Joanne Smith, I would like to introduce Sara Bolton."
- "Joanne Smith, I would like to present Sara Bolton." (more formal)
- "Joanne Smith, have you met Sara Bolton?"
- "Joanne Smith, do you know Sara Bolton?"

After introducing the two people, provide some information that will facilitate the conversation. For example, "Sara just started at a PR firm and given your vast experience in marketing I am sure you will have lots to talk about." The goal is to facilitate a positive connection between the people being introduced and, by providing a topic for immediate discussion, avoid any awkward post-introduction silence.

If you forget a name, don't panic and be honest. Simply say, "I am so sorry but your name has slipped my mind." If someone else fails to introduce you to another person they know, help them out after a couple of minutes and introduce yourself. Most likely they have forgotten your name or the name of the other person. They will appreciate your consideration.

While at dinner, stand up to be introduced or to greet a person you know. In your office, come around your desk to shake hands. When having a group discussion and a person you know enters the group, you should immediately introduce the newcomer. You should introduce yourself whenever you feel the person sitting or standing next to you would be more comfortable knowing who you are.

When receiving a business card at a networking event or during a meeting, don't immediately put it into your pocket or purse. Look at it and perhaps ask a question about it. You want to display interest. Etiquette is about being polite and considerate and, thus, treat the card as you would wish yours to be treated. Make the other person feel important. Making a pleasant comment about the card will also help you to better remember the person. Once back at your office, make some notes on it to remind you of them: the event, a special fact, a unique personal interest, or a common interest is information that will allow you to connect with them at a later time.

Phone Etiquette

With the prevalence of smart phones, it is important to know how to use them in a socially intelligent way. Many people ignore and breach business etiquette by habitually checking for messages, leaving their phones on during meetings, taking calls during meetings, or talking loudly in public areas. The message sent is that the person who is not there takes precedence over the people who are there in person and have taken the time to meet with you. It's called *phubbing* and conveys a general lack of respect.

If you are expecting an important call or email that you cannot miss, tell the person you are meeting with that you might have to step out to take that call or answer the message. If you must answer an unexpected call or email, ask permission to deal with it quickly and excuse yourself. Otherwise, turn off your phone to make a positive impression and show respect.

When in public be conscious of confidentiality issues. Many people still shout when on a cell phone. Be aware if you do and ensure that the conversation remains private. Turn off your phone when dining with clients or work colleagues. If you are under thirty you are most likely more accepting of smartphone use in social settings than people over thirty, the age of the majority of your clients and senior colleagues.

Be careful how you text or email on a smartphone. Since you are typing with your thumbs, read your messages carefully before sending. Typos tarnish your image by making you appear sloppy and inconsiderate of the reader. Prepare a professional signature with your contact information regardless of the device you use.

For conference calls, it is standard protocol for the chair to introduce the people in the room and on the phone, or to ask each person to introduce themselves. Make sure you speak clearly and annunciate fully. Due to the lack of social cues, it is very easy to interrupt someone, fail to address someone, or misattribute a comment. If you do, briefly apologize and move on. It is easy to get distracted when on a conference call in your office alone. Listening is hard. Try doodling to stay focussed and stand up to increase your energy. You will also have more energy and presence in your voice if you speak while standing. Being energized and staying focused shows professionalism and respect for the others on the call.

To summarize, the fundamentals of good smart phone etiquette include

- Avoid habitually checking for messages at meetings
- If you expect an important message let the person running the meeting know
- Turn off your phone when you are with others
- Be aware of privacy and confidentiality when talking to others in public
- If possible, find a private place to talk when in public

ORGANIZATIONAL AWARENESS

Organizational awareness goes beyond knowing the organizational chart or the organization's business objectives. It is about knowing the values and culture of your organization. How are things done? Who is in the loop? Is there any disconnect between what is stated and what is actual? For example, the organization may publicly espouse that a particular skill or attitude is valued but may reward the opposite behaviour in practice. Below is an exercise to highlight your knowledge about those in the workplace who can impact your career. It will be used to walk you through the information that is important to know in developing this type of organizational awareness.

T&T: Influential Other Assessment

Key People to Your Success	Stage of Relationship	Next Steps
1.		
2.		
3.		
4.		

Key People to Your Success

In any organization it is important to know who has authority. Find out who is respected. Who is influential? Who mentors or champions others? Who has informal authority? This is important information to ensure your success in the organization. Knowing who can influence your career is especially key. Think of three or four people who are key to your success and write down their names. Your list can include your direct supervisor, senior people who provide work, colleagues, and perhaps people from other divisions or departments. The important factor is their ability to impact your career.

Stages of Relationship

Now that you have thought of at least three or four people who are influential to your success at work, the next step is to evaluate your stage of relationship with each person. The three stages are: Surrogate, Service, and Solid. In all of these relationships, the aim is to deepen and enhance the relationship until it is Solid. A Solid relationship is one in which you know the person and they know you, where you understand their perspective, you know their passions and goals, and you know what they don't like. To help you determine the stage of each relationship, a brief description of each is included below.

Surrogate Relationship: In this type of relationship, the work or business comes to you due to relationships that others have, and not due to your own direct relationships. This is typically the level of relationship you have as a new hire in any organization unless you own your own business. It is important to note that Surrogate relationships are usually the most unstable relationships as the work does not come directly to you from the source and thus can be funneled to others for a variety of reasons. Your goal should be to provide outstanding service for the person giving you the work so that the relationship can evolve into a Service or Solid relationship.

Service Relationship: This is the relationship you automatically have with any supplier of work, typically your immediate supervisor or boss. They know you and you know them. Consistently great service, coupled with care and concern for both the work product and for the supplier, allows this relationship to develop into a Solid relationship.

Solid Relationship: This is the gold standard in relationships, where mutual respect and caring in turn fosters and nurtures loyalty. You know what is important to the other party, what they like and what they dislike. Should difficult issues or obstacles arise between the parties, they can be worked out more easily due to the level of the relationship. The parties wish the best for each other and want each other to succeed. Your goal is to build Solid relationships with influential others in your organization so that the relationship is one that is stable and can withstand problems that arise.

Possible Next Steps

If you want to deepen the relationship with a person in your organization, think of some activities that they like and would be appropriate for your current relationship stage. You always want to take next steps in a way that is socially intelligent; this rules out using hollow or empty flattery.

When I was an articling student, one of my fellow students sent out a congratulatory email to each of the lawyers who had just been admitted into partnership, whether he knew them or not. Although it may have been well intended, the method (email) and the level of the relationship made the gesture look hollow at best and sucking up at worst.

Below are some suggested activities for getting to know the people who can influence your career.

- Attend networking events and talk with them
- Drop by their office to ask their advice
- Take them to lunch
- Work on a committee with them
- Get involved with their pet project
- Determine how to work with them on a file or project
- Ask a mentor or trusted advisor how to get to know a key person
- Find a way to connect in a SI way

Women have a tendency to avoid powerful individuals even when they can greatly influence careers. Does that tendency apply to you? Do you sit close to the executives in meetings? Of course you want to keep in mind your age and stage, however, if you have seniority and are still not sitting at the table or with those at your level, ask yourself why not. Learn to connect with them in a meaningful way. As a socially intelligent person, you will realize that connection is important to everyone and showing someone respect and interest goes a long way to deepening the relationship.

Watch and Learn

Another way to become knowledgeable about your organization is to watch the people who are influential and have power. How do they communicate in meetings? How do their memos read? Note how they phrase things, especially if they do so in a manner that differs from yours.

How do they use their power? Who is in their circle of influence? How do they make connections and maintain relationships? You don't want to stalk them or tell them what you are doing (that would not be very SI), however, it is amazing what you can learn about others by casually observing them. With time, you will start to see patterns of behaviour and this information will make you much more organizationally aware.

INFLUENCE AND AUTHENTICITY

A very important part of being influential is being authentic. Instead of professing convictions for ideas simply because they are in vogue, you know what you truly believe and value. By knowing yourself and your values, you can be the compass for others, especially in times of great change or uncertainty.

Knowing your values and showing them allows others to know how you think and where you are coming from. And when change is constant, this characteristic of being genuine and consistent is greatly needed. It allows you to gain trust and cooperation, and to create alliances and a circle of influence. Building alliances is a great strength of women that is often underused. Succeeding in a masculine workplace often seems to require going it alone. Paradoxically, male CEOs have their circle of faithful lieutenants who actively support them and are rewarded accordingly. Embrace the power of alliances and develop a circle of influence.

Below is a questionnaire to help you better understand your career values.

T&T: Personal Values Questionnaire

Values are deeply held beliefs that guide a person's actions. Awareness of values will assist you in understanding and achieving a higher level of career satisfaction. This exercise is geared to help you determine and reflect on your personal values.

1. Read the list of values below and determine their level of importance to you.
2. Rate the degree to which each career value guides your actions and reflects your views.
3. Review those you marked *highly valued* and prioritize them.
4. Feel free to add any values that are not listed here and rate them.

Career Values	Highly Valued	Somewhat Valued	Not Valued
Advancement - being able to get ahead, gaining opportunities for growth, and seniority from work well-done			
Belonging- developing close personal relationships with colleagues as a result of work activity			
Public Interaction – having a lot of contact with people in your daily activities			
Being of Service to Others – being involved in assisting and helping others			
Authority – being able to direct and manage the work activity of others			
Respect – working where people are respected and manners are important			
Privacy – working where your private life is respected and kept separate from your professional life			
Fun – working where you can have fun with others and enjoy their company			
Competition – engaging in activities which pit your abilities against others' abilities			
Creativity – working with new ideas and concepts and/or creating projects and activities that do not follow a framework created by others			
Security and Stability - being assured of keeping your job and a reasonable financial reward			

Intellectual Status - being regarded as well-informed and acknowledged as an expert in a given field

Variety – having work responsibilities frequently changed in content, type, and setting

Financial Reward – having a strong likelihood of accumulating large amounts of money or other material gain through ownership, bonuses, or profit sharing

Flexibility – having work that you can do in accordance with your own schedule

Recognition and Appreciation – getting positive feedback and credit for work well done

Purpose – feeling that your work has a bigger purpose, such as helping others or contributing to a greater body of work

Knowledge – increasing your knowledge and understanding about ideas, people, topics or work subjects is of greater worth than financial gain

Diversity - working in an environment that values and embraces diversity in its employees

Travel – travelling for short or long periods of time as part of your work

Independence – being able to determine the nature and process of work without significant direction from others

Integrity – working where your moral interests and moral values are honoured, respected, and shared.

Work/life Balance – working where you have a balance between work and personal life commitments

Pressure – working in time-pressured circumstances where there is little or no margin for error

Solitude – working on files and projects by yourself without much contact with others

When you are finished, list your top 10 values in order of preference. Which of these are essential for you to be satisfied in your career life? Which values would you be willing to compromise, if needed? Did anything surprise you in completing this questionnaire? Any new insights?

To deepen your awareness of your personal and career values, keep track of situations at work where you acted in accordance with them. How did you feel? What about situations where you were being asked to violate them? Knowing when this happens allows you to assess the best way of dealing with the disconnect between your personal values and what you are being asked to do. With this awareness, you may be able to deal with the situation in a way that is constructive and strategic.

Perhaps you can do what is requested in a way that is consistent with your values. If you have enough influence and power, perhaps you can change what is being done so it aligns with your values and still accomplishes the business objectives. But to be able to do this, you first need to know what you value. By knowing your values, you will be better able to be yourself at work and let others see who you are and how you think.

RELATIONSHIP MANAGEMENT

Success relies on both connection and competence, regardless of what is lauded or rewarded by the organization. You may be technically proficient, but at a certain stage or level in your career, other skills become important. Being socially intelligent and politically savvy involves being able to manage relationships well. This particular skill set is a strength for many women due to early gender training. However, this same training teaches girls that conflict and confrontation are to be avoided in order to maintain harmony and relationship. This can create a GBS for women.

Many women deal with conflict by avoiding it or too quickly agreeing with the other party. Masculine culture, in direct contrast, teaches boys to be comfortable with confrontation and competition as part of status and power display. As a result, neither gender approach encourages a positive and constructive way of dealing with conflict. Learning how to respond well to conflict is a tool that everyone should have. It maintains relationships, resolves issues, and, if handled appropriately, enhances your brand.

The following section sets out practical tools and techniques (T&T) for conflict resolution. Five psychological responses to conflict are provided along with descriptions of when to use them. Phrases associated with each are set out for easier implementation. Being able to select and use the most appropriate approach in the circumstance makes dealing with conflict easier and more constructive.

T&T: Five Conflict Modes

The most thorough and relevant framework for dealing with conflict consists of five modes or approaches proposed by psychologists Kenneth Thomas and Ralph Kilmann. The Thomas-Kilmann Conflict Mode Instrument (TKI) is available on-line for assessing which approach you prefer to use.[138] The five modes are: Competing, Collaborating, Avoiding, Accommodating, and Compromising.

All five approaches are equally valid when used appropriately and may be employed in sequence. Each of these five modes can be described according to two dimensions — assertiveness and cooperativeness. Assertiveness refers to the extent to which a person wants to satisfy self-interests (the priority is outcome), while cooperativeness refers to the extent to which a person wants to satisfy the interests of the other person (the priority is relationship). Our preferred, and typically overused modes depend on which goal we value more – outcome or relationship. Most women value relationship over outcome, and thus prefer using cooperative strategies.

Degree of Assertiveness and Cooperativeness for the Five Modesl[39]

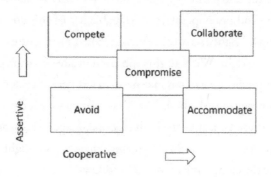

As shown above, Collaborating and Competing are the most assertive modes of addressing conflict, while Accommodating and Collaborating are the most cooperative ones. Compromising lies in the middle of these two dimensions, with Avoiding being the least cooperative and least assertive. Research has shown that the higher up in the organization a person is, the greater the use of the two most assertive strategies – Competing and Collaborating.[140] For individuals in junior positions, the best modes to use are generally the least assertive ones - Accommodating and Avoiding.

Description of Five Modes

Each of the five TKI modes is described below along with phrases that reflect each mode. The phrases can be used to implement the approach and can assist you in recognizing others' approaches to conflict. In reading through the phrases associated with each mode, see if you can determine your favourite. Which phrases seem most comfortable to say? The goal is to get comfortable using all five modes.

Competing: Due to gender training, a competitive approach is underused by most women. Many women feel uncomfortable asserting their position without considering opposing viewpoints. Prioritizing your own interests over those of the other party is at odds with the feminine values of relationship and harmony. This approach is assertive (sometimes even aggressive) and uncooperative. A valuable use of this approach is in standing up for rights, setting boundaries, and directing others when you know you are right. Without this approach in a negotiation or conflict resolution toolbox, a woman may never assert herself even when she is right and her way is the best. The disadvantages with this approach, especially if used often, is the high risk of damage to relationship and the lack of trust and conflict it creates. Phrases you might use when employing the competing mode are as follows.

- "I want you to..."
- "You should..."
- "I am not ... and that is final!"
- "You need to ..."
- "Here is my position... and that is what we are going to do."
- "I expect you to ..."
- "We are going to do what I want or else!"

Collaborating: A collaborative approach is a natural fit for most women as it most closely aligns with feminine values by maintaining a good working relationship in the midst of conflict. You seek a resolution that fully satisfies both parties' interests and maximizes outcomes while at the same time preserving or enhancing the relationship. You identify underlying interests and find options that meet both sets of interests. This mode maximizes both outcome and relationship and allows for buy-in from the other side while obtaining an agreement that satisfies interests. Phrases you might use when employing the collaborating mode are as follows.

- "Tell me what you think about ..."
- "Perhaps we can come up with a solution that works for both of us."

- "That is one option, what about some others?"
- "Help me to understand ..."
- "What are your interests?"
- "I am interested in your thoughts."
- "Let's review all of the options."

Avoiding: With avoidance, you forgo or defer resolving the conflict, a response that is common for a lot of women. However, it is important to use it appropriately and strategically rather than as a default response. Avoiding can take the form of diplomatically side-stepping the issue, postponing or deferring a discussion, letting someone else deal with it, simply ignoring the concern, or hoping time will take care of it. Avoiding is good to use when the issue is minor, when more important items are pressing, or the potential cost of dealing with a conflict outweighs the benefits of its resolution. Also, if others can resolve the conflict more readily, this response should be used. Note that by overusing this response, you won't learn to deal well with conflict. Phrases you might use when employing the avoiding mode are as follows.

- "Maybe we can talk about this later."
- "Sorry but I need to get this done right now."
- "Let me think about it and get back to you."
- "We can't deal with that now."

Accommodating: A person who is accommodating in conflict bows to the interests of others and neglects their own interests in order to maintain or enhance the relationship. It is the response expected of women based on gender stereotypes, and backlash can occur when it is not used. This approach builds relationships and creates a debt that can be used at another time. Accommodation works well to reduce hostile feelings. When overused, others may take advantage and see you as a push-over. The habitual use of this mode may be based on the GBS of a self-limiting mindset that prevents you from standing up for what you want or setting boundaries. Phrases you might use when employing the accommodating mode are as follows.

- "It would be my pleasure."
- "Of course you can do that."
- "Forget about me, how can I help you?"
- "If you feel strongly about it, we'll do it your way."
- "I'm open to whatever you think is best."

Compromising: As another cooperative approach, women sometimes overuse compromising due to gender habits. The key objective is to find an expedient solution that partially satisfies both parties. It involves splitting the difference, exchanging concessions, flipping a coin, or seeking a quick middle-ground position. The goal is to gain something in terms of both outcome and relationship without too much time or effort. It provides for quick resolution. It is great for use where the outcome is of moderate importance and the parties have equal power and strong commitment. Phrases you might use when employing the compromising mode are as follows.

- "Why don't we meet in the middle?"
- "Let's flip a coin."
- "Let's split the difference."
- "If you give me option A, you can have option B."
- "Why don't we do it your way this time and next time we'll do it my way?"
- "You can deal with the first half of the agenda and I will deal with the last half."

T&T: Using the Modes at Work

Reflecting before responding is a good idea, even when time is short. Think about how you would respond to the following situation based on each of the five conflict modes.

> *You've just learned that a report you worked on was given to a senior VP of your division before you approved the final draft. Your name was not included anywhere in the report. The person who handed it in was a project team member who frequently disparages your ideas in meetings but is not above using them in reports or claiming them as their own.*

What do you do? What are the different ways to respond? Should you act immediately or take time to get more info? Here are some options based on the five modes: send a flaming email and copy the senior VP (Compete); have a conflict conversation with the person who submitted the report (Collaborate); delay responding to gather information about what happened, perhaps from alliances and your circle of influence (Avoid); never deal with the issue (Avoid); take the person's name off the next report (Compromise), or just go along with it (Accommodate).

Obviously, some options are better than others. Which one would work best in this circumstance? First evaluate what is most important to you – outcome or relationship? Are both equally important? Do you have low power? Do you care about resolving the issue? These factors will help you decide which mode to use. You may also seek the advice of a mentor or someone from your circle of influence. What do they suggest you do?

A brilliant use of the Avoid strategy was shared by a woman during a seminar who had been involved in this situation at work. Instead of reacting immediately, she waited until an opportunity arose where it would be obvious who had done the actual work. And that occasion arose very soon after. It was thus unnecessary for her to confront or deal with the issue directly. Another very effective way to Avoid is to have others, such as members of your circle of influence or alliances, deal with it for you. That way your trusted colleagues can sort it out for you without you having to complain or explain. This is a very socially intelligent way to deal with conflict and very politically savvy.

Keep in mind that the five modes can also be used in sequence, so if one does not work you might try another. For example, after waiting for someone else to deal with the issue (Avoiding), you may deal with it directly through Compromising where both of you get something but not all that you wanted. Or you might give in and Accommodate to what they want. If the issue is important enough, you may use Collaborating. If you have the power, you know you are right and there is not a lot of time to resolve it, you may resort to Competing - telling the other person what you want done and directing them to do it.

Collaborating is the most sophisticated and effective strategy in conflict resolution and negotiation, and is a natural fit for women. It is based on dialogue to explore the interests and needs of the other person.

COMMUNICATION

Effective communication allows your perspective and ideas to be heard and makes your contributions obvious. It gives you a chance to be persuasive and to work cooperatively with others. Tools and techniques (T&T) for clear and confident communication as well as communication for conflict situations are found in the Communicate chapter.

Another important communication skill that is a key part of social intelligence is being able to disagree while being agreeable. Often, we focus on the part or issue that we disagree about and raise that first. The statements below illustrate how to soften this approach by showing respect and consideration. Such an approach may even serve to protect the other person's feelings and help them save face. People will remember that you were considerate of them and this will allow you to get them on side. A good mantra to use is "hard on the problem, soft on the person."

- "I agree with what you are saying generally but my opinion differs somewhat in what we should do about it."
- "Help me to understand how you came to the solution you are proposing. I am unable to see why the third suggestion is included."
- "We are willing to make many of the changes you have asked for in this contract however there are a few changes we cannot agree to."
- "That makes perfect sense for the most part. It is this point on the third page that is not clear to me."
- "We agree on so much. Let's agree to disagree on that point."
- "Something you said earlier is closer to the way I am viewing the situation."
- "Do you mind if I ask a few questions about this plan so that I can more fully understand your approach?"
- "We agree on 95% of this and it's only that remaining 5% that we need to work out."
- "Your reasons are so cogent and compelling that I don't see how anyone can disagree, however, I do have one concern."
- "I understand what you mean and I agree in principle. In practice, I have one recommendation."

By using these phrases or similar ones, you will be able to express disagreement in a way that allows for continued open discussion. The other person will not shut down nor harbour a grudge due to feeling attacked. That is always the socially intelligent way to proceed.

EXERCISE

QUESTIONNAIRE: ARE YOU SOCIALLY INTELLIGENT?

Read each statement carefully. If the statement describes you, circle T and if the statement does not, circle F. The frame of reference for your responses should be the workplace. The purpose of this questionnaire is to create awareness of your level of skill on each of the five dimensions of social intelligence.

At work I tend to:

1. Size up situations and people quickly.　　T F
2. Recognize when there is a disconnect between what is said and non-verbal behaviour.　　T F
3. Read between the lines to get both the content and subtext of what is being said.　　T F
4. Readily identify shifts in language that mark shifts in emotional states.　　T F
5. Ask questions to understand others' perspectives.　　T F
6. Understand the culture of the workplace and the social codes of business.　　T F
7. Observe others' behaviour without judging or making inferences too quickly.　　T F

Situational Awareness: Total Ts　　=　_____/7

8. Know important organizational information before others. T F
9. Know who is influential in my group and organization.　T F
10. Know the people around me who get things done.　　T F
11. Know what behaviour is valued and rewarded by the organization.　　T F
12. Know the top decision makers and what they are passionate about.　　T F

13. Understand how promotions are obtained and how plum projects get assigned. **T F**

14. Have a solid relationship with those who can influence my advancement. **T F**

Organizational Awareness: Total Ts = _____/7

15. Effectively influence and manage other people's perceptions of me. **T F**

16. Establish credibility with others and not assume that my work speaks for itself. **T F**

17. Make my most important comments and actions memorable to others. **T F**

18. Act in ways that are true to my personal values. **T F**

19. Use verbal and non-verbal language to exude confidence and authoritative presence. **T F**

20. Behave in ways that allow me to be judged as open, honest, ethical, and trustworthy. **T F**

21. Ensure that I am the go-to person for certain types of information. **T F**

Influence and Authenticity: Total Ts = _____/7

22. Try to understand others' perspectives, especially when in conflict with my own. **T F**

23. Handle conflict in ways that maintain relationships and advance my cause. **T F**

24. Consider multiple options and approaches before responding. **T F**

25. Make people feel good about working for or with me. **T F**

26. Pay it forward with others in order to bank favours for when I need them. **T F**

27. Know how to predict, prevent, and protect others from losing face. **T F**

28. Know that both competence and connectedness are essential for success. **T F**

Relationship Management: Total Ts = _____/7

29. Observe how well-respected and savvy colleagues act and communicate in meetings. **T F**
30. Know how to position ideas in a favourable way. **T F**
31. Know how to disagree in a constructive and agreeable fashion. **T F**
32. Use a communication guide that is easy to follow and makes my ideas compelling. **T F**
33. Know how to communicate in a way that is both assertive and connective. **T F**
34. Use multiple techniques to hold the attention of the listener. **T F**
35. Know how to have difficult conversations and resolve conflict constructively. **T F**

Communication: Total Ts = _____/7

To score the questionnaire and determine your level of SI, add the number of questions to which you answered true for each dimension (only T answers are scored). If you score below four on any dimension, examine the skills associated with that dimension in the chart at the beginning of the chapter entitled "SI Dimensions and Relevant Skills" and start setting goals for developing these skills.

WHAT ORGANIZATIONS, LEADERS, AND MENTORS CAN DO

- Increase transparency so that everyone knows what is required to advance and what is rewarded.
- Encourage women to increase their political savvy and organizational awareness, and to develop a circle of influence.

- Provide workshops and training opportunities for women on different strategies for dealing with conflict and when to use them.
- Provide opportunities for women to take stretch assignments and positions on influential committees and to improve their relationships with influential others in the organization.

WANT TO READ MORE?

Albrecht, Karl. *Social Intelligence: The New Science of Success.* San Francisco: Pfeiffer, 2009.

Reardon, Kathleen Kelly. *It's All Politics: Winning in a World Where Hard Work and Talent Aren't Enough.* New York: Crown Business, 2006.

Goleman, Daniel. *Social Intelligence: The New Science of Human Relationships.* New York: Bantam Books, 2007.

THRIVE

There are many gender stereotypes and biases that prevent women from thriving. Believing it is selfish to put yourself first can lead to reduced self care and result in taking care of everyone before yourself. A common gender belief is a woman's place is in the home, even with so many women working outside the home. The result is that working women still do significantly more housework then men - almost 40% more on average.[141] And this belief is not just held by women. Most Americans, men and women, believe that women should be responsible for the majority of the cleaning, cooking, grocery shopping, and children-rearing, even if they work full time. And these responsibilities don't change for women making more money than their husbands.[142] The burden of having two full time jobs – a paying job and the household job – not only impacts gender equality but also significantly affects women's health. Women who work full time are at a greater risk of heart disease, cancer, arthritis, and diabetes than men who work full time.[143]

Another related and equally pernicious belief is that to be successful at work you need to be a super star at home.[144] According to Time magazine, approximately 80% of millennial moms believe that it is important to be the perfect mother.[145] This belief can create Home Control Disease, a syndrome where women focus obsessively on everything about the home and feel the compulsive need to control, manage, and ensure that it is all done their way.[146]

With the many responsibilities women have and are expected to have at home and at work, being resilient and having sufficient energy is even more important for career success. Beliefs about getting ahead such as *harder, stronger, faster*, often serve to reinforce ways of living that wear us down and get in the way of thriving. Arianna Huffington, author of *Thrive*, made it her mission to redefine success to include well-being after smashing her head on her desk from exhaustion and suffering a concussion.[147]

Arianna is not alone. I recently spoke with a young lawyer who suffered a concussion and she admitted it was due to dehydration and long hours of work. Please don't let it get that far in your life. If you routinely suffer from exhaustion just from getting through your day, a change is needed. Don't wait until you experience a major health crisis or a serious accident to start taking care of yourself. I hope the practical suggestions offered in this chapter will keep you from getting close to burnout and will prevent the resulting health issues.

LEARNING TO THRIVE

The focus in this chapter is on managing energy in order to thrive. A large part of well-being for a working woman is being able to manage energy. To manage energy well it is important to know what gives you energy and what drains it. Once you have that awareness you can begin to strategically recharge and reduce the drain. Learning to say "no" in a way that builds relationship is a great way to stop expending valuable energy. Also, taking the time to replenish energy and relax is a key way to keep your energy tank full. This is something that many women don't give themselves permission to do; and if they do, they feel guilty.

To manage energy well also involves being able to reduce negative thoughts and deal with negative emotions. Women tend to ruminate more than men, and that negative voice in our head increases stress and depletes energy. An added benefit of managing your energy well is greater emotional resilience, which allows you to bounce back from negative events.

MANAGE YOUR ENERGY

Do you know what replenishes you? Most people don't and it's important to know. Without this self-awareness about energy, it is very difficult to manage your daily energy flow. This is key to maximizing what replenishes you and minimizing what depletes you. To help you better understand your energy flow and determine your level of self-awareness, a questionnaire is provided below.[148]

EXERCISE

QUESTIONNAIRE: KNOW YOUR ENERGY

Read each statement carefully. If the statement describes you, circle T and if the statement does not, circle F. If you are not sure or don't know, feel free to skip the question.

1. I frequently do an internal check of my energy level.   **T F**
2. I know the relationships that give me energy and the ones that don't.   **T F**
3. Conversation energizes me.   **T F**
4. Being alone recharges me.   **T F**
5. I have certain hobbies that leave me feeling energized.   **T F**
6. I know which aspects of work give me energy.   **T F**
7. I usually feel energized by change.   **T F**
8. Planning is fun and fulfilling for me.   **T F**

9. Working with details typically drains my energy. **T F**

10. I know the eating patterns that drain me. **T F**

11. I engage in creative activities to recharge. **T F**

12. Connecting with others makes me feel alive. **T F**

13. Ideas and theories excite and energize me. **T F**

14. I am aware of my emotions from moment to moment. **T F**

15. I delegate, when possible, work that drains me. **T F**

16. Being in touch with my body helps me know my energy level. **T F**

17. Too much conversation drains me. **T F**

18. I am energized by service to others. **T F**

19. Impulse spending stimulates me. **T F**

20. My inner critic drains my energy. **T F**

21. I use my energy consciously so I have enough to achieve my goals on a daily basis. **T F**

22. I know when my energy is highest (e.g., I know if I'm a morning person or night person). **T F**

23. I consistently get eight to nine hours of sleep a night. **T F**

24. Exercising helps me keep my energy high. **T F**

If you answered true to questions 1, 6, 14, 16 and 22, you are generally aware of your energy state. Questions 2, 3, 4, 5, 7, 8, 9, 10, 12, 13, 17, 18, 19, 20 and 24 deal with activities, so if you answered most of them with either a true or false response versus don't know, then you are aware of your energy in relation to these activities. If you answered true to questions 11, 15 and 21, then you proactively balance energy.

T&T: GET ENOUGH SLEEP

Question 23 in the "Know Your Energy Questionnaire" was added based on recent brain research relating to sleep. Sleep research has indicated that almost all adults need eight to nine hours of sleep each night.[149] This may seem like a lot as most adults in our society are proud of getting less, as if it were a badge of honour. And sleep deprivation can be a real and unavoidable issue for women with young children. The problem with constantly getting less than you need is that you cannot catch up on the weekends or on holidays — the loss is permanent. Adults who have slept six hours can function reasonably well for the first four to six hours of their workday, but after that there is a steep decline.[150] The situation is so dire that Arianna Huffington has declared that we are in the midst of a sleep deprivation crisis. [151]

If you can't get at least eight hours a night, try to top up your sleep time with naps. Grabbing a quick nap reduces your chance of dying from heart disease by 37%, boosts cognitive function, and helps you lose weight.[152] Celebrities such as Heidi Klum, Kendall Jenner, Cara Delevingne, and Katy Perry have all captured their afternoon naps on Instagram. And last year at the Toronto International Film Festival "snooze stations" or temporary nap pods were set up across the city for festival goers to catch some shut-eyes between film screenings. Some spas are even now offering retreats that include napping classes. Arianna Huffington was so committed to people getting enough sleep that she set up nap rooms at Huffington Post. You may discover creative ways for taking naps once you decide to do it.

Suggestions for improving night time sleep include: trying to go to sleep and wake up at the same time each day; developing a 30-minute routine before sleep to relax and get ready for sleep; avoiding exercise late in the evening; turning off all electronic devices 30 minutes before sleep time; and trying to minimize light in the bedroom from electronic devices. There are many apps and gadgets available to measure and improve your sleep each night. One young woman told me her app motivates her to go to bed earlier in order to get a good score in the morning. Find out what works for you to ensure a good night's sleep.

T&T: YOUR ENERGY AT HOME

An innovative way to deal with the energy drain at home is suggested by Tiffany Dufu in her book, *Drop the Ball*. She and her husband created a list of household tasks and then negotiated who would be responsible for each one. This is an effective way to disrupt gender stereotypes and deal with draining tasks at home. Dividing up tasks with your partner and coming up with an agreement that works for both of you is collaborative co-creating at its best. If you are aware of what gives you energy and drains it, you will be able to pick those tasks that you enjoy and that replenish you.

A friend of mine did something similar with her whole family but focused on Christmas. It had all become so much of a production that she dreaded its approach each year. So she sat down with her children and husband and asked them what holiday activities they liked. It turns out that a lot of the things she thought they liked, they didn't. They did them because they thought she liked them. The result was a decluttering of Christmas activities that made it more enjoyable for everyone.

Another way to reduce the energy drain at home is to delegate everything that you can. Most women, perhaps due to the *To Have It All, You Have to Do It All* bias, have problems delegating. If you have this limiting mindset, try to explore the beliefs behind it. It may be due to guilt, lack of trust, or perfectionism. Try going against your instinct and delegate. Dufu calls this "delegating with joy."[153] She describes it as asking someone for help with a higher purpose than the task itself. The higher purpose is allowing you to thrive so you can be your best self. By asking with joy rather than out of resentment, frustration, or even contempt, you create positive energy and conserve the energy you have.

YOUR ENERGY AT WORK

A practical way to become aware of your energy at work is to notice which activities give you energy, which are neutral, and which drain your energy. You may find it helpful to keep a sheet on your desk at work with three columns: Activities that Give Energy (+), Activities that are Neutral, and Activities that Drain Energy (-). As you go through your work day, note those activities that make you feel refreshed and those that tire you quickly. I am a "big picture" person so doing even an hour of putting together tax information for my accountant feels like days of work. By knowing this activity depletes me, I find ways to minimize its impact. The next section provides ideas and techniques for dealing with tasks that drain your energy.

T&T: DECREASE THE ENERGY DRAIN

Once you know what depletes you, look for ways to minimize or eliminate those activities. What you use will depend in large part on your seniority at work. The following are suggestions for decreasing the energy drain first for those who are fairly junior, and then for those who are more senior.

Spread the activity over the day. If you are not yet able to delegate, find a way to spread the draining tasks over the day. Work for a set time on the energy depleting task, then switch to one that is neutral or energizing.

Take breaks. If you are unable to spread a task over time and switch tasks, take breaks. They don't have to be long breaks - doing a mini-meditation for a minute will help. If you can do something that recharges you during the break, even better. You will find that your body intelligence will let you know when to take a break if it is a particularly difficult and draining task. Your body will find excuses for breaks such as coffee, chatting with others, and going to the washroom. Watch for this and listen to it. You will be more productive and make better decisions after taking the break.

Do it when you have energy. As a morning person, I find I can do draining tasks faster and better in the morning. When working as a lawyer on large transactions requiring long hours, I found that I could get so depleted I could not muster the energy to get up and go home late at night. It was just easier to stay and work in a tired fog. I have talked to other women and I was not alone in feeling exhausted and gutted by the end of the day. Recognize when you are at that stage and go home.

Find ways to get help for draining tasks. If you are not detail-oriented, proofing documents may be very draining. Get others, such as your assistant or a colleague, to help you with it where you can. And as you become more senior, learn to hand these tasks off to others.

Here are some ways to decrease the drain when at a more senior level.

Delegate. Delegate whatever tasks can be done by others. Often women don't think to delegate or are held back for psychological reasons. Ensure that you don't delegate anything that furthers your knowledge or expertise.

Negotiate for what you want. Learn how to ask for work on files that you want and with people you enjoy working with. Be clear on what gives you energy and then negotiate those activities on files that align with and foster your career. If this seems like a big leap, do it in small incremental steps, perhaps by first asking for more work that you enjoy. Keep in mind that the alternative is waiting to be given work that others think you should be doing; at a senior level, this is not good for your brand or your energy level.

T&T: LEARN TO SAY NO

This may sound like a sure-fire way to limit your career and halt advancement. However, learning to say no in a way that does not affect the relationship or your reputation for working hard is both strategic and smart. If you say yes frequently to work or activities you don't want to do and that don't advance your career or enhance your skills, try to understand why. Here are some reasons I have heard from clients: I want to help out; I don't want to hurt the relationship; I want to be seen as a team player; I don't want to appear selfish; I want to be liked; and FOMO (fear of missing out).

Say no when the work is draining, when it will take up time better spent on more valuable projects, or when it will not advance your expertise or knowledge. In short, when the benefits are limited. You may also want to say no if you want to work with others in your organization but your time is being unfairly monopolized by one person. From a gender perspective, women tend to volunteer and do lower-level work out of loyalty more often than men. Men are traditionally more strategic in the type of work they do and for whom they do it.

It is important to note that saying no to an influential person early in your career might limit your opportunities for advancement. And if the work will provide you with valuable experience, turning it down could also be a detriment to your career. The key is to be strategic about the things you say no to.

Below are some ways to say no and maintain a good working relationship. They allow you to be clear in an inoffensive way. These strategies show respect while minimizing the possibility that the person asking will feel rejected.

Delay responding with a "let me think about that." This response allows you time to think about the request more fully. If you ultimately say no, the additional time will allow you to think about the type of no you wish to give. This is an appropriate response for people who aren't able to think fast on their feet. It is often best to start with a positive statement before giving this response.

Uncover your yes to say no.[154] With this no, you are actually saying yes to something that is important to you. Keep a list of your commitments so you can stay strong. For example, "I'd like to help with the events committee, but I have committed my time this year to compiling templates for the division."

Offer a lesser yes. With this no, you offer to do something less than or different from what is being asked. For example, "I won't be able to help chair the events committee this year, but I could help organize one of the events."

Offer a yes later. With this no, you show your willingness to help out when the timing is better for you. For example, "I can't help you with the diversity committee right now but in a few months I will have more time. Will you still need help then?"

Offer a different proposal. With this no, you provide an alternative suggestion. For example, "I don't have the time needed to organize the templates for the division, but John has indicated an interest in doing this. Perhaps you could ask him."

Say no with respect. Start with a positive statement rather than the no. This can be done in various ways, but the underlying message is one of respect. For example, acknowledge the person making the request: "You have done such a wonderful job on the events committee this year and I am flattered that you have asked me to chair it for next year, but I don't have the time to do it justice. I am sorry." You could also acknowledge the other person's perspective: "I understand your problem — I have been there." Another option is to show the person you value them: "I appreciate you thinking of me. It sounds like you are really frustrated with finding a replacement."

A comprehensive method for saying no is called *the Sandwich*.[155] It combines several of the suggestions above into one. The top of the Sandwich, or first part of your response, consists of a breezy, sincere apology or praise such as, "I wish I could. Ordinarily I would love to." It is followed by the filling which consists of the crisp, plain, and hearty middle when you say no: "I have other obligations/ deadlines/ commitments/ plans/ meetings." At the bottom of the Sandwich is providing an alternative, such as, "what about Tuesday/ next week/ hiring a temp/ assigning Harry to do that." You may want to rehearse ahead of time what you might say to a request if you don't respond well on the spot.

T&T: INCREASE WHAT REPLENISHES AND RELAXES YOU

Just as important as knowing what depletes your energy is discovering what recharges you. Once you know this you can start to make more time in your day for these activities. Know that working too much can decrease your performance. In the book *Leave No Doubt* about the winning of the men's hockey gold medal at the 2010 Winter Olympics, coach Mike Babcock says the following about over-focusing.

> "You can't analyze, strategize and grind all the time. Day in, day out. It'll wear you down. It'll wear your team down. It will wear down the people around you. That doesn't mean you're not committed or that you lack the right intensity. It means you're a human being. It's OK to change up your focus. Changing your focus isn't being distracted. Changing your focus can be an energy-giving activity."[156]

This is just as true for everyone who works too much as it is for hockey players. In addition to changing your focus, here are some typical energizing and recharging activities.

Talk to others. Ensure that if you talk with close colleagues at work you can trust them to keep what you say confidential. Sometimes we may vent about work events to process what happened, however such venting can easily be taken out of context if relayed to others. In these instances, it is probably better to talk with others outside of work. Cultivate friends that understand and support you.

Take some time alone. If you recharge by being alone, then honour that. Our society is becoming more and more extraverted, so time alone is hard to find. For your mental and physical health, take time to be alone when you need to be. One woman in her early forties told me this suggestion changed her life. She had no time alone at work or at home and, as a result, her health was failing. She made changes so she could be alone at certain times during the day to recharge, and subsequently her heart health improved.

Find engaging activities. Discover activities that charge you up. For me, it was teaching negotiation to law students and public speaking. I came away energized. Discover the activities outside of work that you are eager to do. You may find that it is being on the board of your child's school or helping with fundraising. Find out what energizes you and do it as often as you can.

Go for lunch. For the first few years of my law career I spent lunch hours alone recharging. It helped me, or so I thought, to clear my mind. Then I started going out for lunch with two close colleagues. That hour away was like having a mini-holiday. Being able to forget about work and enjoy good food was refreshing. If this is not possible every day, try to have lunch at least once or twice a week with colleagues. It will not only recharge you, but is a great way to build valuable relationships at work.

Exercise. This is a proven way to clear your head, deal with stress, and build resilience. Do it with others if that motivates you and feels comfortable. Exercising with friends can be both physically beneficial and socially enjoyable.

Make use of rituals. One of my clients revealed that she performs a mini tea ceremony each afternoon. The moment she starts mixing the tea leaves, she relaxes. If you don't have time for such a ritual, being in the moment for the whole time you walk to the kitchen to make tea or get a coffee will make a world of difference.

Employ relaxation techniques. Breathing and mini-meditations are the fastest way to relax. Suze Yalof Schwartz's book *Unplug* includes fifteen very easy daily meditations that take from one to five minutes and have such names as Mood Lifter Meditation, Starbucks Meditation (to use while standing in line getting coffee), and A Quick Shot of Calm. The book also covers other forms of meditation including Aromatherapy, Crystal, and Sound.[157] HeartMath meditation works immediately to reduce stress; it has been shown to significantly reverse the effects of the disease over time. It works quickly using heart connections with the emotional brain to stop strong negative feelings and thoughts.[158] With this type of meditation you focus on your breathing while visualizing someone or something you love. It allows you to be present and experience positive emotions.

Listen to music. Anyone who has listened to music knows that it can have powerful effects on mood, but did you know that music has been found to increase levels of dopamine (the reward neurotransmitter) while significantly decreasing stress hormones? In addition, listening to music generally engages the area of the brain involved in paying attention so it is not surprising that listening to music has been found to increase both concentration and productivity. Thus, music appears to relax, reward, and focus us.[159]

Make it a priority to take time to recharge and replenish, even if only for short periods of time. It will make you more emotionally and physically resilient and, of course, happier.

MANAGE NEGATIVE THOUGHTS

Most of us have an obnoxious inner voice that tells us what we are doing wrong, how stupid we are, how unattractive we are, and how poorly dressed we are compared with others. Sometimes this voice is one that was recorded continuously as a child (maybe that of a parent), and now gets played back to us when we are feeling nervous and apprehensive. I call it the *inner judge* as it is very good at judging and handing out decisions. It has also been called the *inner critic* and the *obnoxious roommate*.[160]

The inner judge is especially active when we are anxious and under stress. Things are always bad and we never live up to expectations. The voice arises out of lower brain activation and makes us particularly alert for threats. It is based on survival mode and not on higher-order thinking or strategy. We are particularly vulnerable to this negative inner dialogue or self-talk when we are tired, hungry, lonely, or stressed. When we are in the grip of the inner voice it can further drain energy, deflate motivation, and demoralize.

Research shows that such a voice does not help us — in fact, it hinders us greatly. It is only through recognizing our inner voice, reducing its influence, and bringing in more positive thoughts that we can perform at our best and become more resilient. So what percentage of time does your mind serve you rather than sabotage you? Research indicates that the tipping point is 75%.[161] This means you want your mind to assist or support you, rather than sabotage you, 75% or more of the time. Interestingly, 80% of individuals fall below this tipping point, so if you are often vulnerable to the inner voice, you are not alone.

Amazing benefits result when you spend 75% of the time or more in adaptive positive thinking versus negative thinking. These benefits include higher salaries, greater success in the arenas of work, marriage, health, friendship, and creativity, and enhanced immune system functioning.[162] Four strategies for reaping these benefits include weakening negative thinking, strengthening adaptive thinking, being more present and mindful, and reducing black-and-white thinking.[163] Each of these strategies is discussed in detail below.

T&T: WEAKEN NEGATIVE THOUGHTS

In order to weaken the impact of negative thoughts, you first need to be aware of them. You need to recognize when your inner critic or judge is operating. When you are hungry, tired, lonely, or stressed, it will be at its strongest and most active. The inner judge is very devious and manipulative, convincing you that you would be less without it. Turn up the volume on this voice so it is very clear when it appears. That does not mean giving it validation. When you turn up the sound of inner negative dialogue, listen to it with detachment. Don't buy into what it is saying. Rather, observe how it functions and how it tries to get you hooked into its way of thinking. By observing it, you will be far less likely to allow it to direct your thoughts and beliefs.

Give your inner judge a name such as Executioner, Destroyer, SOB, or Sourpuss. By naming it, you have identified it for what it does, objectified it, and taken away its validity. Now instead of automatically believing you are not up to the task or you are too full of yourself, you have correctly identified that it is only Sourpuss' opinion. That has to make you smile. And if that doesn't make you smile, start visualizing it as the two grumpy old men in the balcony from *The Muppet Show*. When one woman suggested that in a seminar, all of us had a good laugh. Do whatever works to make you smile or laugh at the inner judge. Creating that gap between you and the negative voice will allow you to view the thoughts more objectively and be better able to discount them.

The importance of weakening this negative inner dialogue cannot be stressed enough. As the inner judge becomes stronger and is given more validity, it can reach a point where it not only sabotages our own thinking but leaks out and sabotages relationships with others. One lawyer I worked with was legally brilliant but also incredibly critical. A female executive from an insurance company finally challenged him in a meeting after he had made enough derogatory remarks about her understanding of the material by saying, "You certainly don't want your client to feel dumb, do you?" Be careful that your critical inner judge does not carry such power that it leaks into your daily interactions. Monitor it carefully and use the tools provided to lessen its power.

T&T: INCREASE ADAPTIVE THINKING

We can increase positive thinking by increasing the volume of our inner coach. Our inner coach is the wise part of us that sees the bigger picture and tells us that all will be well, that the situation is not as bad as it seems, and that we will be able to do what we have chosen to accomplish. It is a voice or perspective that all of us have, but unfortunately it is often not as active or strong as the inner judge. Also, due to the nature of the brain, when the inner judge is most active, the inner coach is silenced. In a lot of workplaces the inner coach's voice is particularly absent.

Perhaps you are thinking that it is a good thing the inner coach's voice is absent. In order to be good at what you do (and the practice of law is a good example), you need to think about all the things that can and do go wrong. However, the inner coach's voice makes us more resourceful and effective when we are under stress. It calms us. In order to be creative and attentive, we need to avoid the downward spiral created by the extreme stress perpetuated by the inner judge. We need to listen to the wise, bigger-picture voice to be able to create solutions to tough problems and situations, to fully explore situations, and to navigate options objectively and fully. Be aware that anxiety paints a false picture of the world and that the mind adds fear. With our inner coach in control, the most urgent actions can be carried out with quiet minds and clear thoughts.

T&T: BE PRESENT

Often when our mind is busy with the hurly-burly of work, we act without consciousness. I recall getting coffee many times and not being aware of what I saw along the way — I only thought about the things I had to do when I got back to my office. I was not being present. Below are some of the ways my clients become present during their busy work day. All of them involve focusing on physical sensations: washing hands in the bathroom and enjoying the feel of the warm water flowing over your hands; exercising and feeling your feet on the treadmill as they take each step; getting tea and being present as you pour the water over the tea and watch the tea infuse into the water; walking down the hall and being aware of what you are seeing and how your feet feel inside your shoes as you walk; drinking a beverage and feeling and tasting the liquid in your mouth; and sitting in a chair and feeling your body against the chair and your feet in your shoes.

Another technique for becoming present is mini-meditation. Being able to meditate for hours is a laudable goal, but one that is typically out of reach for most people. Mini-meditations, involving only a few minutes, are a practical way of bringing the great benefits of meditation into a busy work day. Here is how you do it: look at a picture of someone or something you really love, perhaps a photo of a child, pet, or significant other. It can also be a photo of a place or event that you recall with very fond memories and positive emotions. Continue to look at it for a minute or two. You are meditating. Even smiling at someone in the hallway while being present in that moment is a mini-meditation. Yes, it is that easy. If you want to do more, then do a HeartMath meditation -- focus on your breath while visualizing someone or something you love. It's that simple.

Being present, even for a short time, expands time for me. More specifically, time slows and my awareness seems to expand into the space. In his book *Positive Intelligence*, Shirzad Chamine suggests doing meditations that are short (only seconds at a time) but frequent (hundreds per day). Discover the length and number that work best for you. The goal, regardless of the length of the meditation, is to make it a habit. Your body intelligence, once it experiences the meditations consistently, will start to remind you when it is needed. This meditation habit will increase not only your mental resilience, but your physical and emotional resilience as well.

MANAGE STRONG NEGATIVE EMOTIONS

Being resilient requires dealing well with strong negative emotions. Emotional flooding — when emotions overwhelm — diverts your attention, causes you to reveal information inadvertently, disrupts your thinking, and causes tempers to flare. Suppressing or ignoring emotion is not a solution as it doesn't work. It has been found that suppressed emotion can cause anxiety, impair cognitive ability, reduce memory, increase mindless eating, and increase competitive behaviour. Suppressed emotion can also leak into an interaction through tone, non-verbal behaviour, and attitude.

So what is one to do with strong negative emotions? To behave well in the presence of strong emotions, it is important to know your personal trigger points and have techniques and tools to deal with strong emotions as they arise. Each of these topics is discussed below.

T&T: RECOGNIZE THE TRIGGER

The negative emotions of fear and anger affect interactions and behaviour most often and most dramatically. By identifying the situations or subjects that trigger these two emotions, you can begin dealing with them. Here are some common personal triggers.

Identity Issues: Identities are those stories we tell ourselves about ourselves, and there are as many identities as there are people. Threats to our identity may disrupt our sense of who we are in the world or dash an expectation of who we think we are. Some common identity issues include: *Am I competent? Am I lovable? Am I a good person?* Threats to our identity are profoundly disturbing and can easily knock us off balance. Strong emotions such as anger or fear can surge even without us being aware of the cause.

Core Concerns: We can be provoked when our core concerns are not being met. This can include rudeness, time constraints, disregard for relationships, and challenges to our authority. This can happen when our ideas, thoughts, and actions are devalued or we are not being treated with respect. Perhaps your freedom to make decisions is being impaired. Or you are being treated as inferior to others. Any of these violations of core concerns can result in anger or fear.

Violation of Assumptions: Anger can be triggered by a violation of principles, rules, or assumptions. Common ones are assumptions about fairness, truthfulness, or trust. Often these are hidden biases. Once we recognize the assumption that was violated, we are able to rationally determine if the assumption is valid. Gendered expectations and biases that create gender inequity can easily evoke anger or fear. To bring them into the light, reflect on your negative feelings. Sometimes our emotions show us what is happening before we are consciously aware of it.

Reminder of an Unpleasant Event or Person: It is possible to respond strongly to a person whom we have just met based on that person's resemblance to a person who affected us emotionally in our past. Often this reaction occurs without awareness of the resemblance, so this trigger is particularly hard to identify and understand. If you have gone through all of the other types of triggers and none of them seems applicable, it could be that you are dealing with a resemblance trigger.

There are no absolute ways of protecting ourselves against threats to our identity, or quick fixes for eliminating emotional triggers. However, there are two ways of reducing our strong emotional response. The first is to become aware of our particular identity issues and the second is to avoid the black-and-white thinking that arises from emotion. For example, instead of thinking *I'm either competent or incompetent, lovable or unlovable, good or bad*, it is much more helpful to expand your thinking to include *I can be both wrong and competent*. For more details, see the "Avoid Black-and-White Thinking" section on this topic below.

T&T: DEALING WITH EMOTION

It is important to note that even awareness and recognition of emotions may not be enough to control behaviour. Due to how the human brain works, sometimes very strong emotions, such as extreme fear or rage, may lead us to act before we are even aware of the emotion. Also as most of our blood goes to our extremities when we experience anger (to the hands) or fear (to the feet) for fight or flight responses, our problem-solving abilities are not at their optimum, to say the least.

When strong negative emotions surge it is important to deal with them in a way that is not destructive. By lashing out at the other side or making a decision based on emotion, we may fail to achieve our goals, damage the relationship, and gain a reputation we do not want. Here are some suggestions for dealing with strong negative emotions when they arise.

Take a Break Mentally

There are several helpful techniques that allow us to detach immediately from the thoughts generating the emotion. Seeing the situation or interaction from a distance allows calm rationality to prevail so we can better analyze what is happening. The first group of these techniques involves mental pauses or breaks when you aren't able to take a physical break.

Say "let me think about that" and then use the techniques set out below.

- Use an imaginary pause button. Seeing a big red round button and pressing it while you distance yourself from the immediate exchange will help you to distance yourself mentally.
- Focus on physical sensations in the environment. Listen to the air flow in the room; feel the sensation of your body on the chair, your hand on the table, and the toes in your shoes. Get into your body. All of these will allow your mind to become calm.
- Think of a relaxing scene that you love and that touches you. It may be your backyard in summer, a flower, your child's face, a beach. Any of these scenes will transport you away from the current situation.
- Adopt a relaxed position. Find the tension in your body and relax it intentionally.

Take a Break Physically

Taking a physical break is the easiest and simplest way of dealing with emotion. When you return, you will be in a different place, mentally and emotionally. Here are some suggestions for removing yourself from the situation.

- Go for coffee or lunch.
- Use the bathroom facilities. Run water over your hands to become present and grounded. Use the HeartMath meditation described above while in the stall.
- Schedule the meeting or activity for another time. This can be prefaced by, "I think this is a good time to take a break from this discussion. When would be a good time to reconvene?"

- If you are on the phone, you might say that someone needs you urgently or someone has come into your office and you will call them back. This technique should be used only if you are unable to deal with strong emotions; it should not be used routinely, for obvious reasons.

Breathe

Breathing techniques are very helpful during both mental and physical breaks for allowing the mind and body to get back into balance. Take some deep breaths in through your nose and let the air out slowly through your lips. Or you can let the deep breath out all at once, as if you were sighing. This latter technique allows us to relax. You have to be careful doing this last breathing technique with others, as it may be interpreted by the other side as a sign that you are bored, tired, or extremely frustrated (all of which may be accurate but you don't want to advertise it).

Become an Author

If you can't take a break or don't want to disengage from the conversation, try taking on the role of author and observe the other person's behaviour from that perspective. Get curious. How would you describe the other person's behaviour and the conversation? What attitude, body language, or words are provoking you? How can you convey this to others? This allows you to become detached and observe the interaction objectively. This technique might also allow insight into the type of personal triggers involved.

Avoid Black-and-White Thinking

We often believe that there are only two choices in each situation, such as winning versus losing, candid versus respectful, kind versus honest, perfect versus worthless, loyal versus sell-out, or competent versus incompetent. These choices present simplistic trade-offs that exemplify black-and-white thinking and are particularly destructive when dealing with identities. Identities are at a person's core. If we believe we are flawless, then our sense of self is very vulnerable to feedback or events that contradict what we believe.

For example, if we think of ourselves as competent and we make a big mistake, then black-and-white thinking causes us to think we are totally worthless or incompetent. This type of thinking is based on emotion (all-or-nothing) rather than logic, and can have powerful sway, especially when we are feeling vulnerable.

To reduce black-and-white thinking, recognize when you use it and try to avoid false choices such as "I am the best" or "I am the worst." Becoming aware that there are more than two choices is another technique: "I can make a mistake and still be competent," or "I can accept work from another person and still be loyal to the person for whom I work currently." We are all complex creatures and by increasing the complexity of our identities and avoiding black-and-white thinking, we will be more grounded and far less prone to having our world rocked by challenges to our identities.

Ensure a Balanced Life

To thrive and be resilient, it is important to be in good shape energetically, emotionally, and mentally. The skills set out in this chapter will help you approach the challenges and stresses of life at work in a way that allows for healthy and balanced responses.

An important aspect of thriving is ensuring that the major aspects of life are balanced. Four major areas of life are Health, Relationships, Work, and Play. If there is too much time or energy spent in any one, life becomes unbalanced and resilience lessens. Life balance is like physical balance — constant adjustments are required to stay upright. The chart below provides more detail as to what each quadrant involves and permits reflection on how balanced your life is overall.

Life Balance: The Four Quadrants

RELATIONSHIPS	WORK
Are there people who support and encourage me and are there for me when negative events occur? At work? Away from work? Do I nurture people in my life? Do I connect with and make time for them on a routine basis? Do I take part in my community?	Does my work really engage me? Am I eager to get into what needs to be done at work? Am I challenged in a good way by what I do? How much time do I spend at work per week relative to the time for other quadrants?
HEALTH	**PLAY**
Am I getting adequate sleep most nights? Is my diet based on healthy food or fast food that is convenient but not nutritious? What exercise can I do that is doable over time and that I enjoy that will keep my energy high? Am I monitoring my energy and recharging during my day for maximum resiliency?	Do I have a "fun" list? Do I take time for vacations? Do I celebrate and savour my successes —small or large — or do I just move on to the next file or task? Do I make time to do what I want at least once a week? How can I nurture and sustain that part of me that is playful, curious, and interesting?

As with all personal development, awareness is the first step. Perhaps there is a quadrant that you have neglected due to work demands or pressures. Perhaps you have stopped running or doing other physical exercise due to work and home responsibilities. Maybe it is time to drop the ball and let others do more things. Learn to delegate and negotiate to lessen your load. Or create simple, doable, concrete goals. Perhaps walking up the stairs to work each morning or parking the car farther away from the door become simple, doable goals in the area of health.

The Play quadrant is often the one that suffers most when we are under stress and working long hours. Lack of fun and play can hurt relationships, health, and work. Reward yourself with small things and celebrate even your tiniest successes. An infusion of fun things and attention to enjoyable experiences will contribute to balance and a positive outlook.

WHAT ORGANIZATIONS, LEADERS, AND MENTORS CAN DO

- Model for others how to manage energy and stress well.
- Implement training programs on these topics.
- Create a culture where balance is important and burnout is not the norm.
- Implement a system for ensuring fair workloads such as a weekly method for indicating who is swamped and who has capacity.
- Model how to delegate work to ensure employees receive work that will further their experience.
- Demonstrate to your team that success includes well-being.

WANT TO READ MORE?

Chamine, Shirzad. *Positive Intelligence*. Austin, TX: Greenleaf Book Group, 2012.

Davidson, Richard and Sharon Begley. *The Emotional Life of Your Brain: How Its Unique Patterns Affect the Way You Think, Feel, and Live – and How You Can Change Them.* New York: Hudson Street Press, 2012.

Dufu, Tiffany. *Drop the Ball: Achieving More by Doing Less*. New York: Flatiron Books, 2017.

Huffington, Arianna. *Thrive: The Third Metric to Redefining Success and Creating A Life Of Well-Being, Wisdom And Wonder.* New York: Harmony Books, 2014.

Huffington, Arianna. *The Sleep Revolution: Transforming Your Life, One Night at a Time.* New York: Harmony, 2016.

CONCLUSION

The benefits of gender equality are clear and the arguments, cogent. Moving toward greater gender parity in the workplace is essential for evolving as a society – we cannot go back. Although equality for women on a global scale appears to be a long way off, I am greatly encouraged by the strong will and desire of companies and executives to find viable solutions for reducing gender bias and stereotypes. And I am not alone.[164] I am also heartened to see the large number of women who have climbed to the top of organizations and are now helping other women do the same.

There is growing awareness of implicit bias and a recognition that decisions and actions based on gender blind spots are not effective or beneficial. Ultimately, this heightened consciousness will move us forward to close the gender gap. I have no doubt. We are all awakening to possibilities and seeing a future where everyone is treated equally and respectfully.

Persistence, knowledge and a sense of purpose are very powerful methods for changing attitudes and assumptions. Awareness of the issues is key to motivating men and women to create real change. Here are suggestions for how you can play a part in creating this change.

- *Be a Change Maker.* Hone your social intelligence and, in so doing, become influential. Allow your ideas to be heard and make your value visible. Work from the inside-out for change. Enlist change makers and influential others to help close the gender gap. Many organizations are recognizing the economic advantage that comes with women in leadership positions and on boards. If you are a man seeking to help women and increase gender diversity, hire women. Promote them to senior positions. Research shows that not only will your organization be more profitable, your own reputation will be enhanced.

- *Challenge Unfair Tactics and Gender Bias.* Once you know the rules of the game, you can more easily spot when gender bias is operating. Without such recognition, *everyone* can easily and tacitly buy into it. Once you recognize gender bias – implicit or explicit –diminish its effects by exposing it. Use the techniques offered in this book and teach them to others.

- *Use the Power of Alliances.* Talk to others about what you have seen or experienced. Make it a grassroots endeavor. Turn your friendships into working networks. This is the true power of feminine culture -- to be able to use the collective for change. We have seen in recent months the power of women marching in major cities around the world. Use that impulse to actively create change – for yourself and others. Feminine power, once activated, is immense and unstoppable.

- *Know That Everyone Benefits.* Gender equality has the potential to improve the economy, security, and the overall well-being of a population. This statement is not just a pleasant notion or untested theory but comes directly from research findings. Gender equality reduces poverty and world hunger, expands labour markets to improve employment opportunities for all, and contributes to higher economic growth.[165] In short, gender equality is connected with a higher quality of life for everyone.

- *Help Gender Roles Evolve.* Gender roles are in a state of flux. The patriarchal male role is less acceptable as a norm today and the idea of women as fragile and delicate creatures has been waning for some time.[166] Showing children how to live authentically without the restrictive gender culture programming of past decades is a great challenge for parents but fundamental to achieving gender equity. Allowing children to develop and exhibit their natural traits and abilities, regardless of where they fall on the feminine/masculine spectrum, is the way to ensure that future generations of women and men will let their innate qualities shine and enjoy being who they are.

· *Tap into Your Power.* Recognizing and using your power can mean different things for different women. As discussed in this book, it may involve actively managing a career or figuring out how to *go along to get along* in order to advance and succeed. It may require knowing when to pivot and move to another workplace where the salary is better, the corporate values align, and the work is more fulfilling. Or perhaps you will be empowered to start your own business with totally new organizational structures and policies that disrupt and erase outdated gender scripts.

I am hopeful that with perseverance and awareness we will continue to find ways to contribute to this movement towards gender equality. The way forward differs for each person; however, the overall goal is the same. Writing this book about gender blind spots is my way of contributing to the advancement of gender equality. By each of us working in a way that is comfortable and doable, I know we can create a world where men and women are genuinely and completely equal in their social roles -- with legal and economic parity. By working together, we can ensure that outdated and restrictive gender stereotypes lose their hold so that everyone is able to live authentically and fully.

ACKNOWLEDGEMENTS

This book would not have been possible without the help of many women, to whom I am profoundly grateful. Thank you to

- Amelia Phillips for your insightful feedback on the first draft of this book;
- Rocca Morra Hodge for your support and amazing endorsement;
- Dawn Jetten, Caitriona Robinson, Karen Bell, and Theresa Leitch for being constant champions of my work;
- Betty Ann Heggie for your wise suggestions and being a kindred spirit in the quest for gender equality;
- Rox Bartel, Deborah Levine and Nancy Prenevost for reading early drafts and providing valuable comments;
- Erica Young, Mariana Fonar, Natasha Prasaud, Ratika Gandhi, Gargi Chopra, Sarah Naiman and Sasha Toten for your unending enthusiasm and support;
- Paige Robillard for all of your wonderful assistance, you are the future;
- Donna Goodhand for your invaluable mentorship at the beginning of this journey;

- the Tellwell talent team, Carolyn, Natasha, Rebecca, Jordan, Amanda and Francesca, for your amazing assistance in the publishing process;
- to the young women who attended workshops on this book and who helped to shape and inform its content; and
- to my many clients who shared their insights and experiences with me so I could in turn share them with others.

NOTES

Introduction

1   For the numerous reasons why females will be favoured in the future see, for example, Sallie Krawcheck, *Own it: The Power of Women at Work*. (New York: Crown Business, 2017), 33 and Molly Petrilla, "Women Entrepreneurs are 'More Ambitious and Successful' Than Men," Fortune Magazine, February 29, 2016, accessed April 19, 2017, http://fortune.com/2016/02/29/women-entrepreneurs-success/.

2   Lynne Doughtie, "Inspiring Greatness: Advancing Women Leaders in the Workplace," *Forbes Magazine*, June 13, 2017, 74; For an excellent review of the research on diversity see "Why Diversity Matters", July 2013, Catalyst Information Centre, accessed January 12, 2017, http://www.catalyst.org/knowledge/why-diversity-matters.

3   Tom Schuller, *The Paula Principle: how and why women work below their level of competence* (London: Scribe UK, 2017).

4   Masculine gender training involving denial of emotions and being strong at all times has created a crisis for men according to Jack Myers in *The Future of Men: Masculinity in the Twenty First Century* (New York: Inkshares, 2016).

Terminology and Clarification

5   Gender Revolution, *Special Edition of National Geographic Magazine*, January 2017, volume 231, no 1.

Chapter 1 – Origins

6   Calculated using "your time to gender parity" located in the Global Gender Gap Report 2016, World Economic Forum, accessed January 16, 2017, http://reports.weforum.org/global-gender-gap-report-2016/#read.

7   For a review of the literature on sex differences, and the lack thereof, see Cordelia Fine, *Delusions of Gender: How Our Minds, Society and Neurosexism Create Difference* (New York: W. W. Norton & Company, Inc., 2010) and *Testosterone Rex: Myths of Sex, Science and Society* (New York: W. W. Norton & Company, Inc., 2017).

8   Claire Zillman, "Women are Losing Ambition as Their Careers Progress, Study Finds," *Fortune Magazine*, March 17, 2017, accessed May 7, 2017, http://fortune.com/2017/03/17/women-career-ambition/.

9   As a neuropsychologist, the neuroscience of gender fascinates me. However, close examination of the studies used to support gender brain differences reveals that the evidence is scant, confusing, and in some cases, non-existent. For a brilliant and wickedly funny review of this literature see Cordelia Fine's, *Delusions of Gender*. She will have you laughing out loud.

10   Mahzarin R. Banaji and Anthony G. Greenwald, *Blind Spot: Hidden Biases of Good People* (New York: Delacourte Press, 2013), 61.

11   The Ohio State University Kirwan Institute, "State of the Science: Implicit Bias Review" 2014, Appendix B, accessed July 8, 2017, http://kirwaninstitute.osu.edu/researchandstrategicinitiatives/implicit-bias-review/.

12   Project Implicit, accessed July 8, 2017, https://implicit.harvard.edu/implicit/.

13   Andrea Kramer and Alton Harris, *Breaking Through Bias: Communication Techniques for Women to Succeed at Work* (New York: Bibliomotion, 2016), Kindle edition, Loc 400 of 4406.

14   Pershing, LLC, "Americans Crave a New Kind of Leader – And Women Are Ready to Deliver," February 25, 2012, accessed July 8, 2017, https://www.pershing.com/perspectives/americans-crave-a-new-kind-of-leader-and-women-are-ready-to-deliver.

15   Geert Hofstede, accessed June 15, 2017, https://www.geert-hofstede.com/national-culture.html.

16   Banaji, *Blind Spot*, 13; Fine, *Delusions of Gender*, 211.

17   Fine, *Delusions of Gender*, 211.

18   Fine, *Delusions of Gender*, chapter 20.

19   Fine, *Delusions of Gender*, 218.

20 Tiffany Dufu, *Drop the Ball: Achieving More by Doing Less* (New York: Flatiron Books, 2017), 59.

21 Dufu, *Drop the Ball,* 59.

22 Kerri MacDonald, "Pink or Blue Toys for Girls and Boys," *New York Times,* October 13, 2014, accessed July 8, 2017, https://lens.blogs.nytimes.com/2014/10/13/pink-or-blue-toys-for-girls-and-boys/?_r=0.

23 David Williams, "Men Waste £2000 in Fuel While Lost," *The Telegraph,* August 24, 2010 accessed July 8, 2017, http://www.telegraph.co.uk/motoring/news/7960150/Men-waste-2000-in-fuel-while-lost.html.

24 Fine's books, *Delusions of Gender* and *Testosterone Rex.*

25 Myers, *The Future of Men,* Kindle edition, Loc 1430 of 4697.

26 Angela Saini, *Inferior: How Science Got Women Wrong – and the New Research That's Rewriting the Story* (London: Fourth Estate, 2017), chapter 5.

27 For details see the section "Advantages and Disadvantages of Fast Processing" in the chapter Origins.

28 Lin Bian, Sarah-Jane Leslie, and Audrei Cimpian, "Gender stereotypes about intellectual ability emerge early and influence children's interests, *Science,* Vol. 355, Issue 6323(2017): 389-39, accessed February 21, 2017, http://science.sciencemag.org/content/355/6323/389.

29 Liza Mundy, "Why Is Silicon Valley So Awful to Women?" *The Atlantic,* April 2017, 61.

30 Marshall Goldsmith, *What Got You Here Won't Get You There* (New York: Hachette Books, 2016), 40.

31 My personal observation, based on survey data from seminars and published research findings on personality preferences and negotiation approaches, is that approximately 60 to 70% of both men and women use traditional gender styles and approaches while 30 to 40% of each sex uses gender atypical approaches. Betty Ann Heggie finds similar percentages for males and females in her informal collection of survey data on the use of masculine and feminine approaches (personal report).

Chapter 2 – Expose

32 Shankar Vedantam, *The Hidden Brain: How our Unconscious Minds Elect Presidents, Control Markets, Wage Wars and Save Our Lives* (New York: Spiegel & Grau Trade Paperback, 2010), 99.

33 For details about the use of effective feminine styles, see the chapters Ask and Lead.

34 Pershing LLC, "Americans Crave," 4.

35 Pershing LLC, "Americans Crave," 10.

36 Michael Enright, "For Inflight Emergencies, No Female Doctors Need Apply," *The Sunday Edition*, March 19, 2017, accessed March 20, 2017, http://www.cbc.ca/radio/thesundayedition/doctors-on-planes-the-end-of-the-world-poet-and-therapist-switch-roles-afghan-ambassador-shinkai-karokhail-1.4026266/for-inflight-medical-emergencies-no-female-doctors-need-apply-michael-s-essay-1.4026270.

37 For details see Saini, *Inferior*.

38 For details see Fine, *Delusions of Gender*.

39 Lauren Stiller Rikleen, "Are Women Held Back by Colleagues' Wives?" *Harvard Business Review*, May 16, 2012.

40 Dufu, *Drop the Ball*, 48.

41 Katy Steinmetz, "Help! My Parents Are Millennials: How this generation is changing the way we raise kids," *Time* magazine, October 2015, accessed March 14, 2017, http://wp.lps.org/tnettle/files/2015/03/Help-My-Parents-are-Millennials.pdf.

42 Dufu, *Drop the Ball*, 53.

43 Mundy, "Silicon Valley," 61.

44 Krawcheck, *Own It*, 86.

45 Krawcheck, *Own It*, 188.

46 Eden King and Kristen Jones, "Why Subtle Bias Is So Often Worse than Blatant Discrimination," *Harvard Business Review*, July 13, 2016. https://hbr.org/2016/07/why-subtle-bias-is-so-often-worse-than-blatant-discrimination.

47 Mundy, "Silicon Valley," 69.

48 Krawcheck, *Own It*, 91.

49 Dominic Barton, "It's Time for Companies to Try a New Gender-Equity Playbook," *The Wall Street Journal*, September 27, 2016, accessed February 12, 2017, https://www.wsj.com/articles/its-time-for-companies-to-try-a-new-gender-equality-playbook-1474963861.

50 Iris Bohnet, *What Works: Gender Equality by Design* (Cambridge: Belknap Press of Harvard University Press, 2016), 1.

51 Mundy, "Silicon Valley," 69.

52 Katherine Reynolds Lewis, "NAFE Top Companies: The Way We Work," *Working Mother*, January 23, 2014, accessed November 21, 2017, http://www.workingmother.com/content/nafe-top-companies-way-we-work.

53 Robert Cialdini, *Influence: The Psychology of Persuasion* (New York: Harper Business, 2006).

54 Sady Doyle, "The Trainwreck Files: Hillary Clinton," November 14, 2016, accessed May 3, 2017, https://www.mhpbooks.com/the-trainwreck-files-hillary-clinton/.

55 Katy Steinmetz, "A New Identity," *Time magazine,* March 27, 2017, 48.

56 Krawcheck, *Own It,* 17.

57 Dufu, *Drop the Ball,* 53.

58 See for example Myers, *The Future of Men;* Goldsmith, *What Got You Here.*

59 For a detailed discussion see the chapter Origins.

60 Malcolm Gladwell, "Revisionist History: The Big Man Can't Shoot," June 29, 2016, podcast accessed September 12, 2016, http://revisionisthistory.com/episodes/03-the-big-man-cant-shoot.

61 "As Academic Gender Gap Declines, There is Still Work to Be Done," *The Harbus,* April 25, 2011, accessed February 9, 2017, http://www.harbus.org/2011/gender-gap/.

62 Timothy A. Judge, Beth A. Livingston and Charlice Hurst, "Do Nice Guys—and Gals—Really Finish Last? The Joint Effects of Sex and Agreeableness on Income," *Journal of Personality and Social Psychology* 102 (2) (2012) 390-407, accessed July 8, 2017, http://www.timothy-judge.com/documents/Doniceguysandgalsreallyfinishlast.pdf.

63 See for example David Miler and Diane Halpern, "The new science of cognitive sex differences," *Trends in Cognitive Sciences,* 18 (1) (2014): 37.

64 Colleen Ganley et al., "An Examination of Stereotype Threat Effects on Girls' Mathematics Performance," *Developmental Psychology.* (2013): 1. Advance online publication. doi: 10.1037/a0031412, accessed July 8, 2017, http://andrewgelman.com/wp-content/uploads/2013/04/ganley-et-al.-stereotype-threat.pdf.

65 Hannah-Hanh Nguyen and Ann Marie Ryan, "Does stereotype threat affect test performance of minorities and women? A meta-analysis of experimental evidence," *Journal of Applied Psychology.* 93(6) (2008): 1314-1334, accessed January 10, 2017, https://www.researchgate.net/publication/23489223_Does_Stereotype_Threat_Affect_Test_Performance_of_Minorities_and_Women_A_Meta-Analysis_of_Experimental_Evidence.

66 Andrea Kramer and Alton B. Harris, "Why Women Feel More Stress at Work," *Harvard Business Review,* August 4, 2016, accessed February 14, 2017, https://hbr.org/2016/08/why-women-feel-more-stress-at-work.

67 Kramer and Harris, "Why Women Feel More Stress."

68 Fine, *Delusions of Gender*, 32.

69 Mahzarin and Greenwald, *Blind Spot*, 69.

Chapter 3 – Plan

70 Jenny Blake, *Pivot: The Only Move That Matters Is Your Next One* (New York: Penguin, 2017), 4.

71 Dufu, *Drop the Ball*, 100.

72 For details on how to disrupt gender bias and stereotypes, and what a gender equal society would look like, see Catherine Mayer's *Attack of the 50 Ft. Women: How Gender Equality Can Save the World*. (London: HQ, 2017).

73 Department of Commerce, "Latest Census Data on Education Attainment Shows Women Lead Men in College Completion," March 30, 2016, accessed February 14, 2017, https://www.commerce.gov/news/blog/2016/03/latest-census-data-educational-attainment-shows-women-lead-men-college-completion.

74 Lauren Noel and Christie Hunter Arscott, "Millennial Women: What Executives Need to Know About Millennial Women," Special report by International Consortium for Executive Development Research (ICEDR), accessed March 15, 2017, http://www.icedr.org/research/documents/15_millennial_women.pdf.

75 Krawcheck, *Own it*, 86.

76 Claire Shipman and Katty Kay, *Womenomics: Write Your Own Rules for Success* (New York: HarperCollins, 2009), 112-114.

77 Susie Mesure, "Women head back to work with 'returnships'," *Financial Times*, February 21, 2017, accessed May 2, 2017, https://www.ft.com/content/16ef6eb2-9a8d-11e6-8f9b-70e3cabccfae.

78 Trades Union Congress (TUC) report dated April 2016, accessed March 28, 2017, https://www.hayhow.com/news/business-news/archive/article/2016/April/tuc-study-finds-significant-wage-gap-between-working-fathers-and-childless-men.

79 Avra Davidoff et al., "Making It Work! How to Effectively Navigate Maternity Leave Career Transitions: An Employee's Guide," posted August 19, 2016, accessed February 27, 2017, http://ceric.ca/resource/making-it-work-how-to-effectively-navigate-maternity-leave-career-transitions-an-employees-guide/, 23-24.

80 Davidoff et al., "Making it Work!" 11.

81   Kathleen Kelly Reardon, *It's All Politics: Winning in a World Where Hard Work and Talent Aren't Enough* (New York: Doubleday, 2005), 148.

82   Dufu, *Drop the Ball*, 100.

83   Noel and Arscott, "Millennial Women."

84   Petrilla, "Women Entrepreneurs Are More Ambitious."

85   Blake, *Pivot*.

86   "The 2016 State of Women-Owned Businesses Report" commissioned by American Express OPEN, April 2016, accessed April 4, 2017, http://www.womenable.com/content/userfiles/2016_State_of_Women-Owned_Businesses_Executive_Report.pdf.

87   Krawcheck, *Own It*, 18.

88   Petrilla, "Women Entrepreneurs Are More Ambitious."

89   Krawcheck, *Own It*, 22.

90   This question will be of more importance if you are determining if the fit is right.

Chapter 4 – Ask

91   Dina Pradel, Hannah Riley Bowles and Kathleen McGinn, "When Does Gender Matter in Negotiation?" *Negotiation Newsletter,* Harvard Business School Publishing, November (2005): 4.

92   Linda Babcock and Sara Laschever, *Women Don't Ask: Negotiation and the Gender Divide* (Princeton: Princeton University Press, 2003).

93   Kathleen Harris, "Over Sixty Percent of Millennial Women Say They Don't Know How to Ask for More," Levo.com, April 5, 2016, accessed April 26, 2017, https://www.levo.com/posts/over-sixty-percent-of-millennial-women-say-they-don-t-know-how-to-ask-for-more.

94   Danielle Paquette, "Young women are still less likely to negotiate job offers. But why?" *Washington Post,* July 8, 2016, accessed February 12, 2017, https://www.washingtonpost.com/news/wonk/wp/2016/07/07/young-women-are-still-less-likely-to-negotiate-a-job-offer-but-why/?utm_term=.9068568fd552.

95   Olga Khazan, "Women Know When Negotiation Isn't Worth It," *The Atlantic,* January 6, 2017, accessed July 8, 2107, https://www.theatlantic.com/business/archive/2017/01/women-negotiating/512174/.

96   Sarah Shemkus, "Women Negotiate Salary If They Know It is Negotiable," January 2013, Salary.com http://www.salary.com/women-negotiate-if-negotiable/.

97   For details of this calculation see Linda Babcock and Sara Laschever, "First You Have to Ask," *Harvard Negotiation Newsletter,* January issue (2004): 3.

98   The Muse, "Why Women Must Ask (the Right Way): Negotiation Advice from Stanford's Margaret A. Neale," *Forbes Magazine,* June 17, 2013, accessed July 8, 2017, https://www.forbes.com/sites/dailymuse/2013/06/17/why-women-must-ask-the-right-way-negotiation-advice-from-stanfords-margaret-a-neale/ - 18b309be30a2.

99   Linda Babcock and Sara Laschever, *Ask For It: How Women Can Use Negotiation to Get What They Want* (New York: Bantam Dell, 2008), 259.

100 Pradel, Bowles and McGinn, "When Does Gender Matter?"

101 For a detailed discussion of how to do a body scan, see Delee Fromm, "Emotion in Negotiation," *The Theory and Practice of Representative Negotiation*, ed. C. Hanycz et. Al (Toronto: Emond Montgomery, 2008), 170.

102 Aaron Gouveia, "Salary Negotiation: Separating Fact from Fiction," Salary.com, accessed May 5, 2017, http://www.salary.com/salary-negotiation-separating-fact-from-fiction/slide/4/.

103 Iris Bohnet, a professor at Harvard Kennedy School, did just that when negotiating salary for her full professorship by mentioning both the gender wage gap and the social backlash that comes from women asking directly and negotiating competitively. Bohnet, *What Works,* 74.

104 Kerry Jones, "Gender Can Be a Bigger Factor than Race in Raise Negotiations," *Harvard Business Review*, September 2016, accessed January 12, 2017, https://hbr.org/2016/09/gender-can-be-a-bigger-factor-than-race-in-raise-negotiations.

Chapter 5 – Communicate

105 Deborah Tannen, *Talking From 9 to 5: Women and Men in the Workplace: Language, Sex, and Power* (New York: Quill, 2001).

106 Jessica Bennett, *Feminist Fight Club: An Office Survival Manual (For a Sexist Workplace)* (New York: Harper Wave, 2016), 12.

107 James W. Pennebaker, "Your Use of Pronouns Reveals Your Personality," *Harvard Business Review,* December 2011 issue, accessed May 2012, https://hbr.org/2011/12/your-use-of-pronouns-reveals-your-personality.

108 Phyllis Mindell, *How to Say It for Women: Communicating with Confidence and Power Using the Language of Success* (New York: Prentice Hall Press, 2001), 26.

109 Malcolm Gladwell, *Outliers: The Story of Success* (New York: Little Brown and Company, 2008), 177.

110 Alison Wood Brooks, Hengchen Dai and Maurice E. Schweitzer, "I'm
Sorry About the Rain! Superfluous Apologies Demonstrate Empathic
Concern and Increase Trust," 1:8 *Social Psychological and Personality Science*
(2013), accessed June 2014, http://www.hbs.edu/faculty/Pages/item.
aspx?num=45471.

Chapter 6 – Presence

111 Amy Cuddy, "Your Body Language Shapes Who You Are," TEDGlobal 2012,
filmed June 2012, accessed December 19, 2016, https://www.ted.com/talks/
amy_cuddy_your_body_language_shapes_who_you_are.

112 Amy Cuddy, *Presence: Bringing Your Boldest Self to Your Biggest Challenges*
(New York: Little, Brown

and Company, 2015).

113 See the section, "Use Powerful Non-Verbal Tools" in the chapter Ask.

114 American Psychology Association (2017), "Stress in America: Coping with
Change," Stress in America © Survey, accessed April 22, 2017, http://www.
apa.org/news/press/releases/stress/2016/coping-with-change.pdf.

Chapter 7 – Promote

115 Laura Sabattini, "Unwritten Rule: What You Don't Know Can Hurt Your
Career," Catalyst website, accessed June 20, 2017, http://www.catalyst.org/
knowledge/unwritten-rules-what-you-don't-know-can-hurt-your-career.

116 Andy Coghlan, "We Humans Can Mind-Meld Too," *New Scientist* (July 26,
2010), accessed November 23, 2016, https://www.newscientist.com/article/
dn19220-we-humans-can-mind-meld-too/.

Chapter 8 – Lead

117 J.A. Andersen and P.H. Hansson, "At the end of the road? On differ-
ences between women and men in leadership behavior," *Leadership and
Organization Development Journal*, 32 (5), (2011): 428-441; Daniel Goleman,
R. Boyatzis, and Annie McKee, *Primal Leadership: Realizing the Power of
Emotional Intelligence* (Boston: Harvard Business School Press, 2003).

118 Kevin Lane, Alexia Larmaraud, and Emily Yueh, "Finding Hidden Leaders,"
McKinsey & Company, January 2017, accessed February 9, 2017, http://
www.mckinsey.com/business-functions/organization/our-insights/
finding-hidden-leaders.

119 For more details about this and other techniques to expose gender bias see the
chapter Expose.

120 A. Danielle Way and Joan Marquest, "Management of Gender Roles: Marketing the Androgynous Leadership Style in the Classroom and the General Workplace," *Organization Development Journal* 31(2) (2013):82-94.

121 Deborah Kolb, Judith Williams and Carol Frohlinger, *Her Place at the Table: A Women's Guide to Negotiating Five Key Challenges to Leadership Success* (New York: Jossey-Bass, 2004), 7.

122 Laura Noonan, Madison Marriage and Patrick Jenkins, "Equal Pay and Opportunities for Women in Finance: Why the Hold up?" *The Financial Times,* April 4, 2017, accessed April 7, 2017, https://www.ft.com/content/198abd62-1471-11e7-80f4-13e067d5072c.

123 Lane, Larmaraud and Yueh, "Finding Hidden Leaders."

124 Goleman, Boyatzis and McKee, *Primal Leadership,* 53-69.

125 For a more detailed description of these leadership styles, see Goleman, Boyatzis and McKee, *Primal Leadership,* 53-69.

126 HayGroup, "The Case for Lawyers Who Lead," Philadelphia, 2005, accessed on February 10, 2017, http://www.haygroup.com/us/press/details.aspx?id=2070.

127 HayGroup, "The Case for Lawyers Who Lead."

128 Results from leadership seminars conducted by the author in 2016.

129 Goleman, Boyatzis and McKee, *Primal Leadership,* 53-69.

130 Krawcheck, *Own it,* 67.

131 Karl Albrecht, *Social Intelligence: The New Science of Success* (San Francisco: Pfeiffer, 2007), 126.

132 Kolb, Williams and Frohlinger, *Her Place at the Table,* 62.

133 For more details on this negotiation approach see Rodger Fisher and William Ury with Bruce Patton, ed., *Getting to Yes: Negotiating Agreement Without Giving In,* 2nd ed. (New York: Penguin Books, 1991).

134 Krawcheck, *Own it,* 67.

135 Kolb, Williams and Frohlinger, *Her Place at the Table,* 118.

Chapter 9 – Politics

136 Aviva Rutkin, "Camera spots your hidden prejudices from your body language," Technology News, *New Scientist* magazine, 28 September 2016.

137 The *Kiss, Bow or Shake Hands* series published by Adam's Media.

138 Ralph Kilmann and Kenneth Thomas, "Developing a Forced-Choice Measure of Conflict-Handling Behavior: The MODE Instrument," *Educational and*

Psychological Measurement 37:2 (1977): 309; Joan Mills, Daniel Robey and Larry Smith, "Conflict-Handling and Personality Dimensions of Project-Management Personnel," *Psychological Reports* 57 (1985): 1135. For online assessment go to the Kilmann Diagnostics website at http://www.kilmanndiagnostics.com/ catalog/thomas-kilmann-conflict-mode-instrument.

139　This chart was created by the author based on a chart by Andy Eklund found in the article entitled "Managing Conflict," August 8, 2010, accessed June 19, 2017, http://www.andyeklund.com/managing-conflict/.

140　Kenneth Thomas, Gail Thomas and Nancy Schaubhut, "Conflict Styles of Men and Women at Six Organizational Levels," *International Journal of Conflict Management,* 19:2 (2008): 148.

Chapter 10 – Thrive

141　"Women Still Do More Household Chores Than Men," November 10, 2016, *BBC News,* accessed April 3, 2017, http://www.bbc.com/news/uk-37941191.

142　Taryn Hillin, "Women are literally expected to do all the chores, depressing study finds," *Fusion,* August 23, 2016, accessed April 3, 2017, http://fusion.kinja.com/women-are-literally-expected-to-do-all-the-chores-depr-1793861364.

143　Hillin, "Women are literally expected."

144　Dufu, *Drop the Ball,* 23.

145　Steinmetz, "Help! My Parents Are Millennials."

146　Dufu, *Drop the Ball,* 53.

147　Arianna Huffington, *Thrive: The Third Metric to Redefining Success and Creating a Life Of Well-Being, Wisdom, and Wonder* (New York: Harmony Books, 2014).

148　My thanks to Betty Ann Heggie, who alerted me to this important area of energy awareness and who created several of the questions in this questionnaire.

149　Deepak Chopra and Rudolph Tanzi, *Super Brain* (New York: Harmony Books, 2012), 190; Huffington, *Thrive,* 77.

150　Huffington, *Thrive,* 74-76.

151　Arianna Huffington, *The Sleep Revolution: Transforming Your Life, One Night at a Time* (New York: Harmony, 2016).

152　Julia Seidl, "Day Dream," *Hello Magazine,* June 26, 2017; Arefa Cassoobhoy, "18 Unexpected Ways to Live Longer," WebMD, August 18, 2016, accessed on June 19, 2017, http://www.webmd.com/healthy-aging/aging-body-care-16/

slideshow-longer-life-secrets?ecd=wnl_lbt_092816_socfwd_
REMAIL&ctr=wnl-lbt-092816-socfwd-REMAIL_nsl-ld-stry_1&mb=.

153 Dufu, *Drop the Ball*, 100.

154 For details on this type of "no," see William Ury, *The Power of Positive No* (New York: Bantam Press, 2007) c. 1.

155 Shipman and Kay, *Womenomics*, 100.

156 Mike Babcock and Rick Larsen, *Leave No Doubt* (Montreal: McGill-Queens University Press, 2012), 98.

157 Suze Yalof Schwartz, *Unplug: A Simple Guide to Meditation for Busy Sceptics and Modern Soul Seekers* (New York: Harmony Books, 2017), 144-150.

158 For more information on HeartMath see Doc Childre and Howard Martin, *The Heartmath Solution* (San Francisco: HarperCollins Publishers, 1999) or http://www.heartmath.org/.

159 "Why listening to music is as good as sex," April 12, 2013 *Mail Online*, accessed February 12, 2015, http://www.dailymail.co.uk/sciencetech/article-2308020/How-listening-new-music-really-CAN-make-happy-Scientists-say-hearing-new-tunes-rewarding.html; Dean Burnett, "Does music really help you concentrate," August 20, 2016, *The Guardian*, accessed April 21, 2017, https://www.theguardian.com/education/2016/aug/20/does-music-really-help-you-concentrate.

160 Arianna Huffington spoke about the "obnoxious roommate living in your head" as keynote speaker at the Deloitte Women of Influence Luncheon Series in Toronto (September 11, 2013).

161 Shirzad Chamine, *Positive Intelligence* (New York: Greenleaf Book Group Press, 2012), 7.

162 *Chamine, Positive Intelligence*, 9.

163 Chamine, *Positive Intelligence*, chapter 2.

164 Deborah Gillis, "What Are You Thankful For This Year?" December 19, 2016, Catalyst website.

165 Anika Rahman, "Gender Equality Benefits Everyone," October 5, 2016, Voice of America editorials, accessed May 12, 2017, https://editorials.voa.gov/a/gender-equality-benefits-everyone/3540012.html.

166 Myers, *The Future of Men*, Kindle edition loc. 1494 of 4697.

INDEX

E

Energy
afternoon naps 251
at home 252
at work 253
decrease the drain 253
delegation 252
getting enough sleep 250
learn to say no 255
manage negative thoughts 260
manage your energy 249
recharging activities 258
reducing holiday drain 252
the sandwich way to say no 257
weaken negative thoughts 261
what replenishes and relaxes 257
Equalizing power 132
Etiquette mindset 221
Examples
always be nice 128
not asking 93
politics 217
success of expansive posture 155
Exercises
career management plan 84
communication 144
conflict modes 238
self-promotion 190
social intelligence 227
Exposing leadership bias 194
Exposing gender bias
building alliances 38
correct it 37
name it 36
question it 36
third party questioning 38
try humour 40

F

Fast system processing 4, 5, 6
advantages and disadvantages 6
Fear of standing out 173

Feminine
definition xxii
Feminine communication patterns 121
diminishing endings 135
direct/indirect communication 136
Feminine communication style
equalizing power 132
I as subject 135
passive voice 138
tentative speech patterns 133
undermining starts 134
weakening modifiers 134
when to use subordinate language 140
Feminine culture xxii, 15, 274
Feminine gender habits.
See Gender habits
Feminine social rituals 16
Feminine style
accept what is offered 19
don't ask 19
everyone shares the same values 19
flat power structure 16
Finding the right fit
belief in meritocracy 79
determine reasons for unease 77
gender bias 78
shift in priorities and values 79
staying where you are 79
workplace culture 77
Fitness test. *See* Leadership tests
Five listening checks 208
Frohlinger, Carol 288

G

Gender
definition xxii
Gender atypical
definition xxii
Gender bias. *See* also Common gender biases
definition xxii
unfair tactics xiv

U